ACTION AND REFLECTION
IN TEACHER EDUCATION

ACTION AND REFLECTION IN TEACHER EDUCATION

edited by
GARETH REES HARVARD
PHIL HODKINSON
Exeter University

ABLEX PUBLISHING CORPORATION
NORWOOD, NEW JERSEY

Printed in the United States of America.

Library of Congress Cataloging-in-Publication Data

Action and reflection in teacher education / Gareth Rees Harvard, Phil Hodkinson, editors.
   p. cm.
   Includes bibliographical references and index.
   ISBN 0-89391-897-0. – ISBN 1-56750-058-7 (pbk.)
   1. Teaching. 2. Teachers–Training of–England. 3. Teachers–Training of –Wales. 4. Group work in education. I. Harvard, Gareth Rees. II. Hodkinson, Phil.
   LB1725.G6A628 1994
   371.1'02–dc20   94-9903
                                                                  CIP

Ablex Publishing Corporation
355 Chestnut Street
Norwood, New Jersey 07648

Table of Contents

Preface

Across the developed world, teacher education is once more under the spotlight. This book focuses on recent experiences in England and Wales, where external pressures have highlighted a tension between a technician model of teacher education, in which teachers learn primarily on the job alongside colleagues, and traditional forms of teacher education based in higher education institutions. This tension superficially replicates an old dichotomy between practice and theory.

In response to these tensions and pressures, teacher educators in Britain, as elsewhere, are turning to ideas of reflective practice to attempt an integration of theory with practice. They are doing so in an attempt to reassert a professional view of teachers and teaching. The contributors to this volume all, in different ways, are actively engaged in addressing these issues, often at the level of both theory and practice. There is no overall theoretical framework yet developed that encompasses all the issues and problems raised by these approaches. Consequently, different contributors bring their own perspectives and insights, and many of the chapters are exploratory in nature. It is for the reader to grapple with any inconsistencies, conflicts, or questions this collection raises, and to decide what relevance there is in these British experiences for practice in other countries and cultures.

Throughout this collection, certain key questions and themes recur. There is space here to pick out three only. Firstly, there is the question of balance between work done in school "on the job," and work done away from the workplace, for example in a university. In different ways, most contributors either state or imply that both are necessary. However, the balance and relationship between the two remain problematic. This practical dichotomy is mirrored in the more abstract relationship between theory and practice. It is partly the need to develop wider, non-situation-specific abilities that requires both an off the job component to training, and a theoretical perspective. Yet as Eraut shows in Chapter 5, it is a dangerous mistake to assume that theorizing belongs in higher education, while practice takes place in schools.

Secondly, the contributions to this volume repeatedly draw our attention to teacher education as a partnership activity. As a minimum, this partnership involves the teacher-learner and an external tutor or mentor. With student teachers, the partnership is at least threefold: student, class teacher, and external tutor. In both cases, peers add a further valuable dimension, and several chapters explicitly refer to the appropriateness of collaborative learning activity. Yet a suspicion remains that, too often, such partnerships lack authenticity, being rhetorical devices that hide very uneven power relationships. The development of such partnerships, together with a need to empower students and teachers, requires fresh thinking about the role of the teacher educator.

Thirdly, while classroom performance is rightly a prime focus of teacher education, especially in initial stages, it is important that wider issues are consistently addressed. On one level, performance alone is not enough and needs to be supported by intellectual development. Equally, on a different level, teachers need to critically examine the wider institutional, cultural, and historical contexts in which they work, and understand the impact that such macroperspectives have on the professional role they fulfill. Authors in this volume vary in the attention they give to these issues of breadth, but they are universally implied in their differing explorations of what being a professional teacher means.

In the first chapter, Hodkinson and Harvard outline the recent cultural context of teacher education in Britain. They briefly explain some of the pressures on teacher education and tease out some key theoretical issues that remain to be addressed. They clearly state the value position of the contributors to this volume: that teachers should be professionals, both to meet the needs of the children they educate, and also those of the national economy of which education is part. In Chapter 2, Zeichner considers recent developments in reflective practice in the United States and elsewhere. He describes the ahistorical nature of writing on reflective practice, and therefore the lack of clarity about the theoretical and political commitments underlying specific reform proposals. He classifies some of the major traditions of practice in teacher education, but shows how these are sometimes located in individual courses and are specific to particular countries and cultures. He warns us that some cultural sensitivity is needed when examining reflective practices in teacher education.

Chapters 3 and 4 examine more closely the nature and purpose of teacher reflection as a goal in teacher education. They look beyond whether teaching is reflective or not, noting the particular kinds of reflection that we want to encourage among teacher educators, teachers, and student teachers. They examine some of the necessary conditions for initial and further professional development. Both chapters present models of learning the authors claim can be used to develop teacher education programs. In Chapter 3, Jamieson critically examines the notion of experiential learning, while in Chapter 4 Hodkinson and Harvard explore the currently fashionable concept of competence, and suggest that competing ideologies and institutional constraints can help or hinder the value of such approaches to teachers' professional development.

Eraut, in Chapter 5, specifically addresses the notion of theorizing as a link between public theory, private theory, and practice. He shows that practice always involves the use of theory. The real problem is to improve in students and teachers their ability to critically examine and develop their own personal theories, what he calls to theorize, and to relate those personal to public theories in ways that make the latter useful to them as teachers.

Following these explorations into theory, other contributors examine the overarching concept in teacher education of eliciting teachers' craft knowledge and of designing a framework to help students and teachers assimilate and evaluate the nature of professional knowledge. Various techniques and strategies are described to show how students acquire and go on to test such professional knowledge, often in collaboration with teachers. The various case studies reported here attempt to (a) establish a firm basis on which to conceptualize the nature of teachers' professional knowledge, and (b) show how that knowledge can be represented for student teachers.

In Chapter 6, Brown describes a research project designed to help students learn from experienced teachers, by following observation of lessons with interviews of the teachers concerned. She shows the value of these approaches in helping students gain a more sophisticated understanding of what they see, and suggests principles of procedure to guide the interviewing process.

In Chapters 7 and 8, Dunne and Harvard describe and analyze aspects of a competence-based teacher education scheme. They show how this scheme attempts to develop critical thinking in the students, taking notions of competence beyond performance only. They present a collaborative approach to student teacher education, with a distinct shift in roles for school teachers and university tutors, working in authentic partnership. They question traditional supervision models, and discuss the implications of their model of mentoring, for students and mentors.

Thomas and Bowden, in Chapter 9, describe a project in which external tutors worked with groups of experienced teachers to develop economic awareness as a dimension to other subject work. They show that collaborative working with a tutor or mentor can be effective in inservice training, not just in work with students. In contrast, in Chapter 10, Ackland describes and explores another type of partnership. Here students, teachers and university tutors work together on the evaluation of school-based curriculum developments. Working with students helps the teachers gain a different perspective on what they are doing, and students develop skills of critical evaluation, as well as examining educational activity from a different perspective to that normally experienced on teaching practice.

Chapters 11 and 12 widen the context of teacher education as it is usually considered. Bloomer and Jolly are concerned with teacher education in that part of the postcompulsory sector, which is called *further education* in Britain. Williams addresses the education of teachers from many different countries in teaching English as a foreign language. In both cases, learners are experienced teachers, though often without any relevant initial training. The authors consider, in their contrasting contexts, the importance of basing education on the direct experiences of the teachers, and describe ways in which they have tried to empower the teachers through the educational process.

In the British context, much attention has recently been given to the importance of adequate subject knowledge in teachers. In Chapter 13, McNamara directly addresses this issue and unpicks some of the key theoretical issues implicit in this notion. He highlights some of the advantages and dangers of seeing subject knowledge as the prime factor in initial teacher education.

In the final chapter, Harvard and Hodkinson try to pull together some of the themes and issues that have arisen throughout the book, and to point up some ways forward. To do this, they change the spotlight from the notion of a reflective teacher, to that of a reflective teacher educator. They address the need to change the traditional role of teacher educators and explore the relationships between the approaches championed in this book and different contextual settings for teacher education. They present a personal view of some key requirements if the rhetorical image of teachering as a critically reflective profession is to come a little closer to reality. Inevitably, this raises more questions and problems that the contributors to this book have attempted to address. In this sense, the book is an early, tentative exploration of very confused, largely unknown, but increasingly important terrain.

Taken together, these chapters question whether we have a framework for conceptualizing the knowledge base for teaching. The various method-ologies used to elicit teachers' professional knowledge are derived from different ideologies and presuppose a particular epistemology of practice. Their overriding concern is with the development of a critical, reflective approach to teaching. Each study, from different perspectives, identifies the necessary conditions for collaborative reflective practice between teachers or students and tutors, together with the extent to which such collaboration actually takes place.

CHAPTER 1

Perspectives on Teacher Education

Phil Hodkinson
Crewe and Alsager College of Higher Education
Crewe Campus Crewe, England

Gareth Harvard
Exeter University School of Education Exeter, England

Education is essential for the future of society and the economy, and vast sums of money are spent by governments, employers, and individuals, all investing in the future in different ways. For an increasing number of Western countries, education and training consume a higher proportion of the Gross National Product than defense. All this is uncontentious. What is contentious is the form education should take, and how it is operationalized. One key factor in this operationalization is the education of teachers.

The preparation of teachers and other professional educators is difficult and problematic. One of the reasons is that teaching and learning processes are complex and not fully understood. There is currently a crisis of confidence within teacher education in Britain that is putting these processes under the spotlight. This crisis has resulted in the generation of new ideas and practice, and the reconsideration of procedures previously taken for granted.

TENSIONS IN TEACHER EDUCATION IN BRITAIN

Teacher education in England and Wales is in a state of tension between, on the one hand, proposals for some sort of apprenticeship model, where teachers learn their trade by working in schools alongside more experienced colleagues, and on the other hand, the traditional model, based on the study of academic, educational theory, alongside teaching practice, in

1

a higher education institution. There have been a recent series of publications from right-wing pressure groups (see, for example, Lawlor, 1990; O'Keeffe, 1990) that highlight this dichotomy, presenting a crude stereotypical view of existing teacher education, as if it exclusively involved teaching "irrelevant" theory. The same writers go on to suggest that all this training is both expensive and unnecessary, and to advocate learning on the job only. One influential teacher-educator has also consistently argued for just such an "on the job" approach to initial teacher training (Hargreaves, 1990). The arguments are superficially attractive. Such an approach, it might appear, would insure that training was of direct relevance to the job. It might enable a smoother transition from initial training, through probation, into professional development.

Similar trends can be seen within vocational education in Britain in the emergence of National Vocational Qualifications (NVQs). The NVQ system was introduced to rationalize post-16 vocational qualifications (de Ville, 1986; NCVQ, 1987). The emerging new system is competence based, following, yet different from, American practice in the 1970s (Tuxworth, 1989). This means that the emphasis in training is exclusively on job performance. It is assumed that adequate performance can only take place if it is underpinned by the necessary knowledge, understanding, and skills. Consequently, only the actual performance on the job is assessed. NVQs deliberately separate assessment from learning, stating that the only thing that is important is whether or not a trainee can perform the role for the job, so that it does not matter where or how that performance was learned. Within this NVQ system, the training of *trainers*, whose jobs in many ways resemble those of teachers, is already being addressed (TDLB, 1990). There is much pressure currently, for example, from Her Majesty's Inspectors (HMI), to change teacher training also into an NVQ-type competence-based pattern.

Such approaches to teacher education cannot be easily dismissed. In Britain, many potentially excellent teachers in the past have been denied recognized teacher status simply because they did not hold a recognized teacher qualification. There was, until the recent introduction of experimental, school-based articled and licensed teachers schemes,[1] no means for such people to achieve such status, other than to take a full-time course

---

[1]The British government recently introduced two experimental schemes which allow teachers to take full-time employment prior to achieving qualified teacher status. In the Licensed teacher scheme, schools may appoint unqualified members of staff, for example in shortage subjects. In the more interesting Articled Teachers scheme, beginning teachers are employed as articled teachers for 2 years, during which time they complete appropriate off-the-job training, usually organized by the local education authority in conjunction with a higher education institution.

designed for beginners. The one major exception to this was in further education (see Chapter 11).

There are many dangers with an apprenticeship system, even if competence based. As Solomon (1987) suggested, such a model views teachers as technicians, rather than as professionals. Her view is reinforced by further examination of NVQ developments. Ashworth and Saxton (1990) showed that narrow competences can artificially atomize complex skills and reduce them to mundane mechanical tasks, in which the parts add up to less than the whole. So far, NVQs have succeeded in producing standards of competence mainly at the lower levels, and it is still unclear how the scheme can be expanded to managerial and professional roles (Mansfield, 1989). Candy and Harris (1990) reviewed progress on an Australian competence-based training program for panel beaters. Despite the fact that this was a course for technicians, teachers were still concerned that theory was inadequately addressed. Eraut (1989) reminded us of the importance of theory as a means for practitioners to interpret and criticize their own actions. The same author (Eraut, 1990) suggested that the relationship between competence and knowledge/understanding is more complex than the pure NVQ model assumes, and Black and Wolf (1990) suggested that these complexities increase and become more problematic in more professional jobs. The potential value of competence-based education for professional teachers is returned to in more detail in Chapter 4.

There is a long tradition in Britain of treating teachers as technicians, for example, in some of the attempts to produce "teacher-proof" curriculum packs in the 1970s. The development of the National Curriculum and NVQs continue this process. Both attempt to detail very precisely what teachers will cover, and how it will be assessed. Both deliberately use assessment to control the teaching force and to force teachers to improve "standards." This is to be done by publishing the results achieved by pupils and using these results to evaluate teacher performance. Such approaches fail to understand both the nature of teaching and of education. In many ways, teaching more closely resembles those professions whose development was analyzed by Schon (1983, 1987). Teaching is a complex and multifaceted activity, not a series of simple tasks. Teachers are constantly presented with new and unique situations. Teaching requires wide-ranging professional competence, drawing on a combination of experience, understanding and principles of procedure (Stenhouse, 1975), as well as specific skills. Teaching is also an interpersonal activity, with personalities and relationships at its heart. Although appropriate training can help teachers with such relationships, it should be open-ended and recognize that different teachers teach in different ways. The context within which a teacher works has a major influence on all aspects of the job. This means an essential part of that job has to be to understand the nature of the context and its interaction with both teaching and learning.

As society changes and as curricula change, teaching is a job in constant flux. Teachers need to develop the ability to react constructively to such changes and to be proactive in getting the best for their pupils in situations unforeseen when training programs were designed. Thus, in the early 1990s British schoolteachers must be able to change their approach to the job they do in response to the national curriculum and devolved local management of schools.

This is not to imply that all was perfect with traditional, nontechnician modes of teacher education. Courses sometimes encouraged the learning of theory as if it were fact. On 1-year Postgraduate Certificate of Education (PGCE) courses, this was sometimes the result of pressure of time. Bright graduates skimmed over the surface of educational thinking with a superficiality that could be both frustrating and misleading. On the better paced undergraduate courses, inappropriate assessments sometimes caused theory to be memorized as fact and regurgitated in written examinations. Practical work and group work were sometimes assessed indirectly, through essays, in order to facilitate degree gradings and to strengthen assessment reliability, but at the cost of validity. Sometimes, as with teaching practice itself, practical activities were devalued by being excluded from degree assessment altogether. The result could be that the assessment distorted the course objectives.

There is, however, an alternative view of teacher education, which focuses on the creation of a proactive profession. Teachers, according to this view, need to be empowered to do things for themselves and to think for themselves. There are interesting parallels in other contexts. There are, for example, calls for pupil empowerment to cope with a changing world (e.g., Hopson & Scally, 1981). This has become a central thrust in some recent British educational initiatives, such as the Technical and Vocational Education Initiative (TVEI) and Records of Achievement (ROA) for school pupils. Similarly, there are demands for empowered professionals in health, social services, law, and so on whereas industry demands more flexible and adaptable workers (CBI, 1989).

There are three reasons for advocating such empowerment for pupils. First, there are liberal notions about helping the individual pupil/trainee to make the best of him or herself. Second, there are desires for a more flexible and effective work force, for the benefit of industry, the economy, and the state. Third, there is the need for a more active participatory democracy, in which the advancement of the individual is harmonized with the needs of the community, for example, through the concept of collaborative citizenship advanced by Ranson (1990). These arguments can be amalgamated into a holistic view of empowerment, that has three interrelated elements: (a) personal autonomy, or the ability to think critically for oneself; (b) personal competence, or the ability to do things for oneself and to be enterprising; and (c) community, or the ability to work with and empathize with others (Hodkinson, 1989, 1991).

Educating teachers has dual goals: to enhance the personal, professional growth of the teachers themselves and indirectly that of the learners they work with. It can be argued that, to do this, the same three components are central to teacher education. To be effective and proactive in a changing world, the ability to think critically, both about the work you are doing and the context within which you are placed, is central (autonomy), as are the abilities to perform well in the classroom, to initiate new developments (competence), and to work with others, be they colleagues, superiors, pupils, parents, local employers, other professions, and so on (community).

Problems arise because the three elements are not discrete. The complex interactions between them are crucial to the success of teaching. It is likewise impossible to separate theory from practice, or performance from its context. It follows that any approach to teacher education that tries to do that, or that emphasizes one aspect rather than another, will probably be counterproductive. Yet this is what an apprenticeship system tied to narrow competences will do, because it emphasizes performance and classroom relationships while ignoring critical thinking, theory, and the wider context. Much traditional teacher education, while addressing both autonomy and competence as described above, kept them separated, so that the critical, theoretical courses and performance-focused teaching practice were barely related. The third element, community, is in serious danger of neglect in both traditional academic and apprenticeship approaches.

Such separation of elements and limitation of focus is not inevitable. Much varied work has been done over a considerable period of time, focusing on more integrated models of professional development (see, for example, Fish, 1989). Such approaches attempt to synthesize the elements, rather than rejecting some and concentrating too heavily on others. This volume pulls together some of this work and explores some of the problems, issues, and principles involved in a more integrated approach.

SOME THEORETICAL ISSUES

Teachers bring to the classroom values, beliefs, and experiences that influence everything they do. Recent work suggests that teachers need to be made aware of their existing belief and value systems (sometimes called *schemas*) through critical reflection on both their performances and how they view them.

A *schema* is an organized body of knowledge, a mental structure, or a representation abstracted from experience (Rumelhart, 1980). We use schemas to understand events, objects, people, and feelings, and to respond to them in the most appropriate way we can. Schemas help us to predict events in a reasonably accurate way, but can also be modified to help us interpret and cope with events even more successfully. They also allow us to make selective sense of complex realities, for example, by filtering out "unwanted" information. This filtering process can limit our ability to perceive situations in unfamiliar ways.

The implications of this view of the teacher as reflective practitioner are that teacher educators should establish an understanding, not only of the development of classroom performances, but also of the intellectual processes and structures that mediate them (C. Desforges, personal communication, July 14, 1990). The growth of professional knowledge and teacher competence resides in the schemas and how these are selected and applied in practice (Berliner, 1990; Clark & Peterson, 1986).

Those of us educating teachers need to know much more about how learners' schemas are acquired and develop. Desforges (1989) and Harvard (1990a, 1990b) reminded us that the precise nature of the professionally relevant intellectual processes and mediating schemas is an open question for research. There is as yet an inadequate empirical basis on which to conceptualize how practitioners and student learners select from and store experiences, or how these experiences are structured into professional knowledge.

A crucial part of the job of any teacher is to address the issue of schema development in working with pupils, who also bring preformed schemas to class. For learning to be effective, it should develop from where pupils are, not from where the teacher believes they might be. This is one reason why a technician approach to education is flawed and illustrates some of the complexity and uniqueness of any teaching/learning situation.

How do teachers develop the disposition and ability to reflect critically? Research suggests that such development comes from participating in such critical reflection in partnership with a tutor or mentor (Fenstermacher, 1990; McNamarra, 1990). Such reflection is often most effective for all of us when done collaboratively. Critical reflection will be addressed in more detail in Chapter 2, and the closely related issue of theorizing in Chapter 5.

Teachers engage in a wide range of activities that make up their experience. One aspect is classroom performance, which is both the product of their intellectual structures and the object of analysis by their cognitive processes. Doyle (1990) acknowledged that although a literature on teaching has been accumulating for some time, it is only recently that we have begun to examine systematically the knowledge structures and comprehension processes that teachers use daily to interpret class-room events and reflect on the dilemmas of teaching. This means that to understand how teachers learn the job, it is crucial to have accounts and representations of their practice as it develops over time. These might form key components in a professional profile or record. It is necessary to understand how these practical performances relate to the development of a practitioner's professionally relevant schemas. The record should focus on preparation and evaluation as well as on the performance itself. This will help the professional educator and tutor, where relevant, to understand how the intellectual organization of professional knowledge grows and develops.

However, here is much more to teaching than classroom performance. Teachers also have to plan programs, develop assessment, organize resources, manage and/or work with colleagues, and even become skilled political operators within their own institution (Ball, 1987). Many decisions taken in schools are taken in settings of conflict, where groups and subgroups compete for resources, status, or beliefs. The empowered teacher needs to understand both the political processes and the positions and values of other groups. Teachers also need to understand the values and perspectives of the groups they belong to. For example, Goodson (1983, 1984) showed the importance of subject loyalty to career progression and status. Especially in secondary education, many teachers see their subject as a key component of their identity. Goodson showed that there are many advantages in being associated with a high status subject such as English or Physics, and problems in belonging to a marginal subject such as Rural Science. The differing and unequal sources of power for different groups and individuals have a major impact on all aspects of education. Such aspects of the teacher's role are neglected in the technician view of teaching that presupposes a limited performance, controlled and constrained by others.

The same complex relationship between performance and schema is equally important in these other parts of a professional educator's role. These political experiences can and should also be developed by opening them to critical reflection. However, in some of these areas, this opening up is more difficult to achieve. Although most teachers are aware of classroom performance as something to be professionally developed, many take their micropolitical activities for granted, not always even realizing that they are engaged in them. Teaching is not just about self, a perspective also ignored by the implicitly individualistic technician model of training.

We need to know much more about the nature of teachers' processes for selecting and organizing experience of all aspects of the role. We also need to know how these capacities can be developed. It is essential to challenge the concept of learning that separates what is learned from how it is learned. To learn from experience is to recognize that knowledge is situated, being in part a product of the activity, context, and culture in which it is developed and used. Experiential learning is further explored in Chapter 3.

Another difficulty for the technician model of teaching is that teaching is situated in broad historical, cultural, and epistemological contexts. Reid (1990) gave a graphic illustration of this. He reminded us that, although it is currently impossible to think of schools without the concept of class-rooms, this was not always the case. In the 18th and early 19th centuries, British public schools were run on the monitor system, with up to 100 pupils all taught together in the school hall. Such schools did not have classrooms at all. At a more abstract level, Green (1991) showed that English education has several highly significant "peculiarities," which differentiate its current context from that of any other Western democracy. Once more, the tech-nician model falls short. It assumes that such factors are (a) neutral and (b) unchanging. Neither is correct. Consequently, teachers need the ability to reflect critically about the contexts in which they work. Beliefs and ideol-ogies within broader society are as important to the educative process as the individual schemas of participants.

It is difficult enough for trained professionals to reflect on performance. It is even more difficult to reflect on these broader and less definable contextual characteristics. Experience suggests that two elements are crucial for success. The first is distance, for it is easier to examine the setting when you are temporarily removed from it. The second concerns theory. Theoretical writings of others can help all of us see familiar worlds through different eyes. We are here describing an organic process, in which individual schemas are fed by theoretical perspectives.

The result can be more than changed individual beliefs. One way in which collective understanding grows, and thus new theories emerge, is through the sharing of insights gained. There can be a dialectical relation-ship between practitioner, researcher, and theory. Theory can grow out of reflections on practice, and that practice can change in the light of new theory (Glaser & Strauss, 1967). Once more, the role of tutor to facilitate such processes is crucial. In teacher education there has been a deliberate fostering of these processes for some time. This is often done through teacher research, sometimes called *action research*. This research can focus either on contextual issues or on performance. This volume does not address action research per se. It is well written elsewhere (see, for example, Carr & Kemmis, 1986; Stenhouse, 1975).

Another problem for inservice training and professional development of teachers is the lack of an ethos that values career long professional development. There is currently no clearly articulated model for supporting such long-term development within the British teaching profession. As Tharp and Gallimore (1988, p. 188), in referring to the American context, claimed: the "absence of continuous training and skillful assistance not only frustrates and stunts the growth potential of teachers but also precludes the introduction of new curriculum, and instructional goals."

Teacher education in Britain is fragmented. Initial training is too often a self-contained activity to be completed and forgotten: more a rite of passage than part of a process of personal professional development. The probationary period is little more than an opportunity (seldom taken) to weed out incompetents before they are fully incorporated into the profession. Continuing education for qualified teachers is a mixed bag of inservice education and training (INSET), with occasional higher degrees. It impinges on teachers very unevenly and haphazardly.

These problems are rising on policy agendas in Britain, for example, through the development of staff appraisal systems. The NVQ system addresses similar issues in vocational training, as the focus changes from solving youth unemployment to training throughout working life. *Action planning* is seen, at least in rhetoric, as a lifelong process, in which trainees of any age are aided in identifying their own training needs and in finding appropriate ways of fulfilling them (Stanton, 1990). What we are advocating here is a similar approach for teacher education, in which empowerment becomes central, and the processes engaged in enable individuals, with the help of their supervisors/tutors where appropriate, to develop continuity and progression that makes sense both in the short and medium terms. Our current system already relies on individual teachers to make sense of, and largely take responsibility for, their own professional development. What is needed is an appropriate conceptual framework, with the tools and resources to make this genuinely possible. The tools would include the ability to think for oneself about the job and its contexts, and a "map" of competence and issues to aid that process and to help plan the route, all within a teacher-centered appraisal system. The resources include time, money, appropriate courses, a coherent system of professional development throughout a teacher's career, and, above all, tutorial support.

We must also consider, therefore, the relationship and discourse between the teacher and his or her tutor or mentor. The title *tutor* is chosen advisedly. The role is to help the teacher, whether student, novice or experienced practitioner, to make sense of his or her own role and context. The tutor's role changes from one of didactic presenter (although there may well be particular circumstances when such presentations are required) to one of facilitator and enabler of learning.

This suggests that those with responsibility for educating teachers need to acquire and develop a range of skills previously associated with counselling. These include active listening, open questioning, empathy, and negotiation. They also include confronting, to help learners face up to issues, ideas, or experiences they may prefer to ignore or sidestep. In addition, tutors need to be able to help teachers and trainee teachers assess and evaluate their learning, and to identify priorities for further action. They then need to help provide/develop appropriate situations, resources, and programs of study to enable agreed progress to be made. Within British vocational education, such processes are identified as action planning: in which a trainee is helped by a tutor to go through the stages just outlined. There are dangers of such approaches becoming mechanistic and reductionist. But if used flexibly and imaginatively, an action planning framework can help shift the focus of training onto the individual empowerment of the trainee.

Such an individual focus on learning is not enough. The notion of community as a key element in empowerment must not be lost. Teachers can learn much from each other, provided they are given space and time to discuss and collaborate in the learning process. Although this can, and often does, happen with close colleagues, there is much to be gained from interacting with people from other institutions and backgrounds. Such group seminar work is a long-established part of teacher education, both in INSET and higher degree work. An increasing part of a teacher's role is collaborative, so his or her skills of working with others should be developed. Furthermore, by learning in groups, teachers or trainee teachers can get a sense of what some of their pupils experience in class, and there is a chance that effective pedagogy used with them (the teachers) may rub off. The tutorial role in these group situations remains that of facilitator and enabler.

The relationships between tutor and teacher are paralleled by the relationships between the teacher and the pupils. Teachers present powerful pedagogical models to their pupils. In this sense, the medium is indeed the message. If, for example, a teacher advocates non-racism, but is racist in his or her actions, actions might speak louder than words. If we apply this notion to the idea of empowerment, then a series of potentially dysfunctional relationships can be seen. Pupils cannot easily become empowered if the teacher's role is authoritarian or overly paternal. Pedagogy, assessment, attitudes, and relationships must consistently value and facilitate that empowerment. For teachers to be able to do that, they must have become similarly empowered themselves. The training they receive must partially mirror what they are being expected to do in the classroom, lest authoritarian or paternal tutors reduce empowerment of the teachers and student-teachers they work with. There are also implications for school organization: An authoritarian management structure disempowers individual teachers within a school and may consequently encourage them to be authoritarian in the classroom, thus disempowering their pupils.

EDUCATION AND ECONOMIC PROSPERITY

It is often said that one crucial element in Britain's declining economic performance is an inappropriate education system. For example, Weiner (1981) identified problems for the economy because of negative attitudes to industry, which were linked to class prejudice within society and fostered by the education system. Recent government papers focus on problems supposedly caused by inadequately low staying on rates in education, both post-16 and in higher education (Fowler, 1989). The Confederation of British Industry (CBI, 1989) is asking for more generally skilled and flexible young people to meet the perceived future employment needs. Recent work has shown the fallacy of seeing education as the scapegoat for Britain's industrial problems, and attention is now moving toward problems in employment training and the labor market (Ainley & Corney, 1990; Finegold & Soskice, 1988; Raffe, in press). This new focus on problems within British industry has some interesting educational implications.

Economists and management theorists are increasingly addressing the issue of flexibility in institutions. In a rapidly changing world, firms must be flexible to survive. Finegold (forthcoming) summarized two ideal-type responses to this situation. The first is *competitive flexibility*. This is characterized by the rapid hiring and firing of workers who are employed to do a specific job. There is hierarchical management and a use of mechanization to marginalize labor. Wages are also flexible, possibly through piecework. This he went on to identify with a low-skills approach. Employers do not invest in training workers on short-term contracts. Workers have no real interest in the medium-term well-being of the firm. The result can be poor quality output and loss of time, for example, when workers cannot repair their own production line.

The other ideal type is *flexible specialization*. This is a high-skilled approach in which employees are given considerable job security and some form of share in company responsibility. Emphasis is placed on training because the workforce must be skilled enough to change what they do as circumstances alter. This may involve more developed notions of teamwork, and job rotations. Finegold went on to say that flexible specialization is an appropriate response to long-term demands and pressures on a company, whereas competitive flexibility is a response to short-term demands to meet immediate financial and production targets. He claimed that a flexible-specialization, long-term approach to the problems of change is a crucial element of what he called elsewhere (Finegold, 1991) a *high-skills equilibrium*. By this he meant the ability to compete in world markets by producing high-quality goods through highly skillful processes, rather than trying to compete with Third World countries for low-technology mass production, based on low skills and cheap labor.

This analysis has several obvious implications for education (and therefore for teaching and teacher education), which is an important part of a strategy to move toward a high-skill equilibrium by helping educate highly skilled, empowered, and flexible young people. Furthermore, it is possible to apply the same ideal types to school management. If we do that, we might notice that a combination of inadequate resources, local management of schools, and the requirement that annual budgets are balanced puts cheap inexperience at a premium and increases short-term hiring and firing of teachers (Abrams, 1991). Combine this with a technician ideology, in which training is reduced to "passing" a limited number of competences picked up on the job, and we are describing short-term, low-skill, competitive flexibility. The ruinous consequences could include the disempowerment and lowering of morale of teachers and a gradual decline in educational standards, including the loss of empowerment for pupils, which in turn could contribute to the emasculation of the British workforce and of the British economy.

But teachers deal with people, not parts on a production line. Education has to be long term, because it takes 11 years of compulsory schooling to educate each 16-year-old. If we genuinely value education, a high-skilled, long-term, flexible specialization model is the only moral choice. As this is also of economic importance to the country, the necessary resources must be found. To play their role in developing this high-skills equilibrium, teachers must be empowered professionals, not technicians. For this to be brought about appropriate teacher education strategies are essential. The issues described here and explored in subsequent chapters address this professional, high-skill agenda for teacher education.

REFERENCES

Abrams, F. (1991, July 19). Surge in stop-gap staffing. *Times Educational Supplement*, p. 1.

Ainley, P., & Corney, M. (1990). *Training for the future: The rise and fall of the Manpower Services Commission*. London: Cassell Educational.

Ashworth, P., & Saxton, J. (1990). On 'competence.' *Journal of Further and Higher Education, 14* (2), 3–25.

Ball, S. (1987). *The micro-politics of the school: Towards a theory of school organisation*. London: Routledge.

Berliner, D.C. (1990, September). *Characteristics of experts in the pedagogical domain*.

Paper presented at *International Symposium: Research on Effective and Responsible Teaching*, Fribourg, Switzerland.

Black, H., & Wolf, A. (Eds.). (1990). *Knowledge and competence: Current issues in training and education*. London: COIC, for Department of Employment.

Candy, P., & Harris, R. (1990). Implementing competency-based vocational education: A view from within. *Journal of Further and Higher Education, 14* (2), 38–58

Carr, W., & Kemmis, S. (1986). *Becoming critical: Education, knowledge and action research*. Lewes, UK: Falmer Press.

CBI. (1989). *Towards a skills revolution*. London: CBI.

Clark, C. M., & Peterson, P. L. (1986). Teachers' thought processes. In M. Wittrock (Ed.), *Handbook of research on teaching* (pp. 255–296). New York: Macmillan.

Desforges, C. (1989). Understanding learning for teaching. *Westminster Studies in Education, 12* (2), 17–29.

De Ville, O. (1986). *Review of vocational qualifications in England and Wales*. London: Manpower Services Commission/Department of Education and Science.

Doyle, W. (1990). *How teachers and students manage the experienced curriculum*. Paper presented to International Symposium: Research on Effective and Responsible Teaching, Fribourg, Switzerland.

Eraut, M. (1989). Initial teacher training and the NCVQ Model. In J. Burke (Ed.), *Competency based education and training* (pp. 171–185), Lewes, UK: Falmer.

Eraut, M. (1990). Identifying the knowledge which underpins performance. In H. Black & A. Wolf (Eds.), *Knowledge and competence: Current issues in training and education*. London: COIC, for Department of Employment.

Fenstermacher, G. (1990). *The concepts of method and manner in teaching*. Paper presented at International Symposium: Research on Effective and Responsible Teaching, Fribourg, Switzerland.

Finegold, D. (1991). Institutional incentives and skill creation: Understanding the decisions that lead to a high skill equilibrium. In P. Ryan (Ed.), *International comparisons of vocational education and training for intermediate skills*. Lewes UK: Falmer Press.

Finegold D. (forthcoming). The changing economic context and its relationship with education and training. In D. Finegold, L. McFarland, & W. Richardson (Eds.), *Something borrowed, something blue: Education and training policy transfer between the U.S.A and Britain* (provisional title).

Finegold, D., & Soskice, D. (1988). The failure of training in Britain: analysis and prescription *Oxford Review of Economic Policy, 4* (3), 21–50.

Fish, D. (1989). *Learning through practice in initial teacher training*. London: Kogan Page.

Fowler, N. (1989, November 21). Speech to the CBI Conference, Harrogate.

Glaser, B., & Strauss, A. (1967). *The discovery of grounded theory: Strategies for qualitative research*. London: Weidenfeld and Nicolson.

Goodson, I. (1983). *School subjects and curriculum change*. London: Croom Helm.

Goodson, I. (1984). Beyond the subject monolith: Subject traditions and sub-cultures. In P. Harling (Ed.), *New directions in educational leadership* (pp. 325–341). Lewes, UK: Falmer.

Green, A. (1991). The peculiarities of English education. In Education Group II, *Education limited: Schooling and training and the new right since 1979*. London: Unwin Hyman.

Hargreaves, D. (1990, September 21). Remission on a life sentence *Times Higher Education Supplement*, p. 12.

Harvard G. (1990a). *Developing teacher competence*. Paper presented at International symposium: Research on effective and responsible teaching, Fribourg, Switzerland.

Harvard, G. (1990b). Some exploratory uses of interactive video in teacher education: Designing and presenting interactive video sequences to primary student teachers. *Educational Technology and Training International, 27* (2), 155–173.

Hodkinson, P. (1989). Crossing the academic-vocational divide: Personal effectiveness and autonomy as an integrating theme in post-16 education. *British Journal of Educational Studies, 37* (4), 369–383.

Hodkinson, P. (1991). Liberal education and the new vocationalism: A progressive partnership? *Oxford Review of Education, 17* (1), 73–88.

Hopson, B., & Scally, M. (1981). *Lifeskills teaching.* London: McGraw-Hill.

Lawlor, S. (1990) *Teachers mistaught: Training in theories or education in subjects?* London: Centre for Policy Studies.

Mansfield, B. (1989). Competence and standards. In J. Burke (Ed.), *Competency based education and training.* pp. 26–38) Lewes: Falmer.

McNamarra, D. (1990). Research on teachers' thinking: Its contribution to educating student teachers to think critically *Journal of Education for Teaching, 16* (2), 127–160.

NCVQ. (1987). *The national vocational qualification framework.* London: NCVQ.

O'Keeffe, D. (1990). *The wayward elite: A critique of British teacher education.* London: Adam Smith Institute.

Raffe, D. (in press). Beyond the 'mixed model': Social Research and the case for reform of 16-18s education in Britain. In C. Crouch & Health (Eds.), *Social research and social reform. Essays in honour of A. H. Halsey.* Oxford: Oxford University Press.

Ranson, S. (1990). Towards education for citizenship. *Educational Review, 42* (2), 151–166.

Reid, W. A. (1990). Strange curricula: Origins and development of the institutional categories of schooling. *Journal of Curriculum Studies, 22* (3), 203–216.

Rumelhart, D. E. (1980). Schemata: The building blocks of cognition. In R. Spiro et al. (Eds.), *Theoretical issues in reading comprehension.* Hillsdale, NJ: Erlbaum.

Schon, D. (1983). *The reflective practitioner.* New York: Basic Books.

Schon, D. (1987). *Educating the reflective practitioner.* San Francisco: Jossey Bass.

Solomon, J. (1987). New thoughts on teacher education. *Oxford Review of Education, 13* (3), 267–274.

Stanton, G. (1990). TVEI and individual action plans. In P. Hodkinson (Ed.), *The TVEI extension and the post-16 curriculum.* Oxford: Pergamon Educational Productions.

Stenhouse, L. (1975). *An introduction to curriculum research and development.* London: Heinemann.

TDLB. (1990). *How do you spot good trainers? A consultation document.* London: Training and Development Lead Body.

Tharp, R. G., & Gallimore, R. (1988). *Rousing minds to life.* Cambridge, UK: Cambridge University Press.

Tuxworth, E. (1989). Competence based education and training: Background and origins. In J. Burke (Ed.), *Competency based education and training* (pp. 10–25). Lewes, UK: Falmer Press.

Weiner, M. (1981). *English culture and the decline of the industrial spirit, 1850–1980.* Cambridge, UK: Cambridge University Press.

CHAPTER 2

Conceptions of Reflective Practice in Teaching and Teacher Education

Kenneth M. Zeichner
Department of Curriculum and Instruction
University of Wisconsin-Madison

In the last decade, the slogans *reflective teaching, reflective practitioner, action research, teachers-as-researchers,* and a host of related terms have become fashionable throughout all segments of the teacher education community. These terms have become slogans around which teacher educators all over the world have rallied in the name of teacher education reform. Efforts to make reflective inquiry a central component in teacher education program reforms have included those in the United States (e.g., Clift, Houston, & Pugach, 1990; Cruickshank, 1987; Posner, 1989; Tabachnick & Zeichner, 1991; Valli, 1992), the United Kingdom (e.g., Ashcroft & Griffiths, 1989; Lucas, 1989;), Canada (e.g., Clandinin & Connelly, 1986; Mackinnon & Erickson, 1988; Russell, 1991), Australia (e.g., Gore, 1987; Martinez, 1989, Robottom, 1988; Smith & Sachs, 1988;), Austria (e.g., Altrichter, 1988), the Netherlands (e.g., Korthagen, 1985), Norway (e.g., Handal & Lauvas, 1989), and Thailand (e.g., Thongthew, 1988).[1]

Concurrent with this rapid growth of teacher education program reforms based on the concept of reflective inquiry has been the emergence of a research literature that has sought to describe the nature and impact of program reforms (e.g., Wedman & Martin, 1986; Wubbels & Korthagen, 1990; Zeichner & Liston, 1985;), the processes of teacher reflection and the

---

[1]The concern with facilitating more reflective practice has also been very visible in the more general field of adult education (e.g., Boud, Keogh, & Walker, 1985; Freire, 1973; Mezirow, 1990).

relationships between these thinking processes and teacher development (e.g., La Boskey, 1990; Russell & Munby, 1991), and the conditions that influence the reflective capabilities of teachers (Erickson & Mackinnon, 1991; Grimmett & Crehan, 1990; Kottkamp, 1990; Richert, 1990; Ross, 1990). Amid all of this activity by educational researchers and teacher educators, there has been a great deal of confusion about what is meant in particular cases by the term *reflection*. It has come to the point now where the whole range of beliefs within the teacher education community about teaching, learning, schooling, and the social order have become incorporated into the discourse about reflective teacher education. Everyone has his or her own version of reflective practice in teaching and teacher education (Feiman-Nemser, 1990).

> Terms such as reflective practice, inquiry-oriented teacher education, reflection-in-action, teacher as researcher, teacher as decision-maker, teacher as professional, teacher as problem solver, all encompass some notion of reflection in the process of professional development, but at the same time disguise a vast number of conceptual variations, with a range of implications for the design and organization of teacher education courses. (Calderhead, 1989, p. 43)

Not surprisingly there have been calls recently for efforts to clarify the similarities and differences among attempts by teacher educators and educational researchers to implement and/or study reflective teacher education (e.g., Kremer-Hayon, 1991) and criticism of the lack of attention to the conceptual underpinnings of particular projects such as the recent criticism by Bartlett (1989) of several U.S. efforts.

> The enthusiasm for reflection and teaching in the USA as a research paradigm aimed at developing teacher understanding of practice does not seem to have been matched by a similar enthusiasm for developing a theoretical understanding of reflection, its ideological determination, and how this is to be interpreted and understood. (p. 356)

Varieties of Reflective Practice

Beginning in 1985 with the efforts of Tom in the United States there have been a number of attempts within the teacher education community to clarify the conceptual distinctions among reflective teacher education projects. Tom (1985) argued that there are at least three dimensions that can serve to distinguish reform proposals: (a) differences over which aspects of teaching should be made problematic in teachers' reflections, (b) differences in the model of inquiry that teachers are to employ, and (c) differences with regard to assumptions about the ontological status of educational phenomena.

Tom analyzed many of the existing teacher education reform projects from Australia, the United Kingdom, and the United States that were based on some notion of reflective inquiry, and situated each one on a continuum based on the stance taken in a particular body of work toward each of the three dimensions. For example, Tom described four arenas of the problematic that were emphasized in different programs of work: the teaching and learning process in the classroom, subject matter knowledge, the political and ethical principles underlying teaching, and the society and its institutions. Tom's paper discussed the work of specific people in the field (e.g., John Elliott; Ann and Harold Berlak) in terms of which aspects of teaching they want teachers to make problematic. This chapter provides a very important *internal* analysis of reflective teacher education projects. What Tom failed to do, however, was to relate the differences that he detected in assumptions about what should be made problematic in reflection, and in definitions of inquiry and reality, to broader differences in social theory and political philosophy.

This next step was begun with an important paper by Calderhead (1989) in which an analysis is provided of the different sources of external theoretical influence on various visions of reflective teacher education. Calderhead discussed Dewey's (1933) concept of reflection, Schon's (1983, 1987) ideas about the reflective practitioner, the concept of teaching as a deliberative practice (e.g., Schwab, 1971), and Habermas's (1974) notion of reflection as an element of emancipatory action, in relation to various projects of reflective teaching and teacher education. He concluded from his analysis that concepts of reflective teaching that have been employed in teacher education vary along five dimensions.

> They vary in terms of how they view the process of reflection (e.g., reflection-in-action, curriculum deliberation), the content of reflection (e.g., teachers' own values, societal context, educational theory), the preconditions of reflection (e.g., the attitudes for reflection, the tutorial context in which reflection occurs), and the product of reflection (e.g., effective teaching, emancipation, an understanding of the relationship between values and practice). There is also considerable variance in the way in which concepts have been justified and defended and related to the context of professional education. Reflective teaching has been justified on grounds ranging from moral responsibility to technical effectiveness, and reflection has been incorporated into teacher education courses as divergent as those employing a behavioral skills approach, in which reflection is viewed as a means to the achievement of certain prescribed practices, to those committed to a critical science approach in which reflection is seen as a means toward emancipation and professional autonomy. (pp. 44–45)

The next major attempt to sort out the conceptual confusion with regard to reflective practice in teaching and teacher education came with Grimmett, MacKinnon, Erickson, and Riecken's (1990) presentation of a theoretical framework describing different conceptions of reflection. This analysis rests on differences in the epistemological assumptions in various bodies of work. Grimmett et al. identified three major conceptual orientations to reflective practice based on differences in what is being reflected upon, how the reflective process is engaged, and the purpose of reflection. For each orientation described, they consider the relationship between knowledge and reflection in terms of three categories: (a) the source of the knowledge that is reflected upon, (b) the mode of knowing represented by a particular conception of reflection (technical, deliberative, dialectical), and (c) the use to which knowledge is put as a result of the reflective process (to direct, inform, or apprehend/transform action). This analysis led to the identification of three general conceptual orientations: reflection as instrumental mediation of action—where knowledge is used to direct practice; reflection as deliberating among competing views of teaching—where knowledge is used to inform practice; and reflection as reconstructing experience—where knowledge is used to help teachers apprehend and transform practice.

In the same volume where this framework appeared, Valli (1990a), implying a distinction between technical and moral approaches to reflective practice, identified three approaches to reflective teacher education that emphasize the moral foundations of teaching: the deliberative approach, the relational approach, and the critical approach. Valli distinguished these approaches along three dimensions: the role of reflection in the approach, what content is considered to be worthy of reflection, and how each approach teaches students to evaluate ethical decisions. For example, in the deliberative approach, reflection serves to move students' attention beyond an exclusive focus on technical concerns to consider the moral dimensions of teaching. In the relational approach, reflection provides the grounds for caring relations. Finally, in the critical approach, reflection helps make knowledge problematic and to "give voice" to teachers.

Several other important distinctions among different notions of reflection have been made in the teacher education literature, short of these four ambitious attempts to map the conceptual dimensions of the field. The first distinction is between those programs of work that emphasize reflection as a private activity to be pursued in isolation by individual teachers and those which seek to facilitate reflection as a social practice and public activity involving communities of teachers. The emphasis has clearly been in on the later view even in the United States, where an ethos of individualism typically reigns supreme (Cagan, 1978).[2] There has been clear recognition of the need to provide a social forum for teachers' reflections.

> Lack of social converse actually inhibits the healthy construction of personal beliefs because these only become real and clear to us when we can speak about them to others. Constructive reflection on classroom experience will require us to provide a social forum for discussion. (Solomon, 1987, p. 271)

The recent literature on teacher education is filled with descriptions of projects which seek to engage teachers *with one another* in thinking about the purposes and consequences of their work. Collaborative action research (Lucas, 1988; Robottom, 1988), collaborative autobiography (Raymond, 1990), dialogic writing activities (Maas, 1991), interactive approaches to the supervision of field experiences (Handal & Lauvas, 1987; Ruddick & Sigsworth, 1985), and various forms of structured collegial dialogue among teachers (e.g., Ashcroft & Griffiths, 1989; Berlak & Berlak, 1981; Pugach & Johnson, 1990) are just a few examples of instructional strategies that emphasize the social nature of the reflective process.

Another important distinction that is noted in the literature is between reflective teaching as a detached rational process and as a process imbued with an ethic of care and with passion. Greene (1986) and Noddings (1987) are two of those who have challenged the detached rationality that has dominated the literature in teacher education for a long time, including that on reflective teacher education. Their critiques go well beyond Schon's (1983) criticisms of technical rationality, because the problems they identify, the lack of care, compassion, and passion in actions, can also be a problem in the epistemology of practice that Schon proposes as the new paradigm for conceptualizing reflective practice.

Another distinction that was drawn by Zeichner (1987) is between those programs of work that have emphasized reflective inquiry in individual courses and program components, and those in which entire teacher education programs have been developed and/or redesigned with reflective inquiry as the guiding theme. Although there have been a few efforts to infuse reflective inquiry throughout the entire professional education component of teacher education programs (e.g., Beyer, 1988; Noordhoff & Kleinfeld, 1990; Tetrault & Braunger, 1989), most work of this kind has focused on individual courses and field experiences within a program and institutional structure that remains unchanged (Tom, 1985).

---

[2]Although Bartlett (1989) has charged that work in the United States has ignored the potential for reflective communities, more recent work in the United States (e.g., Bullough & Gitlin, 1991) has shifted away from the typical focus in the United States on reflection as a private activity involving isolated individuals.

One of the most notable characteristics of this emerging literature on reflective inquiry in teaching and teacher education is its ahistorical nature. Other than the efforts that have been made to situate individual projects in relation to the broader theories and world views from which they draw their support (e.g., critical theory), there have been few attempts to either discuss the emergence of the reflective inquiry movement over time or to locate individual projects in relation to the traditions of practice which have characterized the field itself. One consequence of this historical amnesia in teacher education is a lack of clarity about the theoretical and political commitments underlying specific proposals for reform.[3]

Several efforts have been made in recent years to identify the major traditions of practice in teacher education. These include analyses conducted in Australia (Kirk, 1986) the United Kingdom (Hartnett & Naish, 1980), and the United States (Feiman-Nemser, 1990, Joyce, 1975; Zeichner, 1983). Drawing on these frameworks, and on the seminal work of Kliebard (1986) on the development of the public school curriculum in the United States in the 20th century, Zeichner and Liston (1990) identified four major traditions of reform in U.S. teacher education.[4] This analysis was later extended by Zeichner and Tabachnick (1991) to address the specific issue of reflective practice in teaching and teacher education. Four historically based traditions of reflective teaching were discussed in this extension of the original framework: academic, social efficiency, developmentalist, and social reconstructionist. Finally, in a more recent analysis (Zeichner, 1992), this framework was extended again to include a fifth tradition of reflective practice, a generic tradition.

These five traditions of reflective practice in U.S. teaching and teacher education provide a way of situating proposals for reform in relation to the historical forces from which they emerged.[5] It is our belief that this historical perspective of traditions of practice is necessary for understanding the present.

A tradition is an argument extended through time in which certain fundamental agreements are defined and redefined in terms of two kinds of conflict: those with critics and enemies external to the tradition who reject all or at least key parts of those fundamental agreements, and those internal,

---

[3]Richardson's (1990) analysis of the evolution of reflective teaching and teacher education in the United States is one exception to the general ahistorical nature of the field.

[4]Also see Liston and Zeichner (1991) for a discussion of these traditions.

[5]What we have done with regard to traditions of reflective practice in teaching and teacher education is very similar to what Labaree (1990) has done in his analyses of the genealogy of teacher professionalism in the United States. In both cases, there is an attempt to establish the lines of descent which have led to particular reform proposals in the present.

interpretative debates through which the meaning and rationale of the fundamental agreements come to be expressed and by whose progress a tradition is constituted . . . To appeal to tradition is to insist that we cannot adequately identify either our own commitments or those of others in the argumentative conflicts of the present except by situating them within these histories which made them what they have now become. (MacIntyre, 1988, pp. 12–13)

After a brief discussion of the traditions of reflective practice in U.S. teacher education in the section to follow, we will consider the question of the relevance of this analytic framework to the broader international community of teacher educators. Although we must be careful not to apply blindly a set of traditions in one cultural context to other very different situations, it will be argued that the framework of U.S. traditions of reflective practice can be useful as a heuristic for helping non-U.S. teacher educators identify their own traditions of practice.

TRADITIONS OF REFLECTION IN U.S. TEACHER EDUCATION

In our examination of the development of teacher education in the U.S. during the 20th century (Zeichner & Liston, 1990), we concluded that there have been four distinct traditions of practice that have, at least implicitly, guided reform efforts. Although each of these traditions is very diverse (e.g., feminist and critical theory perspectives within social reconstructionism), they also each represent a common commitment to a core set of beliefs. Using this traditions framework, Tabachnick and I (Zeichner & Tabachnick, 1991) identified four varieties of reflective practice in U.S. teacher education: (a) an *academic* version that stresses reflection upon subject matter and the representation and translation of subject matter knowledge to promote student understanding; (b) a *social efficiency* version that emphasizes either the mechanical or thoughtful application of particular teaching strategies that have been suggested by a "knowledge base" external to the practice being studied; (c) a *developmentalist* version that prioritizes teaching that is sensitive to students' interests, thinking, and patterns of developmental growth; and (d) a social reconstructionist version that stresses reflection about the institutional, social, and political contexts of schooling and the assessment of classroom actions for their ability to contribute toward greater equality, justice, and humane conditions in schooling and society. In addition to these four traditions, Zeichner (1992) identified a fifth tradition, a *generic* version of reflection in which reflection in general is advocated without much specificity about the desired purposes and content of the reflection.

Despite the differences in emphasis given to various factors within the different traditions of reflective practice, these traditions are not mutually exclusive. In practice, the traditions overlap and each one attends in some manner to all the issues raised by the traditions as a group. The differences among the traditions are in terms of the emphasis and meaning given to particular factors within a tradition. Through these priorities and particular ways of giving meaning to the issues raised by each perspective, each tradition communicates an allegiance to particular styles of teaching and a rejection of others.[6] With the exception of the social reconstructionist tradition, the traditions reflect a benign view of the social order.[7]

The Academic Tradition

Prior to the existence of formal programs of teacher education in the United States, a classical liberal education was equivalent to being prepared to teach (Borrowman, 1965). As programs for the preparation of both elementary and secondary teachers became established in colleges and universities, the point of view persisted that a sound liberal arts education, complemented by an apprenticeship experience in a school, was the most sensible way to prepare teachers for their work. The academic tradition of reform in 20th-century U.S. teacher education has historically emphasized the role of the liberal arts and disciplinary knowledge in teacher preparation and with the exception of clinical experiences, has belittled the contribution of schools, colleges, and departments of education (e.g., Koerner, 1963). This orientation emphasizes the teacher's role as a scholar and subject matter specialist and has taken many different forms over the years.

---

[6]Some, such as Tom (1991), have proposed a synthesis of the various traditions that treats each one equally. I accept the view that individual teacher education programs need to address all of the traditions. I have also rejected the ideological insularity that characterizes the field and have argued for more dialogue and critique among teacher educators across the various traditions. I reject, though, the ideological even-handedness that Tom (1991) and others have called for, because it denies the inevitable reality that the meaning of each tradition in a program will be different depending on the educational and social philosophies of the teacher educators working in that program. For example, the meaning of the social efficiency focus on the development of technical skills of teaching will be very different in a program that makes the development of generic skills its major goal, than it will be in a program that situates these skills within particular subject areas, in relation to particular conceptions of development, or in relation to the achievement of educational and social equity. The guiding tradition in particular programs will help define the ways in which all of the other traditions are dealt with by teacher educators. There can never be a grand synthesis, as Tom proposes, that washes away ideological differences.

[7]See Zeichner (1991) for an example of how a tradition (in this case social reconstructionism) gives a particular meaning to the issues raised by each perspective.

Recently, Shulman (1986, 1987) and Buchmann, (1984) among others, have advocated views of reflective practice which emphasize the teacher's deliberations about subject matter and its transformation to pupils to promote understanding. Shulman and Buchmann, however, are unlike many others within the academic tradition who have advocated only exposure to subject matter content. Their views represent a challenge to historically dominant notions of academically oriented reform. For example, Shulman and his colleagues in the "Knowledge Growth in Teaching Project" (Wilson, Shulman, & Richert, 1987), have proposed a model of pedagogical reasoning and action, and of the professional knowledge base for teaching, which places the emphasis on the intellectual basis for teaching and on the transformation of subject matter knowledge by teachers. Their model of the professional knowledge base for teaching includes three major categories of knowledge: subject matter content knowledge (what has traditionally been emphasized within the academic tradition), pedagogical content knowledge, and curricular knowledge. Their model of pedagogical reasoning identifies six aspects of the teaching act: comprehension, transformation, instruction, evaluation, reflection, and new comprehension. Both of these frameworks reflect a clear emphasis in their conception of reflective practice on the content to be taught. Shulman's (1987) discussion of representation (an aspect of the transformation process) illustrated this emphasis.

> Representation involves thinking through the key ideas in the text or lesson and identifying the alternative ways of representing them to students. What analogies, metaphors, examples, demonstrations, simulations, and the like can help build a bridge between the teacher's comprehension and that desired for the students? Multiple forms of representation are desirable. (p. 328)

Although this conception of reflective practice does not necessarily ignore general pedagogical knowledge derived from research on teaching, students' understandings and developmental characteristics, and issues of social justice and equity, the standards for assessing the adequacy of the teaching evolve primarily from the academic disciplines.

The Social Efficiency Tradition

The social efficiency tradition of reform in U.S. teacher education, one version of progressivism in American educational thought (Cremin, 1961), has historically emphasized faith in the scientific study of teaching to provide a basis for building a teacher education curriculum. According to contemporary advocates of this view, research on teaching has, in recent years, provided a "knowledge base" that can form the foundation for teacher education curriculum (e.g., Berliner, 1984; Good, 1990).

Feiman-Nemser (1990) identified two different ways in which contemporary teacher educators have interpreted the social efficiency perspective. First, there is a technological version, in which the intent is to teach prospective teachers the skills and competencies research has shown to be associated with desirable pupil outcomes. This narrow interpretation of the social efficiency view emphasizes reflection by teachers about how closely their practice conforms to standards provided by some aspect of research on teaching (e.g., Gentile, 1988).

A second and broader interpretation of the social efficiency tradition, the "deliberative orientation," is one in which the findings of research on teaching are used by teachers, along with other information, to solve teaching problems. According to advocates of this deliberative orientation, the crucial task for teacher educators is to foster teachers' capabilities to exercise their judgment about the use of various teaching skills while taking advantage of research, experience, intuition, and their own values (Zumwalt, 1982).

This broader view of the research–practice relationship in teaching is illustrated by Ross and Kyle's (1987) comments concerning teaching as a decision making process.

> The limits on the appropriate use of teacher effectiveness research must be understood by prospective teachers . . . the most important teacher behavior is the flexibility and judgment necessary to select the appropriate strategy for the particular goal and students involved. (p. 41)

Although this conception of reflective practice does not totally ignore the social context of schooling, issues of equity and social justice, student understandings and developmental characteristics, or subject matter, the emphasis is clearly on the intelligent use of "generic" teaching skills and strategies which have been suggested by research.

The Developmentalist Tradition

The distinguishing characteristic of the developmentalist tradition (another strand of progressivism in U.S. education–Perrone, 1989), is the assumption that the natural development of the learner provides the basis for determining what should be taught to students and how it should be taught. Historically, this natural order of child development was to be determined by research involving the careful observation and description of students' behavior at various stages of development (Mitchell, 1931).

According to Perrone (1989), three central metaphors have been associated with the progressive/developmentalist tradition in U.S. teacher education: teacher as naturalist, teacher as researcher, and teacher as artist. The teacher-as-naturalist dimension has stressed the importance of skill in the observation of students' behavior and in building a curriculum and classroom environment consistent with patterns of child development and children's interests. Classroom practice is to be grounded in close observation and study of children in the classroom, either directly by the teacher, or from reflection on a literature based on such study. The teacher-as-researcher strand of this tradition has emphasized the need to foster the teacher's experimental attitude toward practice and to help teachers initiate and sustain ongoing inquiries in their own classrooms. Finally, the teacher-as-artist element has emphasized the link between creative and fully functioning persons in touch with their own learning and stimulating classrooms.

One contemporary example of reflective teaching practice within this tradition is the work of Duckworth at Harvard University. Duckworth (1987) elaborated a constructivist view of reflective teaching which emphasizes engaging learners with phenomena, instead of explaining things to students at the onset (see also Fosnot, 1989; Sigel, 1990). According to Duckworth, teachers are both practitioners and researchers, and their research should be focused on their students and their current understandings of topics under study. The teacher then uses this knowledge of student understandings to decide the appropriate next steps for their learning, and keeps trying to find out what sense the students are making as the instruction continues.

> The essential element of having the students do the explaining is not the withholding of all the teacher's own thoughts. It is, rather, that the teacher not consider herself or himself the final arbiter of what the learner should think, nor the creator of what the learner does think. The important job for the teacher is to keep trying to find out what sense the students are making. (Duckworth, 1987, p. 133)

This developmental conception of reflective teaching has become increasingly popular in recent years with the growing influence of cognitive psychology in education. Although it does not ignore subject matter standards emanating from the disciplines, research on teaching, and the social and political contexts of schooling and issues of equity and social justice, the emphasis is on reflecting about students and/or on one's own development as a teacher and person.

The Social Reconstructionist Tradition

In the social reconstructionist tradition, schooling and teacher education are both viewed as crucial elements in the movement toward a more just and humane society. According to Valli (1990a), proponents of this approach (which draws on various neo-Marxist, feminist, and critical perspectives) argue

> that schools as social institutions, help reproduce a society based on unjust class, race, and gender relations and that teachers have a moral obligation to reflect on and change their own practices and school structures when these perpetuate such arrangements. (p. 46)

In a social reconstructionist conception of reflective teaching, the teachers' attention is focused both inwardly at their own practice *and* outwardly at the social conditions in which these practices are situated (Kemmis, 1985). How teachers' actions maintain and/or disrupt the status quo in schooling and society is of central concern. The reflection is aimed, in part, at the elimination of the social conditions that distort the self-understandings of teachers and undermine the educative potential and moral basis of schooling.

A second characteristic of a social reconstructionist conception of reflective teaching is its democratic and emancipatory impulse and the focus of teachers' deliberations upon the substantive issues that raise instances of inequality and injustice within schooling and society for close scrutiny. Recognizing the fundamentally political character of all teaching actions, teachers consider such issues as the gendered nature of schooling and teachers work, and the racial and social class issues embedded in everyday classroom actions (Liston & Zeichner, 1990). As one advocate of this perspective argues

> The activities of the classroom frequently carry with them as a part of their own identity, meanings and values that are inherently political . . . some of the most commonplace, seemingly innocent activities of classroom, from segregating students by 'ability,' to discussing U.S. presidents in high school history, to 'individualizing' the curriculum in elementary schools, promote political and ideological interests . . . Since school practice cannot be separated from larger social, political, and ideological realities, they (teachers) must be reflective about the full range of consequences of their actions. (Beyer, 1989, pp. 37, 39, 41)

There are a variety of consequences associated with all teacher actions. Pollard and Tann (1987) identified three such implications: (a) personal—the effects of classroom actions on students' self-images, (b) academic—the effects of classroom actions on students' intellectual achievement, and (c) social—the cumulative effects of school experiences on students' life chances. Although a social reconstructionist perspective involves concern about the personal and academic implications of classroom actions, it is the only one of the traditions that *extends* the analysis to consider the social and political implications of actions as well. It is the only one of the traditions that does not adopt a benign view of the social conditions of schooling.

The third characteristic of a social reconstructionist conception of reflective teaching is its commitment to reflection as a *social* practice. Here the intent is to create communities of learning where prospective teachers can support and sustain each other's growth. This commitment to collaborative modes of learning indicates a dual commitment by teacher educators to an ethic where social justice and equity, on the one hand, and care and compassion, on the other, are valued. This commitment is also thought to be of strategic value in the transformation of unjust and inhumane institutional and social structures, because it is felt that if teachers see their individual situations linked to those of their colleagues, the likelihood of structural change is greater (Freedman, Jackson, & Boles, 1983).

Generic Reflection

In addition to these four traditions of reflective practice in U.S. teaching and teacher education, there has recently been a great deal of advocacy for reflective teaching in general, without much comment about what it is the reflection should be focused on, the criteria that should be used to evaluate the quality of the reflection, or the degree to which teachers' deliberations should incorporate a critique of the social and institutional contexts in which they work. The implication here is that teachers actions are necessarily better just because they are more deliberate or intentional.

> *How* to get students to reflect can take on a life of its own, and can become *the* programmatic goal. *What* they reflect on can become immaterial. For example, racial tension as a school issue can become no more or less worthy of reflection than field trips or homework assignments. (Valli, 1990b, p. 9)

One of the clearest examples of this tendency to advocate reflection in general is found in the Ohio State University materials on Reflective Teaching (Cruickshank, 1987). Drawing on the important distinction made by Dewey (1933) between reflective action and routine action, Cruickshank (1987) argued that teachers need to become more reasoned actors, without at all addressing the issues of the content, quality, and context of the reflection.

> The point is that teachers who study teaching deliberately and become students of teaching can develop life-long assurance that they know what they are doing, why they are doing it, and what will happen as a result of

what they do. Foremost, they can learn to behave according to reason. To lack reason is to be a slave to chance, irrationality, self-interest, and superstition. (p. 34)

In identifying these five different orientations to reflective practice in teaching and teacher education, I am not suggesting that individual teacher education programs can be viewed as pure examples of any one of the orientations. On the contrary, all teacher education programs will reflect some pattern of resonance with the various orientations, emphasizing some and marginalizing others, and defining each one in a way that reflects the particular set of priorities in a particular situation (see Zeichner, in press). Similarly, certain emphases and absences can be detected in any given set of programs or in the reflective teacher education movement as a whole, in terms of the different orientations. The question still remains however, about the usefulness of this analytic framework for understanding approaches to reflective practice in teaching and teacher education outside of the United States. We cannot automatically assume that a set of traditions identified in one cultural context is relevant to understanding other situations.

CONCLUSION

The identification of traditions of reflective practice in teaching and teacher education must, in the final analysis, be based on a study of the historical development of teaching and teacher education in particular countries. Our framework of reform traditions in 20th-century U.S. teacher education grew out of careful study of the U.S. context. What is the usefulness then of this framework to non-U.S. teacher educators?

One way in which the framework can be used is to stimulate similar analyses of reform traditions in other countries. Although there are several existing attempts to develop accounts of theoretical discourse in teacher education across national boundaries (e.g., Kirk, 1986) that do in fact capture some of the common elements in different countries, we need also to begin to understand the aspects of traditions of reflective practice that are unique to specific countries. Tabachnick (1989) discussed some of the problems of misinterpretation that arise when scholarship from one country is imported into another without sensitivity to the cultural conditions in both situations.

Although it is tempting to fit non-U.S. teacher education projects into the category system outlined in this chapter, to do so would distort the meaning of these projects. For example, Korthagen and Wubbels's (1991) account of the approach to reflective teaching at the University of Ultrecht in the Netherlands appeared on the surface to be very similar to the developmentalist notion of teacher reflection espoused by Duckworth (1987) and others in the United States. Beyond these surface similarities, however, there are substantive differences in the projects that relate to the very different histories and structures of education in the two countries.

While these differences in traditions of reflection exist between the U.S. and other industrialized Western nations, they are even more pronounced when we bring non-Western countries into the picture. One example of this is the work currently underway in Thailand (e.g., Thongthew, 1988) to implement reflective teacher education programs that are rooted in Buddhist principles. It is impossible to understand this work in terms of the Western rationality that underlies the reform traditions outlined in this chapter.

Of the four papers discussed in the beginning of this chapter which sought to bring greater conceptual clarity to discourse on reflective teacher education, only the Valli paper limits itself to the context of a single country (the U.S.). Tom, Calderead, and Grimmett et al. all lump together literature and people from several countries in an attempt to map out the conceptual parameters of an international movement. It has been argued here that this approach is misguided, and that more attention needs to be given to the historical and cultural conditions in particular settings. This is not to say that there is nothing that we can learn in one culture that is useful to teacher educators in another. It does say, though, that we need to demonstrate cultural sensitivity when we attempt to make these connections.

Finally, a fundamental message that this chapter attempts to convey to teacher educators of other countries, whatever the differences between these other countries and my own, is that all of us need to begin asking others as well as ourselves more questions about the nature and purposes of teacher reflection as a goal in teacher education. We need to move beyond the current state where reflective teaching by itself is seen as a distinct program emphasis to recognition of the fact that all teachers are reflective in some sense. Given this reality, we must be interested in more complex questions than whether teaching is reflective or not. The important issues are concerned with the particular kinds of reflection that we want to encourage in our teacher education programs, among ourselves, between ourselves and our students and among our students. This message is relevant to teacher educators in every cultural context.

REFERENCES

Altrichter, H. (1988). Enquiry-based learning in initial teacher education. In J. Nias & S. Groundwater-Smith (Eds.), *The enquiring teacher* (pp. 121–134). London: Falmer Press.

Ashcroft, K., & Griffiths M. (1989). Reflective teachers and reflective tutors: School experience in an initial teacher education course. *Journal of Education for Teaching, 15* (1), 35–52.
Bartlett, L. (1989). Images of reflection: A look and a review. *Qualitative Studies in Education, 2* (4), 351–357.
Berlak, A., & Berlak, H. (1981). *Dilemmas of schooling: Teaching and social change.* New York: Methuen.
Berliner, D. (1984). The half-full glass: A review of research on teaching. In P. Hosford (Ed.), *Using what we know about teaching* (pp. 51–77). Alexandria, VA: Association of Supervision & Curriculum Development.
Beyer, L. (1988). *Knowing and acting: Inquiry in idealogy, and educational studies.* London: Falmer Press.
Beyer, L. (1989). *Critical reflection and the culture of schooling: Empowering teachers.* Geelong, Australia: Deakin University Press.
Borrowman, M. (1965). Liberal education and the professional preparation of teachers. In M. L. Borrowman (Ed.), *Teacher education in the U.S.: A documentary history.* New York: Teachers College Press.
Boud, D. Keogh, R., & Walker, D. (1985). Promoting reflection in learning: A model. In D. Boud, R. Keogh, & D. Walker (Eds.), *Reflection: Turning experience into learning.* London: Kogan Page.
Buchmann, M. (1984). The priority of knowledge and understanding in teaching. In L. Katz & J. Raths (Eds.), *Advances in teacher education* (Vol. 1, 29–50). Norwood, NJ: Ablex.
Bullough, R., & Gitlin, A. (1991). Toward educative communities: Teacher education and the development of the reflective practitioner. In B. R. Tabachnick & K. Zeichner (Eds.) *Issues & practices in inquiry-oriented teacher education.* London: Falmer Press.
Cagan, E. (1978). Individualism, collectionism, and radical education reform. *Harvard Educational Review, 48* (2), 227–266.
Calderhead, J. (1989). Reflective teaching and teacher education. *Teaching and Teacher Education, 5* (1), 43–51.
Clandinin, J., & Connelly, F. M. (1986). The reflective practitioner and the practitioners narrative unities. *Canadian Journal of Education, 11* (2), 184–198.
Clift, R. Houston, W. R., & Pugach, M. (1990). *Encouraging reflective practice: An examination of issues & examples.* New York: Teachers College Press.
Cremin, L. (1961). *The transformation of the school: Progressivism in American education, 1876–1957.* New York: Harper & Row.
Cruickshank, D. (1987). *Reflective teaching.* Reston, VA: Association of Teacher Educators.
Dewey, J. (1933). *How we think.* Chicago: Henry Regnery.
Duckworth, E. (1987). *The having of wonderful ideas.* New York: Teachers College Press.
Erickson, G., & Mackinnon, A. (1991). Seeing classrooms in new ways: On becoming a science teacher. In D. Schon (Ed.), *The reflective turn: Case studies in and on educational practice* (pp. 15–36). New York: Teachers College Press.
Feiman-Nemser, S. (1990). Teacher preparation: Structural and conceptual alternatives. In W. R. Houston (Ed.), *Handbook of research on teacher education* (pp. 212–233). New York: Macmillan.
Fosnot, C. T. (1989). *Enquiring teachers, enquiring learners: A constructionist approach for teaching.* New York: Teachers College Press.
Freedman, S., Jackson, J., & Boles, K. (1983). Teaching: An imperiled profession. In L. Shulman & G. Sykes (Eds.), *Handbook of teaching & policy* (pp. 261–299). New York: Longman.
Freire, P. (1973). *Education for critical consciousness.* New York: Seabury Press.
Gentile, J. R. (1988). *Instructional improvement: Summary and analysis of Madeline Hunter's essential elements of instruction and supervision.* Oxford, OH: National Staff Development Council.

Good, T. (1990). Building the knowledge base of teaching. In D. Dill (Ed.), *What teachers need to know* (pp. 17–75). San Francisco: Jossey Bass.

Gore, J. (1987). Reflecting on reflective teaching. *Journal of Teacher Education, 38* (2), 22–39.

Greene, M. (1986). Reflection & passion in teaching. *Journal of Curriculum & Supervision, 2* (1), 68–81.

Grimmett, P., & Crehan, E. P. (1990, April). *Conditions which facilitate and inhibit teacher reflection in clinical supervision: Collegiality re-examined.* Paper presented at the annual meeting of the American Educational Research Association, Boston.

Grimmett, P. MacKinnon, A. Erickson, G., & Riecken, T. (1990). Reflective practice in teacher education. In R. Clift, W. R. Houston, & M. Pugach (Eds.), *Encouraging reflective practice in education* (pp. 20–38). New York: Teachers College Press.

Habermas, J. (1974). *Theory & practice.* London: Heinemann.

Handal, G., & Lauvas, P. (1987). *Promoting reflective teaching.* Milton Keynes, UK: Open University Press.

Hartnett, A., & Naish, M. (1980). Technicians or social bandits? Some moral and political issues in the education of teachers. In P. Woods (Ed.), *Teacher strategies* (pp. 254–274). London: Croom Helm.

Joyce, B. (1975). Conceptions of man and their implications for teacher education. In K. Ryan (Ed.), *Teacher education.* Chicago: University of Chicago Press.

Kemmis, S. (1985). Action research and the politics of reflection. In D. Boud, R. Keogh, & D. Walker (Eds.) *Reflection: Turning experience into learning* (pp. 139–164). London: Croom Helm.

Kirk, D. (1986). Beyond the limits of theoretical discourse in teacher education: Towards a critical pedagogy. *Teaching and Teacher Education, 2,* 155–167.

Kliebard, H. (1986). *The struggle for the American curriculum, 1893–1958.* Boston: Routledge & Kegan Paul.

Koerner, J. (1963). *The miseducation of American teachers.* Boston: Houghton Mifflin.

Korthagen, F. (1985). Reflective teaching and preservice teacher education. *Journal of Teacher Education, 36* (5), 11–15.

Korthagen, F., & Wubbles, T. (1991, April). *Characteristics of reflective practitioners: Towards an operationalization of the concept of reflection.* Paper presented at the annual meeting of the American Educational Research Association, Chicago.

Kottkamp, R. (1990) Means for facilitating reflection. *Education & Urban Society, 22* (2), 182–203.

Kremer-Hayon, L. (1990). Reflection and professional knowledge: A conceptual framework. In C. Day, M. Pope, & P. Denicolo (Eds.), *Insight into teachers' thinking & practice* (pp. 57–70). London: Falmer Press.

Labaree, D. (1990, April). *Power, Knowledge, and the science of teaching: A genealogy of teacher professionalization* Michigan State University, East Lansing, MI.

LaBoskey, V. K. (1990, April). *Reflectivity in preservice teachers: Alert novices vs. common sense thinkers.* Paper presented at the annual meeting of the American Educational Research Association, Boston.

Liston, D., & Zeichner, K. (1990). Teacher education and the social context of schooling. *American Educational Research Journal, 27* (4), 610–638.

Liston, D., & Zeichner, K. (1991). *Teacher education and the social conditions of schooling.* New York: Routledge.

Lucas, P. (1988). An approach to research-based teacher education through collaborative inquiry. *Journal of Education for Teaching, 14* (1), 55–73.

Maas, J. (1991). Writing and reflection in teacher education. In B. R. Tabachnick & K. Zeichner (Eds.), *Issues and practices in inquiry-oriented teacher education.* Philadelphia: Falmer Press.

MacIntyre, A. (1988). *Whose justice? which rationality?* Notre Dame, IN: University of Notre Dame Press.

MacKinnon, A., & Erickson, G. (1988). Taking Schon's ideas to a science teaching practicum. In P. Grimmett & G. Erickson (Eds.), *Reflection in teacher education* (pp. 113–138). New York: Teachers College Press.

Martinez, K. (1989). *Critical reflections on critical reflection in teacher education.* Paper presented at the Fourth National Conference on the Practicum in Teacher Education, Rockhampton, Australia.

Mezirow, J. (1990). How critical reflection triggers transformative learning. In J. Mezirow & Associates (Eds.), *Fostering critical reflection in adulthood.* San Francisco: Jossey-Bass.

Mitchell, L. S. (1931). Cooperative schools for student teachers. *Progressive Education, 8,* 251–255.

Noddings, N. (1987). Fidelity in teaching, teacher education and research for teaching. In M. Okazawa-Rey, J. Anderson, & R. Traver (Eds.), *Teachers, teaching, and teacher education,* (Reprint Series No. 19, pp. 384–400). Cambridge, MA: Harvard Educational Review.

Noordhoff, K., & Kleinfeld, J. (1990). Shaping the rhetoric of reflection for multicultural settings. In R. Clift, W. R. Houston, & M. Pugach (Eds.), *Encouraging reflective practice in education* (pp. 163–185). New York: Teachers College Press.

Perrone, V. (1989). Teacher education and progressivism: A historical perspective. In V. Perrone, *Working papers: Reflections on teachers, schools & communities.* New York: Teachers College Press.

Pollard, A., & Tann, S. (1987). *Reflective teaching in the primary school.* London: Cassell.

Posner, G. (1989). *Field experiences: Methods of reflective teaching* (2nd ed.). New York: Longman.

Pugach, M., & Johnson, L. (1990). Developing reflective practice. In R. Clift, W. R. Houston, & M. Pugach (Eds.), *Encouraging reflective practice in education* (pp. 186–207). New York: Teachers College Press.

Raymond, D. (1990, April). *Focused biographical inquiry in preservice teacher education.* Paper presented at the annual meeting of the American Educational Research Association, Boston.

Richardson, V. (1990). The evolution of reflective teaching and teacher education. In R. Clift, W. R. Houston, & M. Pugach (Eds.), *Encouraging reflective practice in education* (pp. 3–19). New York: Teachers College Press.

Richert, A. (1990). Teaching teachers to reflect: A consideration of programme structure. *Journal of Curriculum Studies, 22* (6), 509–527.

Robottom, I. (1988). A research-based course in science education. In J. Nias & S. Groundwater-Smith (Eds.), *The enquiring teacher: Supporting & sustaining teacher research.* London: Falmer Press.

Ross, D. (1990). Programmatic structures for the preparation of reflective teachers. In. R. Clift, W. R. Houston, & M. Pugach (Eds.), *Encouraging reflective practice in education* (pp. 97–118). New York: Teachers College Press.

Ross, D., & Krogh, S. (1988). From paper to program: A story from elementary PROTE-ACH. *Peabody Journal of Education, 65* (2), 19–34.

Ross, D., & Kyle, D. (1987). Helping preservice teachers learn to use teacher effectiveness research. *Journal of Teacher Education, 38,* 40–44.

Ruddick, J., & Sigsworth, A. (1985). Partnership supervision (or Goldhammer revisited). In D. Hopkins & K. Reid (Eds.), *Rethinking teacher education.* London: Crown Helm.

Russell, T. (1991, April). *Critical attributes of a reflective teacher.* Paper presented at the annual meeting of the American Educational Research Association, Chicago.

Russell, T., & Munby, H. (1991). Reframing: The role of experience in developing teachers–professional knowledge. In D. Schon (Ed.), *The reflective turn: Case studies in and on educational practice* (pp. 164–188). New York: Teachers College Press.

Schon, D. (1983). *The reflective practitioner*. New York: Basic Books.

Schon, D. (1987). *Educating the reflective practitioner*. San Francisco: Jossey Bass.

Schwab, J. (1971). The practical: Arts of eclectic. *School Review, 79*, 493–543.

Shulman, L. (1986). Those who understand: Knowledge growth in teaching. *Educational Researcher, 15* (2), 4–14.

Shulman, L. (1987). Knowledge and teaching: Foundations of the new reform. *Harvard Educational Review, 57*, 1–22.

Sigel, I. (1990). What teachers need to know about human development. In D. Dill (Ed.), *What teachers need to know* (pp. 76–93). San Francisco: Jossey Bass.

Smith, R., & Sachs, J. (1988). It really made me stop and think: Ethnography in preservice teacher education. In J. Nias & S. Groundwater-Smith (Eds.), *The enquiring teacher* (pp. 71–84). London: Falmer Press.

Solomon, J. (1987). New thoughts on teacher education. *Oxford Review of Education, 13* (3), 267– 274.

Tabachnick, B. R. (1989). Needed for teacher education: Naturalistic research that is culturally responsive. *Teaching and Teacher Education, 5* (2), 155–163.

Tabachnick, B. R., & Zeichner, K. (1991). *Issues and practices in inquiry-oriented teacher education*. London: Falmer Press.

Tetreault, M. K., & Braunger, J. (1989). Improving mentor teacher seminars: Feminist theory and practice at Lewis & Clark College. In J. DeVitis & P. Sola (Eds.), *Building bridges for educational reform: New approaches to teacher education* (pp. 63–86). Ames, IA: Iowa State University Press.

Thongthew, S. (1988). Innovative model for teacher education in Thailand. *Proceedings of the First Asia-Pacific Conference on Teacher Education: New directions for a changing world*. Bangkok: Chulalongkorn University.

Tom, A. (1985). Inquiring into inquiry-oriented teacher education. *Journal of Teacher Education, 36* (5), 35–44.

Tom, A. (1991). Whither the professional curriculum for teachers? *Review of Education, 14*, 21–30.

Valli, L. (1990a). Moral approaches to reflective practice. In R. Clift, W. R. Houston, & M. Pugach (Eds.) *Encouraging reflective practice in education* (pp. 39–56). New York: Teachers College Press.

Valli, L. (1990b, April). *The question of quality and content in reflective teaching*. Paper presented at the annual meeting of the American Educational Research Association, Boston.

Valli, L. (1992). *Reflective teacher education: Cases and critiques*. Albany: State University of New York Press.

Wedman, J., & Martin M. (1986). Exploring the development of reflective thinking through journal writing. *Reading Improvement, 23* (1), 68–71.

Wilson, S. Shulman, L., & Richert, A. (1987). 150 different ways of knowing: Representations of knowledge in teaching. In J. Calderhead (Ed.), *Exploring teachers thinking* (pp. 104–124). London: Cassell.

Wubbels, T., & Korthagen, F. (1990). The effects of a preservice teacher education program for the preparation of reflective teachers. *Journal of Education for Teaching, 16* (1), 29–44.

Zeichner, K. (1983). Alternative paradigms of teacher education. *Journal of Teacher Education, 34* (3), 3–9.

Zeichner, K. (1987). Preparing reflective teachers. *International Journal of Educational Research, 11* (5), 565–575.

Zeichner, K. (1991, April). *Teacher education for social responsibility*. Paper presented at the annual meeting of the American Educational Research Association, Chicago, IL.

Zeichner, K. (1992). Conceptions of reflective teaching in contemporary U.S. teacher education program reforms. In L. Valli (Ed.), *Reflective teacher education: Cases and critiques* (pp. 161-172). Albany: State University of New York Press.

Zeichner, K., & Liston, D. (1985). Varieties of discourse in supervisory conferences. *Teaching & Teacher Education, 1*, 155-174.

Zeichner, K., & Liston, D. (1990). Traditions of reform in U.S. teacher education. *Journal of Teacher Education, 41* (2), 3-20.

Zeichner, K., & Tabachnick, B. R. (1991). Reflections on reflective teaching. In B. R. Tabachnick & K. Zeichner (Eds.), *Issues and practices in inquiry-oriented teacher education.* London: Falmer Press.

Zumwalt, K. (1982). Research on teaching: Policy implications for teacher education. In A. Lieberrman & M. McLaughlin (Eds.), *Policy making in education* (pp. 215-248). Chicago: University of Chicago Press.

CHAPTER 3

Experiential Learning in the Context of Teacher Education*

Ian Jamieson
School of Education University of Bath, Avon, England

Few if any would doubt that experience is important in the education of teachers. In common with all of the practitioner professions like medicine, law, or architecture, it is conceded that there are limits to what can be taught directly to students; time has to be set aside for them to acquire some experience of practice. It is at this point that the important questions and qualifications begin. Is any experience to count—and if the answer to this is only "relevant" experience, then what is to count as relevant experience? Is experience enough by itself, or does it need to be structured or supervised in some way? Are there different types of teaching experience students should be exposed to? How much experience do students require to reach minimum levels of competence, or can such questions only be answered on an individual level? What evidence have we that students learn from experience? Are there useful models of experiential learning that can be applied in teacher education?

Before we begin to address some of these questions, it is important that we consider them in the context of current models of both preservice and inservice education. This analysis is largely based on the present situation in the United Kingdom.

As far as the training of student teachers goes there are many impediments to developing an experiential model of teacher education that go

---

*I would like to acknowledge the helpful comments on an earlier draft by James Calderhead and José Chambers.

beyond the idea that students should be exposed to classroom practice. The first impediment is institutional: the fact that initial teacher education is conducted in the academy. The academy, particularly the university, is dominated by knowledge that is abstract, theoretical, conceptual, and propositional. The universities are the home of the historical distrust of the experiences of the senses which has its origin in Plato. To secure knowledge that is dependable, Plato believed, one must move away from the empirical world that our senses come to know and move into the world of abstraction. As a consequence of this, universities, particularly British universities, have resisted the incursions of the practical. Although education alongside law, medicine, business management, and so on have a place in the university system, it has been conceded slowly, and it is still the case that much teaching of these areas, particularly the practical elements, is relegated to lower status nonuniversity institutions.

To this historical legacy we can add one that is particularly applicable to education alone. In the context of teaching in the 19th century in British public schools, from which so many of our images and conceptions of teaching have come, we have to understand the common background and interests of teachers and taught. As Simon (1988) argued,

> The schools, in an important sense, were extensions of the home, largely financed by the parents themselves . . . the products of a close collaboration between parents and teachers. The teachers' pastoral responsibility – in terms of upbringing – was as important, or more so than his (or her) intellectual (teaching) responsibility . . . the process did not require the application of specifically "pedagogical" means. Approaches to teaching were traditional, handed down from generation to generation. (p. 338)

This certainly is one of the origins of the view that teaching consists essentially of the relatively unproblematic transmission of information. It is a view that has particular resonance among the political right. There are several reasons for this. In the first place most of the powerful right-wing pressure groups in the United Kingdom share the same public school experience alluded to by Simon, and they tend to see pedagogy as unproblematic. Secondly, what they see of pedagogy concerns them. They tend to take the view that it lacks intellectual soundness and that it supports a progressive, pupil-centered ideology that is neither effective nor in tune with the cultural values they cherish (Cox & Dyson, 1969; Lawlor, 1990). Thirdly, they are concerned about the quality of the knowledge that is being transmitted as much as by the transmission itself, particularly by nonuniversity educated teachers.

The final institutional problem faced by teacher education in the academy is one of scale. The original model of university education was somewhat akin to that of an apprenticeship. Small numbers of students were inducted into the mysteries of the professions (originally the priesthood). As university education has gradually become "massified," the tendency to acquire secondhand knowledge has grown. It is difficult on organizational grounds alone to resist students spending large amounts of time reading and writing about pedagogy instead of practicing and reflecting on it under the close supervision of a "master teacher." Large numbers conspire with higher education's natural predeliction to abstraction to inhibit the development of a proper vocationalism which fuses the theoretical and the practical.

One final institutional impediment is that many (most?) institutions of teacher education do not themselves have a clearly articulated and corporate view of the activity of teacher education. It is assumed, for example, that those teachers whom they recruit from schools as "excellent teachers" must have the skills of teacher educators despite the fact that the one activity deals with children and the other with adults. Sometimes there is a failure to recognize that there are some differences between adult learners and children as learners, or, if the difference is recognized, it is assumed that experts in the one can easily transfer their skills to the other. To this child/adult (pedagogy/androgogy) distinction we can add another: Schools are still dominated by getting children to "know that," whereas initial teacher education is much more concerned with "knowing how." This has fundamental implications for models of teaching and learning which are rarely clearly articulated and acknowledged.

It would be wrong to argue that the impediments to experiential learning in initial teacher education all stem from its location in higher education. There are three other countervailing forces. The first relates to the relative lack of a clearly articulated and disseminated theory of experiential learning. As we show, such a theory does exist, and writers like Kolb (1984) have done much to develop and popularize the earlier seminal work of Lewin (1951). In the last five years in the United Kingdom there have been a considerable number of straightforward guides on experiential learning that have taken us far beyond the simplicities of the slogan "I hear and I forget; I see and I remember; I do and I understand" (Dennison & Kirk, 1990; Gibbs, 1988; Weil & McGill, 1989). Such guides do have the merit of articulating a possible theory of action, but whether such guides can of themselves help students or teachers develop expertise in experiential learning is another matter. It may be the case that students must actively experience "experiential learning" with the help of a mentor or facilitator in order to acquire the necessary skills of reflection on action.

Even supposing that teacher trainers had access to such a theory, and that it had clear implications for teachers, there is little doubt that many student teachers would have resisted such models. The vast majority of students who elect for teacher training have been the successful products of an education system based on didacticism. Most of them have found this mode of teaching and learning unproblematic (and because of the streaming, banding, and setting arrangements in English secondary schools, they have largely been insulated from those students who did find it difficult). Most of their experience of teachers is of people teaching successfully in a didactic fashion. They have undergone what Lortie (1975) called an *apprenticeship of observation*. This argument is predicated on the assertion that English schools have been largely based on didactic modes of teaching. There is plenty of evidence to confirm such a view for the recent past (Galton, Simon, & Croll, 1980; HMI, 1979), but what of the belief that more "progressive" methods have penetrated secondary schools through national developments like Technical and Vocational Education Initiative (TVEI; a national, multimillion-pound initiative in curriculum change instituted in 1973 which has stressed, among other things, more flexible teaching and learning styles)? On the best available evidence that we have it would be fair to say that news of the revolution is premature (Barnes et al., 1987). Although TVEI has probably been effective in placing teaching and learning styles on the agenda of secondary schools, and the reform of the 16+ examination General Certificate of Secondary Education has certainly encouraged more student-centered learning, there has been no wholesale transformation. The "didactic contract" between teacher and taught, which allows classroom life to proceed smoothly, remains largely intact. This is important to the debate, because if the reality of schools was such that they demanded the teaching skills associated with active learning from students on teaching practice, and of new entrants to the profession, this would place enormous pressure on teacher training institutions and their students to conform.

When one turns to the education of practicing teachers, some of the barriers to the development of experiential learning are similar. The first is that inservice education is very often organized and taught by those in universities and other institutions of higher education; indeed, the very same people who are engaged in initial teacher education often teach inservice courses as well. Higher education, at least in the United Kingdom, has also set the agenda for the further education and training of teachers. Teachers have traditionally chosen from a menu of courses that placed a high premium on the transmission of knowledge. The courses were also located away from pupils and classrooms in the academy.

During the course of the 1980s this model of inservice training began to decline for a number of reasons not strictly germane to this chapter. Three changes are relevant to the arguments being advanced here. First, consequent on change in the way in which inservice education was funded, teachers' employers, the Local Education Authorities (LEAs), began to cease the funding of teachers on long courses in higher education. Secondly, and partly as a consequence of this first change, LEAs and teachers began to formulate some of their own agendas for inservice training. Finally, we have seen the growth of school-based inservice provision, much of which builds on the present experience of teachers in their classrooms. Many of the conditions described here are conducive to the development of experiential learning models of working, and there is little doubt that the action research/teacher as researcher model of development has begun to flourish under these conditions. The major impediments to this development are the very short periods of time given to inservice training in this model, which as we shall see does not fit the demands of experiential learning; the assumption that very large numbers of teachers can be pushed through this model of training, and finally the fact that much inservice is still in the hands of those who have a transmission model of learning.

THE LIMITS TO DIDACTICISM

In the previous section we set out a range of arguments to demonstrate the resistances to experiential learning in teacher education conducted in the academy. Against this we have to counterpose the view that, in the context of the practical professions, which include teaching, didacticism simply doesn't work. Perhaps the two most widely known exponents of such a view are Revans (1982) and Schön (1983), but they have many followers who have produced a good deal of empirical evidence to suggest that the basic thesis is sound (e.g., Steinberg & Caruso, 1985). The Schön/Revans thesis can be summed up as follows. Higher education is the major center of technical rationality, that is, knowledge about the way the world is, based on scientific principles of enquiry. This knowledge is encoded in what we know as the academic disciplines. From out of the relevant disciplines comes a relevant theory of action. In the case of teaching, the relevant disciplines would be the discipline that is to be taught and the disciplines that contribute to pedagogy and the general context of teaching (largely psychology, sociology, and philosophy).

Why is it asserted that this model does not work? We might begin by noting that practitioners themselves are sceptical about the contribution of theory and didacticism to the development of their practical competence in the classroom. The major problem is that the disciplines produce their knowledge at a level of abstraction (as theories, models, etc.), so that no clear lines of action can possibly be deduced from these that would fit the very large number of contexts (and teacher/pupil/subject configurations within contexts) met in teaching. Furthermore, the major disciplines that empirically relate to action in teaching, psychology, and sociology do not possess consensual or dependable bodies of knowledge that would even permit accurate deductions of action.

A THEORY OF EXPERIENTIAL LEARNING

The defects of a crude experiential model of learning were made very clear by Huxley:

> Nature's discipline is not even a word and a blow, and the blow first: but the blow without the word. It is left to you to find out why your ears were boxed. The object of artificial education is to make good these defects in Nature's methods. (1893, p. 85)

What experiential learning theory attempts to do is to devise models of learning from experience that make it effective. It accepts Huxley's view that mere exposure to experience is insufficient. Left to their own devices, student teachers at least do not always embrace the dictum "I do and I understand"; very often they declare "I do, and I'm even more confused!"

It is difficult to put forward a succinct definition of *experiential learning*. It is often defined as learning in which the learner is directly in touch with the realities being studied, and makes use of that direct contact to acquire changed insights that are carried forward to subsequent encounters with other realities. It is to be contrasted with learning in which the learner reads about, hears about, talks about, or writes about these realities but keeps this process separate, in both time and location, from lived contexts in which the learning thus acquired is apparently put to use.

This definition needs to encapsulate three slightly different referents for experiential learning, all of which are relevant for student and experienced teachers. The first refers to the planned provision of experience related to what is being learned. This is encapsulated in the idea of "teaching practice." The second refers to the provision of contrived experiences from which it is expected that learners will derive learning of a more general nature, and which are often thought to be helpful simply because they draw on the vividness of action. Various forms of simulations, role plays, and microteaching come under this category. Finally, we have experiential learning, which can be seen as a mode of operating within experiences in which the actor has developed modes of operating that allow him or her to look habitually for the learning that is available.

The most common model of experiential learning is that developed by Kolb (1984). Kolb's contribution has been as a synthesizer. The origins of his model, which is reproduced in Figure 3.1, can be seen in the work of several people. At the turn of the century John Dewey outlined a learning

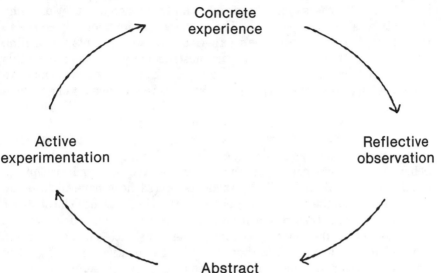

Figure 3.1. The Experiential Learning Cycle. From *Experiential Learning: Experience as the Source of Learning and Development,* by D.A. Kolb, 1984. Englewood Cliffs, NJ: Prentice-Hall. Copyright 1984 by Prentice-Hall. Reprinted by permission.

process that went from problem selection and observation to design solution, development, and testing. The American social psychologist Kurt Lewin was the first to conceptualize learning into a stage cycle of concrete experience, reflective observation, abstract conceptualization, and active experimentation.

In Kolb's model the learning cycle begins with experience. In fact to start here glosses over some important considerations that are prior to this point. In the context of initial teacher education, two things usually happen before this stage. Firstly, experiences are very often "set up" for students. This can involve *selecting* experiences, for example, selecting certain schools or certain groups of children for teaching practice. Alternatively, experiences can be *constructed*; for example, simulations of certain common situations encountered by teachers can be set up by the students' mentors. In the second place, students are usually briefed before the experience about its purpose, what to expect, what to look out for, pay attention to, and so on. In inservice models of working, teachers are often asked to bring with them recent examples of "experiences" so that the group and the individual can work on them.

It is significant that, in the model, the experience is merely the beginning of the cycle. It is followed by three further stages that are equally vital to learning. The next of these stages is reflective observation. In this stage the experience is analyzed, interrogated for meaning, and reworked if necessary. Teachers typically ask why children reacted as they did, why that action caused that reaction. The analogy that immediately comes to mind is that of reworking one's experience of seeing a play or a film. Following the stage of reflection comes abstract conceptualization. At this stage the particular experience is contextualized and attempts are made to generate some tentative hypothesis about classes of events of the type experienced. This usually involves developing some second-order concepts that abstract from the particulars of a specific experience. Thus teachers go from the realities of particular classrooms with particular configurations of pupils and tasks to some tentative contingent models of classroom behavior. It is worth noting that the academy and the academic disciplines often *begin* at this point; if the students or teachers have little or no experience, then they inevitably get lost in the abstractions. The abstract conceptualizations they create are different in at least one crucial respect from those of the disciplines—they have been constructed by the teachers themselves and form part of their "theory of education/pedagogy." The final stage of the learning cycle involves testing out these new concepts and theories in new situations, active experimentation in Kolb's terms, and so the cycle goes round again. One application of this model in initial teacher education is described in Chapter 6 of this volume.

Kolb did recognize that different learners will find different stages of the model more or less easy depending on their individual learning styles. Kolb and his followers tried to match up individual learning styles with the experiential learning cycle, which is shown in Figure 3.2.

The divergent learning style emphasizes concrete experience and re-

(ACCOMMODATOR)	EXPERIENCE	(DIVERGER)
Can carry out plans		Imaginative, good at generating ideas
Interested in action and results		Can view situation from different angles
Adapts to immediate circumstances		Open to experience
Trial and error style		Recognises problems
Sets objectives		Investigates
Sets schedules		Senses opportunities
EXPERIMENTATION		**REFLECTION**
Good at practical applications		Ability to create theoretical models
Makes decisions		Compares alternatives
Focusses efforts		Defines problems
Does well when there is one answer		Establishes criteria
Evaluates plans		Formulates hypotheses
Selects from alternatives		
(CONVERGER)	CONCEPTUALIZATION	(ASSIMILATOR)

Figure 3.2.   Learning Styles and the Experiential Learning Cycle. From *Learning by Doing: A Guide to Teaching and Learning Methods*, by G. Gibbs, 1988, London: FEU. Reprinted by permission.

flective observation. Individuals with this style are called *divergent*, because they perform better in situations that call for the generation of alternative ideas and interpretations. Students with this style, argued Kolb, are most likely to be found in the humanities and liberal arts.

In the *assimilative* style the learning predispositions are toward abstract conceptualization and reflective observation. The strengths of this model lie in the ability to reason inductively, to create theoretical models, and to assimilate disparate observations into an integrated whole. The stress is not on the application of theories but rather on the requirement that they are logically sound and precise. Students with this learning style tend to be found in mathematics and the natural sciences.

The *convergent* learning style relies primarily on the dominant learning abilities of abstract conceptualization and active experimentation. The strength of this learning style lies in the ability to solve problems and apply ideas in a. practical way. Individuals with this learning style are referred to as *convergers*, because they perform best when there is a single correct answer to a question or problem. Students who have convergence as a dominant learning style are often specialized in the physical sciences.

The final learning style referred to in this model is labeled *accommodative*. The strength of accommodation lies in its ability to accomplish successfully plans and tasks in situations marked by uncertainty. Accommodators are good at adapting themselves to changing circumstances. Students who have a strong accommodative learning style are often specialized in areas like business studies.

Shiro (1978) attempted to translate Kolb's model of learning styles into teaching styles (see Figure 3.3).

It is most useful to view Kolb's work as the production of a very useful heuristic device in thinking about experiential learning. There are a number of important questions it raises that are unanswered. The first relates to the key concept of learning style. It is not clear what the psychological status of such a construct is. At times there is an implication that such things are innate, but even if this is the case, such a position would need to recognize that habituation to a particular discipline in which certain kinds of learning styles are traditionally dominant also has an important effect. The second question relates to Kolb's use of the idea of stages in the experiential learning model. We should view the idea of the stages heuristically, because in reality the separation of the action and reflection upon it is an artificial separation in relation to most forms of activity. Becoming better at learning from experience requires us to recognize the thinking that takes place inside the doing, and *then* to include a consideration of that blend of thinking and doing in a subsequent and additional reflective phase. This is captured by Schön's idea of "reflection on reflection-in-action." Some people have interpreted Kolb's stages

TEACHER TYPES

EXPERIENCE

TYPE FOUR TEACHER	TYPE ONE TEACHER
Role: Colleague	Role: Facilitator
Intent of Teaching: to enhance a better vision of what society can be.	Intent of Teaching: to further individual growth according to the needs of each child.
Measure of Teacher Effectiveness: getting students to act upon their visions.	Measure of Teacher Effectiveness: facilitating student growth and development.
Purpose of Student Evaluation: to measure students' progress with respect to abilities.	Purpose of Student Evaluation: to diagnose student abilities so as to facilitate growing.
Concept of Knowledge: knowledge gives the student the ability to interpret and to reconstruct her/his society.	Concept of Knowledge: knowledge gives personal insights, it derives its authority from the meaning it has to its possessor.

EXPERIMENTATION_____ | _____REFLECTION

TYPE THREE TEACHER	TYPE TWO TEACHER
Role: Manager	Role: Transmitter
Intent of Teaching: to prepare students to perform skills they will need in society.	Intent of Teaching: to advance students within the discipline.
Measure of Teacher Effectiveness: efficiency in getting students to achieve skills.	Measure of Teacher Effectiveness: accuracy in presenting the discipline.
Purpose of Student Evaluation: to certify to clients that students have certain skills.	Purpose of Student Evaluation: to rank order students for future advancement of the discipline.
Concept of Knowledge: knowledge gives the student the ability to do certain things ... capability for action.	Concept of Knowledge: knowledge gives the student the ability to understand certain things.

CONCEPTUALIZATION

Figure 3.3. Characteristics of preferred teaching styles (adaptation based on Shiro, 1978).

as though we always need to start with concrete experience and move round the learning cycle clockwise. This is not necessary either logically or empirically, as Kolb himself acknowledges. It is obviously common to start with concrete experience but also possible to start with abstract conceptualization or active experimentation.

The third question raised by Kolb's model, which is particularly pertinent for teachers, is whether a model developed in the context of adult learners applies equally to children. In other words, the model may have a good deal to say about the process of teachers' learning, but can it be applied equally well to the learning of their pupils? This is an important question, because teacher educators in the UK are now beginning to use the model to developed a more "balanced" portfolio of teaching styles. This is well illustrated by Figure 3.4, which is taken from some inservice material developed by Bell (1990).

THE IMPLICATIONS OF EXPERIENTIAL LEARNING THEORY FOR TEACHER EDUCATION

Experiential learning theory has several important implications for the education of teachers. In the first place it stresses that teachers, like everybody else, learn in different ways, but that we all have dominant learning styles. So experiential learning modes are going to be easier and more attractive to some teachers than others. We can go further than this; if Kolb is correct in associating learning styles with the learning of particular academic subjects, then in the context of teacher education this will mean that, *ceteris paribus*, teachers of mathematics and science will

ASSIGNMENT

Review or plan a lesson or topic of your choice using the Kolb model and the quadrants below.

Lesson/topic: . . . . Yr grp . . . . Ability . . . .
Objectives (briefly) . . . .

ENTHUSIASTIC	IMAGINATIVE
(Lesson opportunities for: - open-ended experimentation - pupil-initiated activity - pupil trial and error - etc.)	(Lesson opportunities for: - imagination - innovation - divergent thinking - etc.)
PRACTICAL	LOGICAL
(Lesson opportunities for: - practising skills - doing structured practical work - showing practical applications of knowledge - etc.)	(Lesson opportunities for: - pupils to think logically - acquiring abstract information - concept acquisition - etc.)

Write the various activities/phases of your lesson in the relevant quadrants. Review what you have written and if the content of any one quadrant is weak - think of activities which you could use to strengthen it.

Figure 3.4. An inservice activity for teachers (adaptation based on Bell, 1990).

find this model of learning more difficult than teachers of (say) English and the humanities. Such differences can be exacerbated if teachers in maths and science take an epistemological view of their subjects as linear constructions of knowledge that are essentially abstract and decontextualized. There is little doubt that, until relatively recently, such a view was dominant among teachers of math and science.

How student teachers are taught in their initial training may also have some implications for models of teaching and learning that they take with them to their classrooms. All other things being equal, if students are exposed to experiential methods in training, they are more likely to employ these methods in their practice. And *all* subject teachers can use such models. It is interesting that the two subject areas that have developed the ideas of constructivism in children's learning most fully have been math and science (Driver, 1983; Hoyles, 1989). Perhaps this is because math and science found the greatest difficulties in engaging pupils in their subjects and most crucially getting them to *think* scientifically and mathematically, and constructivism, getting students to experience particular problems and then construct their own solutions, was seen as a way of accomplishing this. We return to the problems of didacticism. In certain pupils it can produce adequate performance in routine tests, but so, it is argued, it does not appear to produce a deep level of understanding that allows them to perform well in new contexts.

One of the messages of initial teacher training ought to be that, because pupils learn in different ways, then teachers ought to adopt a variety of teaching strategies so that particular students are not disadvantaged. Set in the context of the dominance of didactic modes in schools, this has usually translated itself into a plea for the development of more active modes of teaching and learning. We have suggested, following Kolb, that learning style might be related to ability in various subjects, but it is also likely that, independent of any subject effect, some students learn more effectively from experience than others. In other words, some have an "experiential learning set." An interesting finding from a study of a simulation (a particular form of experiential learning) was that those students "who seemed to gain least from the experience differed from those who gained most in displaying less empathy, preferring symbolic methods of learning (reading and writing) to listening and experiencing, and liked independent work more than group instruction" (Lee & O'Leary, 1971). Student teachers then need to acquire the skills of teaching in the experiential mode, and they will clearly be helped in this endeavor if they themselves are exposed to this mode during their training.

If we think about teachers teaching in the classroom, we immediately focus on the role of the teacher. A question that puzzles many is, What do teachers actually do when they are operating in the experiential mode?

This is a question also faced in teacher education; how do teacher educators promote learning from experience in their students?

It is possible to recognize two ideal-typical models in existence. In the first model we see a mere illusion of experiential learning. Students are "given" or "put through" experiences so that they may discover the "right answers," much as rats are driven through a maze until they find the correct path. One can see this model most clearly in school science, when pupils undertake strictly controlled experiments to "prove" accepted theories. This method has been dubbed *recipe science* (Bentley & Watts, 1989). Similarly in teacher education students are sometimes put in microteaching situations to demonstrate certain points the tutor believes are important. One of the defining marks of this form of experiential learning is that it is dominated by the tutor or teacher; control rests with him or her just as it does in didactic teaching.

In the other model of experiential learning the student is in control of learning, trying with the help of the tutor or teacher to make sense, his or her sense, of the experience, and to integrate it into a personal stock of knowledge. Returning to our school science example, this would mean getting pupils to test their own hypotheses about scientific phenomena, setting up their own experiments and considering their own results in the light of their own and conventional theories.

This second model recognizes the obvious truth that only learners can learn and that the role for the tutor/teacher here is as a facilitator of learning. In learning to teach, this is a very important point. Those who can teach, who appear to student teachers as competent performers, often "know more than they can say"; they possess what Polanyi (1958) termed *tacit* and Oakeshott (1975) *practical* knowledge. There is considerable evidence to show that most competent teachers cannot in fact conceptualize and explain what it is that they do that makes them successful (Furlong, Hirst, Pocklington, & Miles, 1988). At best we get either decontextualized "tips for teachers" generalized from *their* experience and delivered didactically, or highly context-bound specific explanations of why such a strategy worked *for them* in that particular situation.

Student teachers are in a particularly difficult situation, because they have to handle very complex classroom situations with relatively little knowledge or experience. What exactly do these students need experience of? We could follow Tom (1985) in specifying four arenas of the teaching situation that can be the subject of experience and reflection because they are problematic. He specified these as: the teaching–learning process, subject matter knowledge, political and ethical principles underlying teaching, and educational institutions within their broad social context. In an alternative formulation Laboskey (1991) argued that preservice teachers need knowledge and experience about teaching context, processes, attitudes, and subject content. In her view the neglected area, and one that is crucial for teacher success, is beliefs, values, and attitudes.

These formulations reveal the enormous complexity of the teaching-learning process. Student teachers and serving teachers very often attempt to cope with this complexity by simplifying it, and one of the first steps in this process is an attempt to categorize situations. Different writers described this categorizing in different ways. Some have found the idea of "images" of situations useful following work in cognitive psychology, which had found application in the study of chess playing and medical diagnosis (e.g., Brewer, 1987). Specifically in the context of teaching, Berliner (1987) argued that experienced teachers have more elaborate *schema*, that is, networks of knowledge for understanding practice, and a repertoire of *scripts*, that is, knowledge that guides routine responses. So in planning schoolwork, teachers draw upon different kinds of knowledge—about pupils, subject matter, school context, and educational aims—to generate a new category of knowledge, which Wilson, Shulman, and Richert (1987) termed *pedagogical content knowledge*. These scripts or schemata are acquired in a complex way. Some students and teachers are able to pick up a very great deal merely by watching competent practitioners and by going through teaching experiences. One thing that clearly helps is acquiring a range of diverse teaching experiences, and there is an important message here for experiential learning in general and teacher education in particular. The wider the range of experiences, the more likely it is that students will learn and understand what strategies work (Woolf, Kelson, & Silver, 1990). There is a sense in which this variety of experience is the individual version of the disciplines approach to knowledge. It could be argued that some of the well-known and developed schemas, for example, the experiential learning cycle model itself, have been developed by trying them out in a very wide range of situations and contexts to test their validity and reliability—far more than any individual teacher could possibly undertake. Thus it is quite false to counterpose knowledge acquisition through the disciplines with the development of a personal "knowledge-in-action," as Schön does. As Gilliss (1988) persuasively argued, "it is not a matter of having either the knowledge that Technical Rationality produces or the knowledge that Reflective Practice produces, but more a case of having both forms of knowledge, each informing the other" (p. 45).

The merit in Schön's argument is that he stresses the importance of professionals acquiring the ability to reflect on their practice and to learn from it in a way that allows for the production of new schema/scripts and for the modification of existing scripts. His reflection-in-action is at the center of experiential learning theory; the model reflects a second order ability to acquire and apply practical knowledge that is separate from that practical knowledge itself.

What is reasonably clear is that if students or serving teachers are unable to acquire a sufficient number of robust scripts, they will be under a great deal of stress in the classroom and are at risk of early burn out and certainly subject to feelings of classroom incompetence. But there are other sorts of dangers with this model, particularly if the scripts or schemas have been acquired without an adequate and rigorous reflection process. The main danger is that, once acquired, teachers will develop an unthinking reliance on the script and fail to recognize the strangeness of each new classroom encounter. The second problem is that so powerful are many of the images and schemas acquired experientially that, once acquired, they can be very difficult to modify. We all know that when their practice is challenged, many teachers will justify their own claims on the basis of experience, and it can be difficult to get them to reexamine the nature of that experience or to avail themselves of different experiences.

The tutor as facilitator has a fundamentally important role in helping students and teachers become reflective practitioners. Probably the first task is to develop in teachers a view of their own abilities and competencies. A useful way of seeing this is shown by Dubin's (1962) model of competence and incompetence in human learners (Figure 3.5).

A major job for the tutor is to assist the teacher to know what it is he or she does not know. Clearly the worst situation is to deal with teachers in cell 3–unconscious incompetence, and the ultimate goal is cell 2–conscious competence. A major goal in initial teacher education, however, is

	1	2
Competent relative to particular skills or knowledge	Unconscious competence *(not interested in this particular learning)*	Conscious competence *(requiring learning in new areas)*
	3	4
Incompetent relative to particular skills or knowledge	Unconscious incompetence *(in need of learning but unaware of the need)*	Conscious incompetence *(very suitable for learning)*

Figure 3.5. Competence and incompetence in human learners (adaptation based on Dubin, 1962).

cell 4, to make students aware of what it is that they are not good at and then help them acquire the skills and opportunities to become competent. A major way of doing this is through metacognition – a recognition of the centrality of the learner in the learning process, and the belief that awareness of one's own mental processes, and the ability to reflect on these, are central to effective learning.

Tutors can support these metacognitive processes in a number of ways: first, by the careful construction and selection of experiences that will test the areas of a student's competence and reveal those areas of relative incompetence. The tutor also needs to ensure that, once new skills and knowledge have been acquired, they are practiced. There seems increasing evidence in favor of some sort of cognitive information-processing model of learning, which suggests that information is first processed in short-term memory that only has a limited capacity. It is only if the learner pays active attention to the contents of short-term memory through "rehearsal" or constant repetition that it can be transferred to long-term memory.

Not only is varied practice important, but so also is the environment in which the experience takes place. It needs to be one where risk and safety are combined with perhaps the balance changing as the student teacher becomes more proficient and confident. Risk is always necessary, because only through a new situation with some element of risk in it is learning possible. But it also needs to be an environment where "mistakes" are not penalized but rather are seen as sources of learning. In experiential learning, getting it wrong is a necessary part of getting it right. It follows from this that a key role for the teacher trainer is that of coach and provider of feedback. The tutor also needs to be somebody who can offer alternative explanations to the student to account for behavior – explanations drawn from the disciplines, his or her own experience, or the experience of colleagues and fellow students. Of course in the end the students and teachers must construct explanations that seem reasonable to them, and develop their scripts accordingly. A major source of these will be their own experiences, but they must also be confronted with other "reasons" emanating from other people's experiences, some of which will be codified by the traditional disciplines of education.

Three other things seem important if teacher education is to construct an experiential learning community. Teaching is very often a lonely profession in which reflection-in-action has to be developed in a solitary way. There is little excuse for this in initial teacher education, which should try to establish collaborative modes of learning. Students can learn a great deal by observing and giving feedback to each other, and by discussing and making sense of their experiences together. From the experiential learning model it also follows that time for reflection is vital. As Rogers (1985) argued

> teacher education, and indeed teaching itself, is often a hurried, time-dominated activity. One learns to deal with daily crises, but seldom has time to search for the meaning inherent in events. Thus there is need to stand back, examine events from a number of perspectives, to apply theory to practice, and indeed, practice to theory. (p. 252)

Thirdly, teachers need the opportunity to present their perceptions, their theories and models, and their scripts to others. The requirement to present (represent) is itself important, whether it be verbally, iconically, or symbolically, because it forces teachers to clarify in their own minds the nature of their experiences and their perceptions of them. It also places them in the (semi) public domain, and this opens them up to challenge and reinterpretation. Finally, this process offers more scripts for fellow students or teachers to examine.

The final implication of experiential learning theory for teacher education lies in the area of assessment. Everybody who teaches knows that how the assessment process is conducted has a big influence on how teachers behave and how pupils learn. In schools student teachers quickly realize, even supposing that they were not already aware of it, and experienced teachers certainly know that the assessment model is one dominated by the reproductive mode; that is, pupils are encouraged to reproduce received wisdom, not their own knowledge and experience, but essentially the knowledge and experience of others. Such an emphasis means that there is considerable pressure for pupils to engage in what the Gothenberg school calls *surface processing* as opposed to *deep processing* (Marton & Säljö, 1976). In surface processing, texts are skimmed for facts that pupils are likely to be asked to reproduce in examinations. Pupils are not encouraged, at least by the assessment, to fully integrate the meaning of the texts into their own experience and theories.

These prevalent models of assessment in schools have two major effects on students undergoing teacher training. In the first place it means that students entering teacher education establishments do so with learning strategies that are likely to have been influenced by their experiences of assessment both at school *and* in undergraduate education. They will be lucky if they have not acquired the routine of surface processing. In the second place they will quite likely go out on teaching practice in schools in which the reproductive assessment model is still extant. This will not encourage them to explore experiential learning strategies, which are unlikely to be very effective in producing masses of facts for reproduction in tests and examinations.

Fortunately initial teacher education in the United Kingdom has largely moved away from such modes of assessment, although the recent interest in the idea of competence, including in some versions "competency checklists," could produce surface-processing-type approaches to learning in student teachers. It should be clear that the concept of the reflective practitioner requires an assessment model that has a major function of diagnostic feedback to students. The dilemma is that institutions of teacher education also have a public duty to protect the school system from people who have not reached minimum competence standards. There is a well-known difficulty in trying to design assessment systems that serve both purposes. The problem is less marked in inservice education. In the first place much of the work here is not assessed, and even where it is, for accreditation purposes, the assessment mode is very often congruent with the reflective practitioner model.

CONCLUSION

There is little doubt that experiential learning has a great deal to offer teacher education. Versions of the model have been influential in developing the reflective practitioner model in initial teacher education and the teacher researcher model in inservice teacher education. Experiential learning models are about empowering teachers in the sense that they are giving teachers the tools to create and recreate their own professional knowledge. What we have to insure is that our models of experiential learning are robust and that they help teachers create reliable and valid professional knowledge.

The major site where we judge professional knowledge is in the classroom; experiential learning in the development of teacher competence should be judged in the light of enhanced pupil learning. It is already clear that experiential models are having an effect. Because the model argues that people have different learning styles, it suggests that teachers should develop a portfolio of teaching styles in order that all pupils should be fairly treated. This argument has been extended to suggest that all learning styles have their strengths and weaknesses and are more or less suited to different tasks and situations. It follows from this proposition that teachers should consciously act to develop the full range of learning styles in young people. In terms of the wide range of skills and knowledge required in being a teacher, it also follows that teachers themselves should try and develop in themselves the full range of learning styles.

At this juncture it is probably the case that experiential learning theory focuses too much on classroom processes. Yet, if teachers are to become "extended professionals" in contrast to "restricted professionals" (Hoyle,

1974), then they will need to develop theories-in-action not merely for the classroom, but for the wider communities of staffroom, school and community. Ideally both student teachers and experienced teachers should be working on real professional problems forming what Revans would call an *action learning set*. The end result of this process, which Revans referred to as *system gamma*, is a process that involves "the symbiosis of a person changing a situation (action) and of the person being changed by this action (learning)" (Revans, 1982). One of the major advantages of this model is that it uses "experiences" and experiential learning to blend together preservice and inservice education.

REFERENCES

Barnes, D., Johnson, G., Jordan, S., Layton, D., Medway, P., & Yeomans, D. (1987). *The TVEI curriculum 14-16*. London: Training Agency.

Bell, G. (1990). *Learner centred teaching* [mimeo]. *London: Royal Society of Arts.*

Bentley, D., & Watts, M. (Eds.). (1989). *Learning and teaching in school science: Practical alternatives*. Milton Keynes, UK: Open University Press.

Berliner, D. C. (1987). Ways of thinking about students and classrooms by more and less experienced teachers. In J. Calderhead (Ed.), *Exploring teachers' thinking*. London: Cassell.

Brewer, W. F. (1987). Schemas versus mental models in human memory. In P. Morris (Ed.), *Modelling cognition*. Chichester, UK: Wiley.

Cox, C. B., & Dyson, A. E. (Eds.). (1969). *A black paper*. London: The Critical Quarterly Society.

Dennison, B., & Kirk, R. (1990). *Do, review, learn, apply: A simple guide to experiential learning*. Oxford: Blackwell.

Driver, R. (1983). *The pupil as scientist*. Milton Keynes, UK: Open University Press.

Dubin, P. (1962). *Human relations in administration*. Englewood Cliffs, NJ: Prentice-Hall.

Furlong, V. J., Hirst, P. H., Pocklington, K., & Miles, S. (1988). *Initial teacher training and the role of the school*. Milton Keynes, UK: Open University Press.

Galton, M., Simon, B., & Croll, P. (1980). *Inside the primary school*. London: Routledge & Kegan Paul.

Gibbs, G. (1988). *Learning by doing: A guide to teaching and learning methods*. London: FEU.

Gilliss, G. (1988). Schön's reflective practitioner: A model for teachers? In P. P. Grimmett & G. L. Erikson (Eds.), *Reflections in teacher education* New York: Teachers College Press.

HMI. (1979). *Aspects of secondary education in England: A survey by HM Inspectors of Schools*. London: HMSO.

Hoyle, E. (1974). Professionality, professionalism and control in teaching. *London Educational Review, 3, 2.*

Hoyles, C. (1989). Paradoxes in mathematics education in the 1980s. In E. Clough & J. Nixon (Eds.), *The new learning*. London: Macmillan.

Huxley, T. H. (1893). *Collected essays* (Vol. III). London: Macmillan.

Kolb, D. A. (1984). *Experiential learning: Experience as the source of learning and development*. Englewood Cliffs, NJ: Prentice-Hall.

Laboskey, V. (1991, March). *A conceptual framework for reflection on pre-service teacher education*. Paper delivered at the Conceptualising Reflection in Teacher Development Conference, University of Bath, England.

Lawlor, S. (1990). *Teachers mistaught: Training in theories or education in subjects*. London: Centre for Policy Studies.

Lee, R. S., & O'Leary, M. A. (1971). Attitude and personality, effects of a three-day simulation. *Simulations and Games, 2*, 43–50.

Lewin, K. (1951). *Field theory in social sciences*. New York: Harper and Row.

Lortie, D. C. (1975). *Schoolteacher*. Chicago: University of Chicago Press.

Marton, F., & Säljö, R. (1976). On qualitative differences in learning: 1. Outcomes and processes. *British Journal of Educational Psychology, 46*, 4–11.

Oakeshott, M. (1975). *On human conduct*. Oxford: Oxford University Press.

Polanyi, M. (1958). *Personal knowledge*. London: Routledge & Kegal Paul.

Revans, R. W. (1982). *The origins and growth of action learning*. Bromley, UK: Chartwell-Bratt.

Rogers, V. (1985). Ways of knowing: Their meaning for teacher education. In E. Eisner (Ed.), *Learning and Teaching the Ways of knowing* Chicago: National Society for the Study of Education.

Schön, D. (1983). *The reflective practitioner*. London: Temple Smith.

Shiro, M. (1978). *Curriculum for better schools: The great ideological debate*. Englewood Cliffs, NJ: Educational Technology Publications.

Simon, B. (1988). Why no pedagogy in England. In R. Dale, R. Fergusson, & A. Robinson (Eds.), *Framework for teaching*. London: Hodder & Stoughton.

Steinberg, R. J., & Caruso, D. R. (1985). Practical modes of knowing. In E. Eisner (Ed.), *Learning and teaching the ways of knowing* (Yearbook of the National Society for the Study of Education). Chicago: University of Chicago Press.

Tom, A. (1985). Inquiring into inquiry-oriented teacher education. *Journal of Teacher Education, 36*, 5.

Weil, S. W., & Mc Gill, I. (Eds.). (1989). *Making sense of experiential learning: Diversity in theory and practice*. Milton Keynes, UK: Open University Press.

Wilson, S. M., Shulman, L. S., & Richert, A. E. (1987). "150 different ways" of knowing: Representations of knowledge in teaching. In J. Calderhead (Ed.), *Exploring teachers' thinking*. London: Cassell.

Woolf, A., Kelson, M., & Silver, R. (1990). *Learning in context: Patterns of skills transfer and training implications*. Sheffield, UK: TEED, Department of Employment.

CHAPTER 4

Competence-Based Learning in Teacher Education

Phil Hodkinson
Crewe and Alsager College of Higher Education Crew, England

Gareth Harvard
University of Exeter School of Education

The use of *competence* in education is not new. During the 1970s much competence-based work was developed in the United States (Tuxworth, 1989). As indicated in Chapter 1, the concept was revitalized in Britain in the late 1980s, especially in the field of vocational education and training. This new British work is analyzed in terms of two different underlying ideologies, which are then used to explore the applicability of a competence-based approach to the professional education of teachers.

The term *competence* was defined in the British vocational context by the De Ville Report (De Ville, 1986), from which the new, competence-based National Vocational Qualifications (NVOs) developed. This suggested that competence consisted of three interlinked components: knowledge, understanding, and skills. Whatever the job, it was argued, appropriate attainment in all three was essential for effective performance. Competence was seen as an indivisible integration of the three. This whole is then subdivided for practical purposes into units and elements of competence, each of which in turn integrates knowledge, understanding, and skills. This definition is a useful starting point for our analysis, but the actual relationship between skills, understanding, and knowledge within this umbrella term is complex and problematic (Black & Wolf, 1990; Burke, 1989).

However, the meaning given to competence, the way it is operationalized, and its power as an educational device vary according to the belief systems within it is located. We use the term *ideology* for such implicit belief systems, but without the Marsian implications of social control with which the term is often associated (Apple, 1979). The contention here is that there are two different ideologies that underpin the notion of competence at the levels of theoretical conceptualization and practical operation. We call these two ideal-type ideologies *behavioristic* and *interactive*. In reality, most competence schemes contain elements of both. What matters is which dominates.

THE BEHAVIORISTIC IDEOLOGY OF COMPETENCE

The behavioristic ideology takes a largely external-realist ontology. That is, it assumes that that reality is external to the individual and objective in nature. This is linked with a positivistic epistemology, seeing knowledge as acquired through objective investigation, so that, for example, science is a means of advancing our understanding, continually narrowing the gap between what we know and what actually is. When applied to the notion of competence, such an ideological stance focuses attention on the statement of competence as of crucial importance. The NVQ in Britain places great emphasis on the careful analysis of occupational roles, in order to determine what the "correct" elements of competence are (Jessup, 1991). This work is controlled by industry-led bodies that represent and are drawn from major employers in the field, who therefore give validity to the selection and definition of particular elements. The links with a positivistic theoretical framework are shown by this assumption that competence can be objectively discovered and defined, together with the importance placed on so doing.

We chose the label *behavioristic* rather than *positivistic* to emphasize another feature of this ideology: its view of how people learn. Behaviorism sees learning as a response to external stimuli, in which the learners are passive in the learning process responding to their environment and to others. Such a view of learning places emphasis on teaching. It is associated with transmission models of teaching and learning, in which knowledge is poured out of one person (the teacher) and into the other (the student). It sees skill acquisition as the result of an unproblematic combination of instruction and practice. A more complete picture of the traditional procedures of teaching often associated with this ideology can be found in Levin and Allen (1976).

If taken literally, the definition of competence given earlier implies such a behaviorist position, because it views the link between understanding and performance as linear and unproblematic. In the NVQ system, appropriate performance of a role is taken as proof, for assessment purposes, that the necessary knowledge, understanding, and skills must be there.

The assumption is that there is one correct understanding, without which performance is impossible.

The behaviorism in NVQ approaches to competence can be seen in other ways, too. NVQ procedures are only concerned with assessment of outcomes. There is no specification of teaching or learning, because they claim that it does not matter how role competence is learned. All that matters is that it can be demonstrated. The assumptions that teaching is (a) unproblematic and (b) to be judged purely on the measurement of outcomes in performance derives from behaviorism. All NVQ outcomes are expressed and measured in behavioral terms. What matters is identifying the appropriate behaviors and measuring or assessing them.

Ashworth and Saxton (1990) give a thorough analysis of some well-rehearsed problems connected with such a behavioristic view of competence, and their paper warrants studying in full. They suggest that elements of competence can fragment or atomize an occupational role, so that the sum of the parts adds up to less than the whole. This is made worse when the elements are used primarily for summative assessment. The constant search for statements that can be reliably and validly assessed can lead to the reification of the statements, which becomes ends in themselves, as groups spend endless hours trying to get them "right."

The deeper and more fundamental difficulty of using competence within a behavioristic ideology is that this view of learning is flawed, presenting an oversimplified assumption that learning is a one way process which artificially separates the learner from the context of learning. These issues can be explored further if we now examine the alternative interactive ideology.

AN INTERACTIVE IDEOLOGY

From this perspective, reality is not given and "out there," but is the product of man as a social being. Symbolic interactionists such as Goffman (1961) and Berger and Luckman (1966) argued that humans generate knowledge and a view of "reality" through social interaction. From this perspective, advancing our understanding is not seen as narrowing the gap between what we know and some external objective reality. Kuhn (1962) suggested that, rather than moving toward truth in a linear way, the history of science actually consists of a series of paradigm shifts, as one reality is substituted for another, in a series of "scientific revolutions." From this perspective, the search for the definitive elements of competence to fit an occupational role becomes little more useful than the hunt for the holy grail, because there will be no absolute objective role in the first place. Rather, the role will be defined by the perceptions of actors, which in turn will be the product of their culture, history, and interactions with others. The nature of role also depends on the context in which it is placed, including the unequal power relations between participants. Views of the role will often be contested. This can be easily seen in relation to teaching, and the conflicts between views of the teacher's role as that of a technician or that of a professional were briefly described in Chapter 1. Furthermore, from an interactionist perspective, roles, meanings, and perceptions change as a result of dynamic interactions between actors that are related dialectically to changes in context and culture.

Such a view of knowledge is complemented by current work into how people learn, which also begins from an interactive position. Rumelhart (1980), among many others, sees learning as the use and development of schemas. A *schema* is a mental representation of a set of related categories. When we come across something new, we select one of our repertoire of schemas to make sense of it. Unlike a behavioristic perspective, schema theory sees learning as an interaction between the learner and the learned. The same speech, heard by a socialist and a capitalist, can be seen by both as supporting their case. This is because both use their own schemas to filter out the bits that do not support their own positions. There is a striking parallel here with the way Kuhn views the history of science. He claims that scientists use paradigms to filter out what is relevant in exactly the same partial and distorting way. From this perspective, what we learn depends at least as much on our beliefs and existing understanding (schemas) as it does on the way we are taught. Learning is a dialectical process, in which our use of schemas filter reality as we know it, and the schemas themselves are changed by contact with new stimuli, contexts, or experiences.

Learning is not just about interactions between people, but also about the interactions between people and their environment. Resnick (1987) suggested that this is one way in which learning outside school differs from most formal learning within school. In addition, she suggested that learning outside school usually involves the use of tools as an integral part of the learning process, whereas learning in school often emphasizes pure mentation. She went on to claim that learning in school would be much more efficient if we modeled it more on everyday learning outside. She did, however, give one important warning. What she called "learning outside school" is situation specific, whereas education has to be engaged in generalizable understanding, capable of application and development in new and often unforseen situations.

Brown, Collins, and Duguid (1989) claimed that it is impossible to separate learning from its context. All cognition, they said, is situated. What you learn cannot be separated from the activity you are engaged in while learning, or from the context or culture in which the learning takes place. From this point of view, isolating a statement of competence is nonsense. Not only does the context determine how the competence is performed, it also determines what the competence statement actually means to the performer, the trainer, and the assessor. Even in the same physical setting, other aspects of the personal context will be different for each individual, so it is quite possible, even likely, that all will understand the statement differently. Furthermore, although the written statement takes on the identity of an external fixture, competence in practice, however it is understood, is constantly evolving in a dialectical relationship between performers, actions, and culture. By *culture* we mean the historically rooted system of established beliefs and values from which no person or performance can be isolated. Furthermore, the performer, actions, and culture themselves are not fixed but dynamic. From such a perspective the use of competence looks inappropriate, being based on a fundamental misunderstanding of the learning process.

However, even from this interactive perspective, competence is not so easily dismissed. The use of a competence-based system has enabled NVQ in Britain to move the emphasis in vocational learning out of the classroom and into the working environment. We recently visited one college of further education where the hairdressing department had moved over to an NVQ approach. All learning was centered around a salon, where customers came to have their hair cut. Trainees learned by cutting hair under the supervision of the instructor. Theoretical studies were related to the practical work that arose in the salon. Each trainee worked as an individual and as part of a group. This salon, without ever having read the paper by Brown et al., was consciously trying to create a genuine culture of hairdressing, to provide authentic hairdressing activity, and to integrate conceptual development with them. As if following Resnick, cognition was shared rather than purely individual, and tool manipulation was central to the learning process. Although no one in the salon knew what a schema was, there was a genuine attempt to develop learning as individual development, with the learners sharing responsibility for how they learned, for the sequence of tasks undertaken, and for the pace at which learning took place. There appeared to be an implicit recognition that the same learning experience might produce very different outcomes for different students.

The developments described are not accidental outcomes, but are part of the official rhetoric of NVQ (Jessup, 1991). The use of competence facilitated these changes in several ways. The removal of large, knowledge-based syllabi made traditional rote learning of facts, including theories-as-facts, largely superfluous, and greatly reduced transmission teaching. The existence of statements of competence gave trainees a language with which to understand their learning and negotiate with tutors about needs and methods. It gave them shared ownership of course objectives and assessment criteria, reducing their dependence on the tutor. However, NVQ training of the type described runs serious risks of being situation specific. Candy and Harris (1990), commenting on similar Australian experiences, found that teachers felt theory was being neglected. Yet, the use of theory is vital if learning is to be generalizable beyond the situation where it took place.

Within NVQ, therefore, evidence of both ideologies can be found. However, it is the behaviorist ideology that is dominant. This is because the system is completely assessment led, and the derivation, nature, and supposed acquisition of competence are all positivistic and behavioristic. In considering teacher education, it is necessary to explore what competence would look like if the interactive ideology dominated.

AN INTERACTIVE MODEL OF COMPETENCE

As with the behavioristic NVQ definition, we begin with the notion of competence as holistic. But here it is the nature of learning that becomes the center of the model, rather than being excluded and taken for granted. Competence becomes a dynamic process, rather than an outcome. Our model of competence is shown in Figure 4.1. Competence includes teacher performances, whether in the classroom or other settings, together with the teacher's intellectual processes and knowledge structures or schemas. All three are seen within a cultural context with which they interact. The behaviorist view of competence restricts it to performance only.

This interactive model of competence looks at ways of monitoring how professional knowledge is organized. It also examines the nature of thinking and learning processes for selecting and organizing experience. More specifically, it resembles Ryle's (1949) notion of *intelligent practice*, in which one performance is modified by its predecessor, rather than being a replica of its predecessors. To judge a performance as intelligent or not, we must look beyond performance itself. We have to inquire into the capacities, abilities, skills, and dispositions of which the performance is an example. Ryle concluded that knowing how is a disposition that can take many forms, including an amalgamation of covert and overt exercises, imaginative inquiry and practice.

Our model of competence looks beyond performance by incorporating the propensities and abilities competent performer is exercizing. It examines the nature of understanding as part of knowing how. One necessary condition for understanding or critically evaluating performance is some mastery in the processes and procedures to be evaluated. But this is not to say that the capacity to perform and appreciate performance necessarily

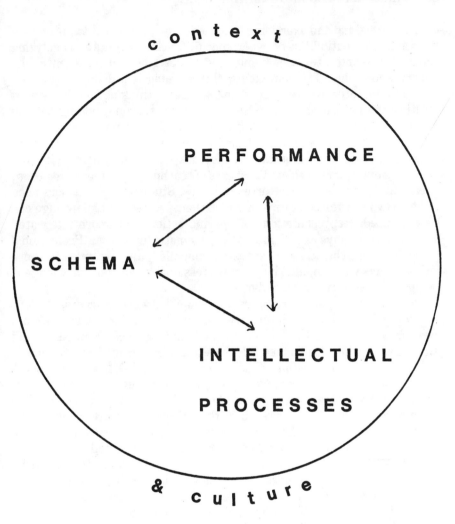

Figure 4.1.

involves the ability to formulate criticism. Similarly, the ability to understand a performance does not involve the same degree of competence as
the ability to do it. So if we wish to develop teachers as professionals, with
the ability to understand and critically evaluate what they do, we need to
focus on how they learn. Our model of competence helps to describe and
explain how professionally relevant knowledge is acquired and developed
in specific conditions and context.

   Learning, in this model, consists of the progressive development of
schemas and intellectual processes by actively linking experiences to
previous knowledge by adding more detail of a range of specific teaching

events, by making and exercising informed judgements about appropriate links and incompatibilities between specific teaching events and analyzing the language and categories being used to describe and represent pedagogical knowledge. The context for this learning is a dialogue between learner and tutor to help focus the learners' thinking. This involves eliciting the nature of their existing schemas, refining, adding to, and challenging them, in the context of improving teacher performance.

Thus, student teachers, while learning, must demonstrate how they are relating practice to schemas and intellectual processes by identifying and analyzing exemplars of selected aspects of teaching, by categorizing those events in discourse and written evaluations. Students and teachers need to be shown the various forms in which their professional knowledge can be organized. Representations of specific actions and more integrated activity can be physical, diagramatic, schematic, or verbal. Professional knowledge, or schema must be tested, amended, and extended in these various ways while monitoring how professionally relevant knowledge is being progressively structured over time.

We believe that the working relationships between teachers, student teachers, and tutors or mentors are improved when they work within a clear framework for the development of students' pedagogic skills and strategies. Within this framework there must be a continuous testing of practitioners' schemas against practical experiences. When all participants can jointly explore the language and categories they use to talk about selected aspect of teaching there is a better chance of being able to refine and develop the way in which teachers think about their work. In our model of teachers' professional learning actions and activity, verbal and mental actions are constantly being worked on and reconstructed. Working on explicit representations of situated knowledge in particular contents can be a means of developing professionally relevant knowledge schemas.

Our concern with intellectual processes refers specifically to the nature and development of deliberation and judgment as more complex expressions of competence. These can be practiced in discourse with student teachers, by requiring them to construct a "practical argument" (Fenstermacher, 1986), in which they test and monitor how they reason about teacher actions and carefully examine how this process informs their thinking and planning of future teaching episodes.

These approaches involve tutoring student teachers in cognitive modeling activities that show how performance and schema are related, and now "schemas and intellectual processes become powerful mediators of experience and determinants of action" (Desforges, 1989, p. 23). This involves students or teachers in representing their practical knowledge as an explicit representation so that it can be analyzed and interpreted for more strategic planning, teaching, and evaluation. It is strategic in that performance is being modified by what has gone on before. In this sense, effective learning is not just constructive: it is intentional. It begins as a collaborative activity but, ultimately, is directed at the learner's self-guided activity and constructive self-explanation.

Part of this process of growing professional independence is the constant challenging of teachers' understanding by presenting alternative perspectives, explanations, and theories. These play an essential part in the dialogue between teacher-learner and tutor. Professional teachers need to develop the ability to absorb and/or confront research findings and what Eraut (1989) called *publicly available theories*.

> Publicly available theories – Piagetian Theory, Symbolic Interactionist Theory, Human Capital Theory, etc. – are systems of ideas published in books, discussed in classes and accompanied by a critical literature which expands, interprets and challenges their meaning and their validity. (p. 1)

Without direct engagement with such theory, we risk a situation in which the accumulated knowledge of generations is ignored, and personal idiosyncracies go unchallenged.

Our model suggests that understanding is a part of knowing how and demonstrates that this can show itself in different ways. We need to recognize the different capacities and abilities that teachers need to (a) demonstrate competent performance, (b) witness and understand observed performances, and (c) critically evaluate performance. By attending to these various facets of growth of teacher competence, we are more likely to develop their capacity to monitor how they organize professionally relevant knowledge over time, interpret contradictions, and articulate different kinds of challenges so that they become conscious agents in their pedagogy (Britzman, 1989).

THE USE OF COMPETENCE APPROACHES IN TEACHER EDUCATION

A comparison of what has been said about competence so far with what was said about teacher education in Chapter 1 makes our basic position quite clear. A behaviorist model of competence is logically and practically linked with the view of teacher as technician, with which we strongly dissent. Such a position is a dangerous oversimplification and misunderstanding of learning, teaching, and what education should be about. The interactive model of competence just outlined has much in common with our conception of the teacher as a proactive and empowered professional. The key questions, therefore, concern the extent to which an explicitly competence-based model of teacher education based on an interactive ideology is appropriate in the development of professional teacher, and what its limitations are. One example of such a program is described and analyzed in Chapters 6 and 7 later in this volume. Here, we are concerned with general principles.

Teacher education, especially the initial education of teachers, is centrally concerned with performance, and with enabling teachers to perform better in a range of situations of which the classroom is only one. One advantage of competence-based schemes is that elements of teacher performance are made explicit. There are two criteria for the selection of statements of competence. Firstly, such statements of competence should be closely related to the roles teachers have to perform, or they will be meaningless. However, from an interactive perspective, there is no single externally verifiable role, nor is there one set of "correct" statements of competence. In an interactive approach, teachers should be reflective and critical in their performance. As Jamieson (Chapter 3) suggested, teachers as learners need to understand themselves better, and such self-reflection and self-awareness can be seen as key aspects of performance.

By accepting a plurality of valid units of competence, we are freed from the damaging and distorting reification of the statements. We can also invoke the second criteria for their selection: their usefulness as a learning tool. Appropriate competence statements provide teachers with a language to make sense of their practical experiences, and to facilitate dialogue about teaching and education. They can facilitate diagnosis of strengths and weaknesses in performance, enabling attention to be focused in appropriate areas. Competence statements enable learning and assessment to be shared between learner and tutor, which is essential if the teacher-learner is to become a partner in learning and be empowered, which in itself is a necessary condition for continued learning once formal instruction is completed.

It will be clear by now that we are strong advocates of an interactive competence-based approach to teacher education. However, this is not to say that teacher education should consist of nothing else. If only because of our lack of knowledge about how people learn and the contested nature of almost all educational, psychological, and sociological theory, it would be foolish and dangerous to base all our practice on one theoretical framework. It would also be a mistake to focus the whole of teacher education on performance, important though that is.

One of the dangers of such a narrow focusing on performance was demonstrated by Hargreaves (1989). He showed that there are two alternative sets of explanation for what HMI consistently identify as poor, overly didactic transmission teaching. The official view, he said, is that such poor teaching is explained by three factors: inadequate personal qualities in teachers, inadequate pedagogical skills, and inadequate subject knowledge (see also McNamarra, Chapter 13). If we accept this analysis unquestioningly, then the first is an issue of recruitment, the second an issue either of recruitment or initial training, and the third is an issue where competence-based training might help improve standards of performance. However, Hargreaves offered an alternative explanation that suggests that the limited nature of transmission teaching is a result of intelligent, motivated, and competent professionals making rational responses to the context in which they work. As he said: "Teachers, like other people, are not just bundles of skill, competence and technique; they are creators of meaning, interpreters of the world and all it asks of them" (p. 58). He analyzed in detail several situational factors which pressure teachers to adopt these transmission approaches. They are:

1. The control purposes that transmission teaching serves in managing large cohorts of pupils in restricted physical space;

2. Its appropriateness for circumstances of low resource levels and severe material constraints;

3. Its compatibility with a mandated curriculum, whether this is governmentally set or determined by a public examination system;

4. Its association with particular subject specialisms and, elsewhere, its availability as a fall-back strategy for those teaching outside the secure boundaries of their own specialism;

5. The minimal effort demands it makes upon teachers who have lowered their investment in teaching due to career blockage and status denial;

6. Its suitability for, and protection by, the conditions of teacher isolation, where external criteria of professional competence are ostensibly met and inducements to change are absent (p. 70).

What Hargreaves showed is that teacher performance in the classroom cannot be improved or changed significantly by focusing on the performance only. This would amount to an overindividualized view of teaching—another manifestation of the "blaming the victim" syndrome. Thus, if one teacher manages to teach effectively and imaginatively despite the contextual problems but another does not, the fault must always be found in the personal performance and competence of the one who does not.

The critical reflectivity implicit within an interactive model of competence, that in turn includes culture and context as part of its frame, can avoid the worst dangers of individualization in ways that a behaviorist model does not. However, as with the symbolic interactionist school of sociology from which it is partly drawn, the model does largely ignore the larger historical, political, and economic dimensions of the society in which we all live, work, and learn; if teachers are to be genuinely empowered they must be made to be aware of these macroissues, and enabled to make their own sophisticated judgments of them. They need to be able to question the validity and appropriateness of society in terms of values and ethics, as well as their own pragmatic performance. Hargreaves reminded us that the two are linked.

Too rigid adherence to even an interactive competence model would open up teacher education to the same criticism that Alvis (1991) made about progressive education and the new vocationalism in Britain. He claimed that what are basically child- or learner-centered approaches to education constantly fall into the trap of taking the existing society in which we live as an unproblematic, an uncontested given. This is disempowering for the learner and may serve to foster the aims of the new right in preserving elitism and an ideology of individualism so graphically illustrated when Margaret Thatcher, while Prime minister of Britain, claimed there was no such thing as society.

Linked with this issue is another, concerned with the relationship between theory and practice. Young (1990) suggested that recent changes within teacher education, from an academic-discipline-based approach to a focus on issues and practical problems, leaves the relationship between theory and practice unchanged. He suggested that we need to address this relationship through three steps:

> First, we need to recognize and understand the 'theories' that students or teachers have for making sense of their practice. This is the element of reflecting on practice in any successful educational experience. Second, we need to assess the theories that have been developed by those with time to reflect and research. This is not a passive activity, but requires the clarifying of agreed purposes between student and teacher which then become the criteria for examining the "theories". Third, we need to develop strategies that enable the "theories" of the two kinds to interrogate each other. (p. 18)

The use of competences within an interactionist ideology concerns the first step, but the use of competence statements alone does not guarantee it. The real power of an interactive model of competence presented here is that, unlike the behaviorist model, it explicitly focuses on learning rather than on the measurement of outcomes. An essential part of this model is the interaction between learner and tutor, between learner and other teachers, between learner and pupils, and between learner and peers. Young reminded us that the theoretical work of educational academics has to be a vital ingredient in this process. Such theoretical perspectives facilitate personal schema development and change and are vital in the development of critical perspective. An interactive view of competence follows Young in that it stresses engagement with such theoretical perspectives, rather than separating them out as sometimes happens in both overly academic and overly practical courses.

It follows from Young's analysis that there will need to be specific coverage of theoretical issues in order to engage in his second step. This may well be done partly in didactic ways through reading and lectures, but must go on to involve teacher-learners actively using an interactive approach. It would need to be "off the job," to give distance from the situationally specific arena of performance. Although such studies would sit uncomfortably alongside a behaviorist competence approach, they simply add to and enrich interactive competence. What is more, the interactive model of competence outlined here will be helpful in engaging in Young's third step, which is the cross-interrogation of his two types of theory through the ongoing dialogue between teacher-learner and tutors and peers, aided by the exposure of personal schema to criticism.

CONCLUSION

In this chapter we tried to examine the potential of competence-based approaches to the education of professional teachers. The conclusion, as with so many things, must be that it is neither good nor bad per se. The meaning of a competence approach varies enormously depending on the ideology adopted. The behaviorist approaches of NVQ, while bringing some benefits in terms of relating learning to the practice of the workplace and reducing transmission teaching, is inappropriate for professional education, because of its unrealistic view of learning, its concentration on the situationally specific, and its view of the teacher as a technician working in a taken-for-granted context. Competence derived from an interactive perspective would not only avoid most of the worst excesses of a behaviorist approach, it would also facilitate reflective practice and enable the engagement between practice, implicit personal theory, and external academic theory. Crucial to this conception of competence is the deliberate focus on the learning process.

We also showed that such a competence-based approach is not enough. It can be a valuable part of teacher education, alongside other elements that are equally important, such as the critical examination of broader contextual and ideological issues. The criticality developed in professional teachers must go beyond performance and engage in macroissues at a level of ethics and value judgment. Such approaches will inevitably attract strong opposition from the intellectual right. In distancing ourselves from their stance, we must not surrender too much ground by allowing them to colonize competency approaches as their own. Rather we need to contest the meaning of competence and define it in an interactive ideology, as a key part of a teacher education provision.

REFERENCES

Alvis, J. (1991). The strange fate of progressive education. In Education Group II, *Education limited: Schooling, training and the new Right in England since 1979*. London: Unwin Hyman.

Apple, M. W. (1979). *Ideology and the curriculum*. London: Routledge and Kegan Paul.

Ashworth, P. D., & Saxton, J. (1990). On competence. *Journal of Further and Higher Education, 14* (2), 1-25.

Berger, P. L., & Luckman, T. (1966). *The social construction of reality: A treatise on the sociology of knowledge*. New York: Doubleday.

Black, H., & Wolf, A. (Eds.). (1990). *Knowledge and competence: Current issues in training and education*. London: CDIC.

Britzman, D. P. (1989). Who has the floor? Curriculum, teaching and the English teacher's struggle for voice. *Curriculum Inquiry, 19* (2), 143-162.

Brown, J. S., Collins, A., & Duguid, P. (1989). Situated cognition and the culture of learning. *Educational Researcher, 18* (1), 32-42.

Burke, J. (Eds.). (1989). *Competence based education and training*. Lewes, UK: Falmer.

Candy, P., & Harris, R. (1990). Implementing competence-based vocational education: A view from within. *Journal of Further and Higher Education, 14* (2), 38-58.

Desforges, C. (1989). Understanding learning for teaching *Westminster Studies in Education, 12*, 17-29.

De Ville, D. (1986). *Review of vocational qualifications in England and Wales*. London: MSC/Department of Employment.

Eraut, M. R. (1989). *The acquisition and use of educational Theory by beginning teachers*. Unpublished mimeo.

Fenstermacher, G. (1986). Philosophy of research on teaching: Three aspects. In M. C. Wittrock (Ed.), *Handbook of research on teaching* (3rd ed.). New York: Macmillan.

Goffman, E. (1961). *Encounters: Two studies in the sociology of interaction*. Indianapolis: Bobbs-Merill.

Hargreaves, A. (1989). Teaching quality: A sociological analysis. In B. Cosin, M. Flude, & M. Hales (Eds.), *School, work and equality*. London: Hodder and Stoughton.

Jessup, G. (1991). *Outcomes: NVQs and the emerging model of education and training*. Lewes, UK: Falmer.

Kuhn, T. (1962). *The structure of scientific revolutions*. Chicago: University of Chicago Press.

Levin, J. R., & Allen, V. L. (Eds.). (1976). *Cognitive learning in children*. New York: Academic Press.

Resnick, L. B. (1987). Learning in school and out. *Educational Researcher, 16* (9), 13-20.

Rumelhart, D. E. (1980). Schemata: The building blocks of cognition. In R. Spiro, B. C. Brice, & W. F. Brewer (Eds.), *Theoretical issues in reading comprehension*. Hillsdale, NJ: Erlbaum.

Ryle, G. (1949). *The concept of mind*. London: Penguin Books.

Tuxworth, E. (1989). Competence based education and training: Backgrounds and origins. In J. Burke (Ed.), *competence based education and training*. Lewes, UK: Falmer.

Young, M. (1990). Bridging the theory/practice divide: An old problem in a new context. *Educational and Child Psychology, 7* (3), 14-22.

CHAPTER 5

The Acquisition and Use of Educational Theory By Beginning Teachers

Michael Eraut
University of Sussex

This chapter is a revised version of a paper given to a UCET conference in 1985 on the role of theory in PGCE courses. Since that time the relationship between theory and practice appears not to have been further elucidated but to have been covered up by new labels and old accusations. The concept of the "reflective practitioner" (Schon, 1983, 1987) has gained wide currency, but the role of theory in guiding or informing the process of reflection has yet to receive the attention it deserves. The radical right has suggested that the teaching of theory is not only irrelevant but subversive, and argued for taking teacher training out of higher education and locating it only in schools. The idea that much mid-career teacher education should involve "action research" has become quite popular, whereas the role of theory in such work has been little discussed. Theory has even been identified as a mechanism used by academics to assert control over practitioners (Elliott, 1991).

This chapter argues that more heat than light is created by perpetually contrasting theory with practice, and by assuming that there is only one kind of theory. We need to introduce student teachers to different kinds of theory, to share with them the discussion about using theory in practice and inferring theory out of practice, and to develop their capacity to theorize about what they are doing. As Russell (1988) reported:

> We are increasingly convinced that the image one holds of the relationship between theory and practice can significantly influence understanding of the

69

personal learning process, at every stage in one's development of the professional knowledge of teaching. (p. 33)

Both the concept of theory and the process of theorizing must be demystified.

The chapter confines its attention to educational theory and does not cover teachers' knowledge of subject matter, important though this is. Thus the theories under discussion will relate to classroom events, to school policy and practice, and to the effect of influences across the school's boundary with the community.

I shall begin by providing definitions of two key terms, *theory* and *theorize*, as these are fundamental to my analysis. Theory is used in both a public and a private sense. Publicly available theories – Piagetian theory, symbolic interactionist theory, human capital theory, and so on – are systems of ideas published in books, discussed in classes, and accompanied by a critical literature that expands, interprets, and challenges their meaning and their validity. By extension, the term *theory* is generalized to include collections of such individual theories whose identity is proclaimed by the title of a course or a location in a library. Private theories are ideas in people's minds which they use to interpret or explain their experience. These may be private versions of publicly available theories, or they may not be traceable in any publicly available form. Their use may not be explicit, indeed they may only be inferred from observing someone's behavior; but they must be at least capable of explicit formulation.

My definition of *theory*, therefore, is framed to allow for both public and private theories, and extended to include a valuational element in addition to interpretation and explanation:

> *Educational theory* comprises concepts, frameworks, ideas, and principles that may be used to interpret, explain, or judge intentions, actions, and experiences in educational or education-related settings.

This definition excludes the use of theory to mean something opposed to or apart from practice; because this leads all too easily to the absurd conclusion that an idea is only "theoretical" if it never gets used.

My definition of the term *theorize* also needs justification, because in common usage to theorize is to construct a theory. I shall be arguing below in some detail that both the complex and unique nature of practical situations, and the manner in which publicly available theories are formulated, makes the routine application of such theories to practice impossible. Using a theory involves giving it a contextually specific meaning, so there is always an element of reinterpretation or reconstruction; and the intellectual effort is often at least as great as in constructing a private theory. Thus it is unhelpful to suggest that the construction of private theory is significantly different from the reconstruction of public theory. Accepting this argument allows me to define *theorize* in much more general terms:

> To *theorize* is to interpret, explain, or judge intentions, actions, and experiences.

Given the many ways in which people "pick up" ideas, and their tendency to forget where they got them, it would be exceedingly impractical to adopt a definition of *theorize* which depended on the nature of the source or even on knowing whether an idea was original or not. Both putting public theories into use and reviewing private theories already in use involve the process of theorizing; and the distinction between them is not always clear.

Theory may be acquired from many different sources, for example, precourse experience, school experience, student colleagues, university teaching, and reading. Teaching strategies of beginning teachers are generally acknowledged to be strongly influenced by their earlier experiences as pupils. People tend to teach, or in a few cases to avoid teaching, in a similar manner to that in which they themselves were taught. Similarly, student teachers already possess a considerable quantity of theory before they even begin their courses. Their reflections on their own experience of schooling are not the only important component of this theoretical preknowledge. Many other aspects of their lives will have contributed to their "knowledge of people" and their "theories of human behavior." Such theories need not be clearly formulated nor even explicitly stated to influence their later behavior as teachers. Moreover, there are many ideas about education freely circulating in the press, on television, and in everyday conversation to which they are unlikely to be immune. These last may have been subjected to at least some critical argument, but it is doubtful, apart from those cases where relevant material was included in first degrees, whether any of this theoretical preknowledge will have been subjected to any systematic reflection and scrutiny. To what extent, then, we may ask, should a PGCE course aim to make explicit this precourse personal knowledge so that it may be criticized, built on, or evaluated? At Sussex, this process begins with a student autobiography[1] handed in on arrival and is linked to reflection on early observation. The most extensive program of reflection on prior experience, however, is reported by Korthagen (1988), from Utrecht, where it is also linked to their concurrent learning of their main subject of mathematics:

---

[1]See Grumet (1989) for a more prolonged autobiographical approach.

Two aspects are particularly noteworthy. First of all, learning to reflect is not limited to the pedagogical component of the programme. It is also a recurring principle on the mathematical side. Students are encouraged to reflect not only on the subject content, but also to consider the way in which they help or cooperate with others, as well as their awareness of feelings, attitudes and personal goals. Thus the mathematical side of the programme and the specific professional preparation are closely linked.

A second major aspect of the programme is that reflection is stressed even before students embark on their practical teaching. The idea behind this is that student teachers can be armed against socialization into established patterns of school practice. The student teacher must first gain some idea of who he or she is, of what he or she wants, and above all, of the ways in which one can take responsibility for one's own learning. The first period of student teaching can be one of extreme stress, in which the prime concern is simply to 'get through'. This is not an auspicious moment for learning the art of reflection. Prospective teachers must already have at their disposal sufficient powers of reflection to enable them to evaluate the influence of these personal concerns on the way in which they themselves function in the classroom. (pp. 38–39)

Although most of this chapter is concerned with theorizing about one's own classroom experience, other school-based sources of theory should not be forgotten. Beginning teachers encounter other teachers' theories, even pupils' theories, whether or not they recognize them as such. These also could be examined with benefit. Clark (1986) reported that:

Research on teacher thinking has documented the fact that teachers develop and hold implicit theories about their students about the subject matter that they teach and about their roles and responsibilities and how they should act. These implicit theories are not neat and complete reproductions of the educational psychology found in textbooks or lecture notes. Rather, teachers' implicit theories tend to be eclectic aggregations of cause-effect propositions from many sources, rules of thumb, generalizations drawn from personal experience, beliefs, values, biases, and prejudices. . . . And teachers' implicit theories about themselves and their work are thought to play an important part in the judgements and interpretations that teachers make every day. (p. 5)

Greater understanding of the origins and functions of teachers' theories about pupils, about knowledge, and about teaching and learning could help bring the process of socialization into the profession under greater critical control.

It would also be healthy if we regarded the acquisition of theory from books in a similar kind of way. We tend to take for granted that our students know what kinds of theory and theorizing are found in different sorts of text, and fail to help them evaluate the theories embedded in "nontheoretical" curriculum and methods books. Teachers tend to mine such books for practical knowledge and absorb without criticism the persuasive rhetoric in which such knowledge is often couched.[2] Surely the critical use of different kinds of books is important for beginning teachers' acquisition of theory?

If a major aim of PGCE courses is to enhance the theorizing capacities of our students, that is, their ability to acquire, refine, evaluate, and use theories for the improvement of their practice, then it is essential for them to have some knowledge and understanding of the theorizing process itself. Unless they can conceptualize the task of learning to theorize, they are unlikely to develop the capacity to do so. Moreover, without some discussion and reflection on personal experience of professional knowledge and learning, the nature of the theorizing task may be misunderstood. Indeed there is a danger that it is perceived as other-oriented rather than self-oriented, completing written assignments to pass the course or talking in seminars to give the tutor a good impression and get good references. Beginning teachers also need to acquire some understanding of the role which theorizing can play in various aspects of professional practice, to have some knowledge of where and how other teachers have used it, for what purpose, and with what effect.

Such practical questions as when to theorize and for how long, what factors to consider, when and how to get another opinion, how to focus and organize one's thinking, what evidence to consider reasonable, when to trust and when not to trust one's early thoughts, have considerable influence on the benefits accruing from the theorizing process. These need to be discussed at some stage, because they affect people's ability to assert a useful degree of control over their own theorizing (their metacognition). It is also important to discuss the essentially practical nature of theorizing if students are to develop a sensible perspective on it (i.e., some practical wisdom).

It is misleading, however, to describe theorizing as a skill, because the repetitive element is far too slight. It probably improves with practice, but such practice is unlikely to be of a routine variety. Kuhn (1974) argued, in the case of science, that it is not by linguistic rules that science attaches its language to nature, but rather by means of exemplars. It this were also true of education, then students' knowledge of theorizing would consist primarily of those exemplars they had become familiar with. These would provide a knowledge of the theorizing process that could be applied through further intuitive generalization, and there would be no need to

---

[2]Cf. Anderson's (1981) critique of Schools Council project manuals, and my own work (Eraut Goad, & Smith, 1975) on assumptions embedded in pupils' materials.

look for any special forms of reasoning that could be labeled as *theorizing skills*. Indeed such is the power of conceptual frameworks that problems of theorizing are more likely to arise from the limited range of perspectives we bring to seeing practice and to representing what we see, than from any lack of ability to reason.

In order to extend the range of perspectives we bring to the interpretation of practice, we need more concepts and ideas to think with. Although some may be derived from reflection and discussion of personal practice, others can be obtained from the domain of public theory. But what is the likelihood that public theory will be called upon in this way? This brings us to a practical paradox. If public theory is taught but does not get used, it gets consigned to some remote attic of the mind, from where it is unlikely to be retrieved as it is already labeled *irrelevant*. But if public theory is not taught, teachers' ability to theorize is handicapped by their limited repertoire of available concepts, ideas, and principles. To resolve this dilemma, we must examine more closely the processes by which public theory gets used.

THE ACQUISITION AND USE OF DISCIPLINE-BASED THEORY

Traditionally, higher education has accorded priority to discipline-based theories and concepts, derived from bodies of coherent, systematic knowledge. Historically, those disciplines regarded as relevant to education have been psychology, philosophy, sociology, and occasionally history. The validity of these disciplines does not depend on their professional application, but their relevance to beginning teachers has been increasingly questioned. Though it is usually possible to argue that discipline-based knowledge connects with practical situations in the sense of contributing some understanding of them, this does not establish any priority. The problem with public theories in general is that they tend to remain in educational discourse, be discussed, criticized, and written about without affecting practice. They may not ever get used. Hence, before we try to decide what theories should be included in PGCE courses, we need to understand rather more about how and when such knowledge might get used.

Broudy, Smith, and Burnett (1964) defined four categories for describing how knowledge acquired during schooling is used in later life, namely replication, application, interpretation, and association. These can also be applied to the use of discipline-based theories by beginning teachers. The replicative mode of knowledge use is rare in PGCE courses, being confined to derivative approaches to essay writing (strongly discouraged) and examinations (does anyone still have them?). The applicative mode has been long regarded as important, but support for the notion that theory derived within discipline-based inquiry can be directly applied to practice has dwindled over the last decade. Indeed many authors now argue that such a relationship between theory and practice is impossible (Hirst, 1979; McIntyre, 1980; Tom, 1980). Instead we are offered the notions of grounded theory, practical principles, and craft knowledge, which are both directly derived from and readily applicable to practice. These ideas will be further examined in the next section.

The interpretative use of theory has become increasingly prominent in discussion of theory–practice issues, so let us consider some of its implications. First, the complexity of educational settings usually insures that a very large number of concepts and ideas are potentially relevant. So on what grounds does a person select? Is it according to utility or ethical principles, or is it governed by more intuitive criteria like personal preference or fittingness? Second, how does a discipline-derived concept or idea come to be seen as relevant? Either because interpreters make their own linkages to practical situations, or because some previous user of the theory has demonstrated relevance for a situation construed as similar. Without such examples, and without the ability or disposition to draw fresh concepts into their theorizing, beginning teachers are likely to relegate areas of theory to storage. Thirdly, both the selection and the use of ideas are likely to be influenced by existing conceptual frameworks. Some teachers will be more inclined to use certain ideas than others, and they may not be aware of the reason. Finally, the process of interpretation is reversible. The meaning of a concept is largely carried by knowledge of examples of its use, so that an individual's understanding of the concept is expanded, perhaps even altered, by each new example of its use. The converse of using existing theory to interpret practice is allowing practice to reshape theory, a relationship that is nicely expressed by Piaget's twin concepts of assimilation and accommodation. Thus if we wish to encourage the interpretative use of discipline-based theories, we need to consider the following points:

1. The use of an idea depends not only on it being "in mind," but also on it being perceived as relevant because examples are known of its use in similar situations.
2. The selection of an interpretation is influenced by existing conceptual frameworks that may derive primarily from prior experience and not be at all explicit.
3. These frameworks may change through accommodation to new experiences, but the process is slow, gradual, and uncertain.
4. The interpretative use of theory necessarily involves theorizing, for which many beginning teachers may have neither the skill nor

the disposition unless their training is somehow able to provide them.

The associative use of theory is rarely discussed, but a few examples will illustrate how powerfully pervasive it can be. The accountability debate has been not only about power, but also about images: the school as a garden, the school as a club, the school as a factory. Progressive education, in particular, has been powerfully presented in terms of images: and accounts of progressive classrooms are notable for their image-making as opposed to analytic qualities. Special education, on the other hand, is dominated by medical rather than horticultural images – classification according to handicap rather than need and the diagnosis–treatment approach to individualization. Still other images are conjured up by terms like *core, basics, pastoral,* or *interface.* Even the process of learning itself is frequently discussed in metaphoric terms (Reddy, 1979):

It is very difficult to put this concept into words. (p. 312)

Everybody must get the ideas in this article into his head by tomorrow. (p. 315)

You have to absorb Plato's ideas a little at a time. (p. 319)

PRACTICAL KNOWLEDGE AND PRACTICAL PRINCIPLES

Those types of knowledge that are derived from practice and validated in practice are variously described as practical knowledge (Oakeshott, 1962) or craft knowledge (McNamara & Desforges, 1979; Tom, 1980). This encompasses process knowledge or "know-how"; specific knowledge about particular people, situations, decisions, or actions; and generalized knowledge of the type Hirst (1979, 1985) has called *practical concepts and principles.* However, the nature and status of this practical knowledge is by no means agreed, and its separateness from discipline-based knowledge may be more apparent than real. Four major issues for debate are the explicitness of practical knowledge, its generalizability, its scope, and its morality.

Oakeshott (1962), following Aristotle, made a clear distinction between technical knowledge and practical knowledge. Technical knowledge is capable of written codification; but practical knowledge is expressed only in practice and learned only through experience with practice. Some kinds of practical knowledge are uncodifiable in principle. For example, knowledge that is essentially nonverbal – the tone of a voice or musical instrument, the feel of a muscle or a piece of sculpture, the expression on a face –

cannot be fully described in writing. Verbal performances, such as teaching or advocacy, which are not fully scripted beyond a brief set of notes, cannot be reduced to simple technical descriptions. Even scripted performances, like those of an actor or pianist, take on their special character because interpretations of quality require the repeatable elements such as the memorization of the script and the reproduction of the sounds to be reduced to instinctive routine.

However, to recognize that uncodifiable practical knowledge exists need not imply that stored written knowledge is irrelevant to such situations. Performances may be written about and discussed by critics and colleagues, and there is a tradition of criticism of nonverbal activities like art and music, which, though perhaps overrated, is certainly not futile. The problem lies in the complex, often tenuous, relationship between comment and action. Moreover, as already suggested, the unscripted and intuitive nature of many verbal activities makes attempts to describe or criticize them equally difficult. Argyris and Schon (1974) noted how divergence between comment and action still persists when commentator and actor are the same person. They argue that professional actions are based on implicit "theories in use," which differ from the "espoused theories" used to explain them to external audiences or even to the actor himself. Self-knowledge of performance is difficult to acquire, and self-comment tends to be justificatory rather than critical in intent.

Argyris and Schon regarded making implicit "theories in use" explicit and thereby open to criticism as the key to professional learning, but they were talking about experienced practitioners. The question persists as to how much professional know-how is essentially implicit, and how much is capable with appropriate time and attention of being described and explained. Moreover, it is easier to follow the Argyris and Schon model in their selected context of management than in classroom teaching. Most managerial decisions can be described as *cool*—there is time to reflect and deliberate; whereas while classroom decisions are *hot*, in the midst of the action, and intuitive (Jackson, 1971). The problem of making classroom knowledge explicit is clearly much greater.

A useful approach to the questions of the generalizability of practical knowledge is provided by Buchler's (1961) analysis of *method*:

Whoever is said to act methodically (1) chooses a mode of conduct (2) to be directed in a given way (3) to a particular set of circumstances (4) for the attainment of a result. These four simple factors required by the conjunction of 'art' and 'method' can each assume different forms. The mode of conduct adopted may consist in (1a) established practice, in (1b) established practice modified by idiosyncratic technique, or in (1c) essentially idiosyncratic, private practice. Whatever procedure is adopted, it may be utilized (2a) strictly and in accordance with prescription, or (2b) loosely, variably, and with a discretionary relation to prescription, or (2c) uniquely, in consequence of predominant reliance on insight. The circumstances under which the procedure is utilised may be (3a) definitely classifiable circumstances, or (3b) circumstances ranging from the expected and classified down to the minimal circumstances that would allow the procedure. And the result toward which the activity aims may be (4a) an envisaged or familiar type of result, or (4b) an indefinite result accepted as such in terms of desirability, or (4c) a relatively novel result. These forms are not exhaustive, but their possible combinations help to explain the differences that prevail when we speak variously of the art of surgery, the art of writing fiction, the art of management, the art of building, or the art of swimming. (pp. 32–33)

Commenting on Bentham's concept of a "tactic faculty," Buchler distinguished between two possible meanings:

One of these has to do with a prepared order eligible for application to appropriate circumstance; the other has to do with a power of adjusting practice to variable circumstances. The one emphasizes a fund or store of techniques whose function is anticipatory; the other emphasizes resourceful practice precisely in the face of the unanticipated. (p. 34)

According to the model of practice that is believed to be desirable, the process of professional education will need to take a very different form. A combination of (1a), (2a), (3a), and (4a) leads to an emphasis on methodic training, coaching, and planned activity; whereas a combination of (1c), (2c), (3b), and (4c) leads to an emphasis on variety of experience, responsiveness, invention, and quick reading of a situation as it develops. The former can bypass theory by teaching methodic procedures from an apparently atheoretical perspective; the latter is likely to emphasize the primacy of personal experience.

Between these two extremes lies the possibility of method that is adapted to suit both user and situation. Although teachers are expected and encouraged to develop their own personal method, this is usually viewed in terms of selection from recognized methods followed by adaptation to create a personal style. Only rarely would the method itself be seen as novel. The process requires that student teachers be prepared to modify and experiment with the methods they have chosen to use, that they are encouraged to do this, and that they are provided with appropriate feedback. Adaptation to situation, however, requires rather different treatment. It is little help merely to agree that it is desirable to adapt method to suit particular pupils and particular circumstances, for there remains the problem of precisely how it is to be done.

This leads us back to decision making as an aspect of teacher behavior to which our attention is frequently drawn, and whose effectiveness clearly depends on the knowledge and know-how the teacher brings to each individual situation. Because much of this knowledge comes from experience with previous situations, its use must involve at least some degree of generalization. Some idea, procedure, or action that was used in a previous situation is considered to be applicable to the new one. The nature of this generalization process, however, may vary in both scope and explicitness: at minimum Situation B is perceived as similar to Situation G and handled in the same sort of way; at maximum, some practical principle is consciously applied, which is thought to be valid for all situations of a certain type. Semiconscious patterning of previous experience may also occur, making it difficult for the professional to trace the source of, or even to clearly articulate, the generalisation he or she is using.

In this context it is important to note that recent research on human inference (Nisbett & Ross, 1980) has shown that it has many limitations. For example, Tversky and Kahneman (1973) found that in judging the relative frequency of particular objects or the likelihood of particular events, people are influenced by their relative accessibility in the mind. In particular the immediate perceptual salience of an event influences the vividness or completeness with which it is recalled. Thus, a teacher making a judgment about a child's behavior or potential is more likely to remember some incidents than others and to attach more weight to some kinds of evidence. Learning to read a situation and adapt one's behavior accordingly is likely to be promoted by reflective theorizing, whether or not the behavior is perceived as principle based or rule following. But such reflection is also susceptible to error, unless it is brought under proper critical control.

Teachers are also particularly vulnerable to what Ross (1977) has called the *fundamental attribution error*—the tendency to attribute behavior exclusively to the actor's dispositions and to ignore powerful situational determinants of the behavior. He suggests that this "dispositionalist theory" is woven into the fabric of our culture, with "situationalist" thinking being confined to social scientists. Hence we need to introduce beginning teachers to sufficient social science theory to enable them to place teaching within its situational and institutional contexts, what Zeichner and Lipson (1987) referred to as *second level reflection*.

Another issue that remains to be solved is the scope of practical knowledge or, what matters more for many practical purposes, the scope of those practical principles that can be derived from it and made explicit. How feasible are the aspirations of those who hope to codify teachers' craft knowledge? It is not difficult to find maxims or practical tips to pass on to beginning teachers, but what do they all add up to? Can we envisage a situation where the sum of such advice specifies at all precisely what a teacher ought to decide, even if one assumes there is basic agreement on aims and values? Wittgenstein pointed out that no set of rules can completely prescribe a decision, because there remain further decisions about when a rule is applicable and when it is not. But this theoretical limit of prescription seems very remote when we have nothing resembling a comprehensive set of rules. Can an amorphous collection of practical principles be said to constitute a grounded theory of practice, or is this mere wishful thinking?

Other philosophers have focused on the way in which practical knowledge incorporates moral principles. The Whites (1984) disclosed the complex nature of the relationship when they define *successful practice* as "that practice which is achieving justifiable aims in an acceptable way." However, although moral principles must be involved in deciding what aims are justifiable and what methods are acceptable, these may not be made explicit. As Petrie (1981) suggested, "Norm-regarding behaviour can be in accordance with implicit or unconscious rules, if we stand ready to correct deviations from the norm and recognize our mistakes" (p. 89). If one questions teachers about where and when they are called upon to resolve moral issues, they are likely to cite critical incidents involving the conduct of individual pupils and teachers; the moral principles underlying the teaching process itself are often taken for granted. Nevertheless, moral principles *are* embedded in practice; and it is because we believe teachers *ought* to recognize them, discuss them, and evaluate them that we seek to include such activities in initial training courses.

THE INFLUENCE OF CONTEXT ON THE THEORIZING PROCESS

In an earlier article on teacher learning during inservice education (Eraut, 1982), I argued that such learning is highly dependent on the context. Much PGCE and INSET teaching is based on the rarely challenged assumption that knowledge is first acquired and then subsequently, if circumstances permit, used. But there is a fundamental flaw in this assumption—the hidden premise that it is the same knowledge in each case. This can only be true of the replicative and applicative modes of knowledge use. Even within an academic context, if somebody encounters a new idea in a lecture, book, or seminar, and then later refers to it in an essay or project, can we say that learning about the idea was confined to the moment of the original encounter? Some learning is associated with new input, some with new use; and some, no doubt, with the period in between, when there may be reflection on input or contemplation of use. Not only does an idea get reinterpreted during use in accord with the reciprocal relationship between theory and practice we discussed earlier, but it may even need to be used before it can acquire any significant meaning for the user.

Theory is not stored in the mind in isolated and decontextualized form: It derives meaning and richness from connections with other ideas and associations with a variety of situations. The form the knowledge takes is strongly influenced by the ways in which it has been used, and this creates barriers to transfer between dissimilar contexts. We could ask, for example, whether the prolonged use of an idea in an academic context gives it a framework that inhibits its transfer to the school context–a mental analogue of that well-known phenomenon of "functional fixedness."

So let us consider carefully what learning to use ideas in various PGCE contexts involves. Within higher education, ideas may be used in writing, in formal discussion and in informal conversation. Where there is academic writing in essay format, both teachers and students (other than scientists and mathematicians) are well used to the conventions–specialized language, profuse citation, validation according to traditional disciplines or established fields of study, attention to several perspectives, and so on. The purposes of other kinds of writing, for example, extensive entries in course files, may be much less clear; so too might the criteria by which such writing is to be judged. Could the hidden curriculum ever become: "Provided you keep within acceptable limits, it's not what you think or do but the way you write about it that counts"? Theorizing in written form can also cause problems, because it leaves the students on their own just when they are most in need of help. Moreover, because the written form is rarely found among practicing teachers, it appears inauthentic and is unlikely to be used after qualification. We tend to take it for granted that writing for a wider audience enhances the theorizing process, but this may not necessarily be true. Teaching is primarily an oral culture.

Similarly, the way in which theory is used in formal discussion is strongly influenced by the communication process involved. Both group pressures for consensus and arguments between opposing members can lead to ideas being clothed in emotional language and used for their immediate impact on the discourse, to justify a viewpoint rather than clarify a meaning. Good preparation for staffroom politics, perhaps, but not good professional learning! Another problem arises when importing classroom experience into university-based discussions. To be anecdotal is easy, but to give sufficient contextual information for group theorizing is both time-consuming and risky for the individual involved. Not all students can provide the required quality of reporting, nor indeed can many experienced teachers. Given the personal nature of theorizing, we also ought to ask ourselves whether the group discussion provides the best way of developing it. For example, does it give all but one or two students sufficient practice in making it part of their own natural way of thinking? How about other forms of groupwork? Would it not be valid criticism to suggest that most PGCE courses give too much attention to the acquisition of theory and too little to helping students to use it?

Within schools, beginning teachers undergo three main kinds of experience which may or may not be closely related. They listen to, and sometimes participate in, *teacher discourse* about pupils, about school or department policy or about classroom practice. They *observe teachers and pupils* in classrooms, corridors, staffrooms, and other settings. They *practice teaching* with some guidance, receiving comments on lesson plans, being observed, engaging in postlesson discussion, and contributing to a logbook or course file. In some PGCE courses they also have the opportunity within a day or two to discuss what they have heard, seen or done in school back in the university setting. All these experiences can promote theorizing, particularly when this is encouraged by school as well as university tutors; but there are major contextual constraints.

First, there is the comparative rarity of professional discourse in many schools, particularly about classroom matters. Indeed, in most staffrooms the hidden agenda seems to be how to talk about the classroom without giving away any information that could possibly be used as a basis for criticism. That generating such discussion is difficult has been noted by McNamara and Desforges (1979), although there have always been some schools and departments where talk about teaching is common. However, the problem remains that the further away from the classroom, the more decontextualized such discussion becomes and the more difficult for the discussants to share meanings. In the absence of what Lortie (1975) called a *technical culture of teaching*, there is no common language of talk about classrooms; and the communication of meaning is dependent on shared experiences which can provide common points of reference.

Discourse about pupils, however, has traditionally played an important part in the training of primary teachers; and it has been linked with classrooms through observational studies of pupils. One possible explanation is that discourse about pupils is acceptable, even common, in primary schools, perhaps because it carries less threat than talk about teaching. Another is that student teachers have excellent opportunities for collecting information about individual pupils and studying how they learn. There is probably scope for more such work in secondary schools. The main problem here is not so much the lack of theorizing – labeling is a form of theorizing, for example – but the need to bring that theorizing under proper critical control.

Students' access to policy talk is likely to be limited, unless there is a series of joint seminars with their school-based tutors. These days, however, they are increasingly likely to encounter policy documents. To understand the significance of both spoken and written policy discourse, they will need to know something of school micropolitics and of policy-related communication between the school and external groups. This is virtually impossible on a PGCE course unless students spend considerable time in one school. Moreover, do we not need to examine more carefully how theory is used in policy discourse: Does it add meaning, does it mystify the audience, or is it simply a convenient source of justification? Another problem arises from the inevitable gap between policy and practice, between what people say and what they do. When policies are characterized by explicit reference to educational principles, this difference between rhetoric and reality can lead to rejection of those principles or to a kind of cynical and amoral pragmatism.

The second major contextual constraint on theorizing in schools arises from the nature of teaching itself. Learning to become a teacher and cope in the classroom involves developing routines and short-cuts, internalizing classroom decision making, and reducing the range of possible ways of thinking to manageable proportions. There are too many variables to take into account at once. This leads to intuitive grasping of certain communal practitioners' concepts (Buchmann, 1980) before they can be brought under proper control, although apparently more valid theoretical ideas get consigned to "storage" and never get retrieved.

Another difficulty, which I discussed earlier, is that theoretical ideas usually cannot be applied "off the shelf"; their implications have to be worked out and thought through. The busy teacher or student teacher may not easily find the time. Thus the functional relevance of a piece of theoretical knowledge depends less on its presumed validity than on the ability and willingness of people to use it. This is mainly determined by individual professionals and their work contexts, but is also affected by the way in which the knowledge is introduced and linked to their ongoing professional concerns.

THE DISPOSITION TO THEORIZE

Finally, we come to the most important quality of the professional teacher, the disposition to theorize. If our students acquire and sustain this disposition, they will go on developing their theorizing capacities throughout their teaching careers, they will be genuinely self-evaluative, and they will continue to search for, invent, and implement new ideas. Without, it they will become prisoners of their early school experience, perhaps the competent teachers of today, almost certainly the ossified teachers of tomorrow. Calderhead (1988) wrote:

Recent research on student teachers tends to suggest that their teaching relies heavily on the images of practice that are acquired from past and current experiences in schools. These images can be taken and implemented uncritically. The evaluation of practice might remain at a superficial level and knowledge bases which could potentially inform practice be little utilized. Furthermore, the school, and sometimes college, ethos might support a conception of teaching which does not encourage and may even impede an analytical response to one's own teaching, leading in some cases to opinionated or self-defensive approaches to professional learning. As a result, student teachers' learning could quite quickly reach a plateau where teaching has become routine, conservative and unproblematic. (p. 62)

So what factors are likely to affect the disposition to theorize; and what can we do to promote it?

First let us consider Fuller's developmental model of the process of becoming a teacher, which she derived from a longitudinal study of the concerns of beginning teachers (see Figure 5.1).

At the beginning student teachers' concerns may be distributed over stages 0-3, with attention to 2 when starting class teaching and attention to 3 when taking small groups of pupils. As and if they develop competence and confidence, they begin to acquire significant concerns at stages 4-5, though the earlier stages are likely to remain prominent for some considerable time. However, student teachers, or indeed qualified teachers, who are still struggling to manage their classes may be unlikely to accommodate these later stages of concern.

I.	Early Phase	0	Concerns about self (nonteaching concerns)
II.	Middle phase (competence)*	1	Concerns about professional expectations and acceptance
		2	Concerns about one's own adequacy: subject matter and class control
		3	Concerns about relationships with pupils
III.	Late phase (professionalism)*	4	Concerns about pupils' learning what is taught
		5	Concerns about pupils' learning what they need
		6	Concerns about one's own (teacher's) contributions to pupil change

*Added by the author.

Adapted from *Personalized Education for Teachers: An Introduction for Teacher Educator*, by F. Fuller, 1970, Austin: R & D Center for Teacher Education, University of Texas. Reprinted by permission.

Figure 5.1. *Model of teacher development.*

Insofar as this model is true for British PGCE students, and I suspect it is true for many but not for all, there are important implications for theorizing about classroom practice. Neither public theory nor requests for experience-based theorizing are likely to be taken seriously unless they engage with student concerns that are current. Hence, one might argue that early in the course student theorizing will need to address competence concerns; while the more advanced professional concerns are considered later.

However, in addition to teacher development we have to consider the process of professional socialization. Beginning teachers may need to theorize about Middle Phase concerns, but competent experienced teachers cope with them semiautomatically. It is only the Late Phase concerns that demand theorizing from experienced teachers as well. But in many educational settings only minimal attention is paid to these professional concerns. So there is little demand for theorizing, which then gets identified with the beginning teacher phase – something to be grown out of instead of something to be grown into. How then do we prepare our students for continuing professional growth in unthinking schools?

First, I believe we have to share the problem with them from the outset. The nature of their moral commitment needs to be clarified and the issue of professional identity continually discussed. Second, they need to encounter theorizing in school settings and gain some understanding of its potential role – if not in their practice school, then in some other school. Third, they need to have some knowledge of alternative courses of action, without which planning or evaluating becomes a routine from which practical theorizing is likely to be excluded. To provide such knowledge should be the responsibility of the curriculum component of a PGCE course; though a discussion of the nature of a choice between two alternatives might well be part of a theorizing course. Fourth, they have to develop realistic views about theorizing that are not impossible to realize when they become full-time teachers. Then, finally, they need to have some experience of success in theorizing, to be helped to see what and how they have learned, not to see themselves as deficient in comparison with academic models. Both writing and formal discussion may easily acquire the negative significance of time away from practice, which will be exacerbated by any personal difficulties with these types of communication. Moreover, lack of self-knowledge may lead to students being unaware of the extent of their learning and assuming the least possible benefit.

The other main influence on the process of learning to theorize is the relationship between lecturers and teacher tutors in the practice schools. Even on well-coordinated courses, students have to negotiate meanings and expectations with each group separately. Thus, the institutional separation presents a structural symbol of what both sides tend to call a *theory–practice gap.* Theorizing becomes what one does in university for the lecturers, not what one does in school. Is it not then important for there to be continuing discourse between teachers and lecturers on both sites to demonstrate their shared commitment to theorizing? Such discourse would also be a valuable staff development activity for both parties, a necessary complement to "recent and relevant experience." At the end of an article describing the many problems of an experienced teacher education program, planned jointly by teachers and teacher educators, Lanier (1983) gave an attractive account of just such a process:

> Discussions sometimes grew out of material selected by teacher educators for its apparent general importance to education (for example, studies of child development, teacher expectations, the changing nature and structure of American families, the complex organisation of modern institutions including the school). Other times discussions grew out of practical problems and interests of classroom teachers (for example, How can one motivate youngsters to read? How does one help apparent under-achievers? How can one encourage greater respect among youngsters of different races?). Thus, the teacher educators made the initial judgements about the formal knowledge that they thought *might* be worthwhile and then let their shared examination and discourse with teachers determine whether or not it was useful in helping them understand and think better about the problems and practice of teaching. The teachers, on the other hand, made the initial judgements about the concrete problems that they thought were worth serious attention, and then let their shared examination and discourse with teacher educators determine whether or not they could justify actions in light of public and general criteria, rather than by personal and unexamined preferences alone. The prevailing approach was continually to use conceptual tools in examining fundamental beliefs and ideas, whether they emanated from formal *or* practical knowledge. The movement was back and forth, from the abstract to the concrete, and from the practical to the theoretic. Questions of how much attention and when to shift attention from one emphasis to another were continually open for consideration and negotiation. (pp. 145–146)

REFERENCES

Anderson, D. C. (1981). *Evaluating curriculum proposals.* London: Croom Helm.

Argyris, C., & Schon, D. A. (1974). *Theory in practice: Increasing professional effectiveness.* San Francisco: Jossey-Bass.

Broudy, H. S., Smith, B. O., & Burnett, J. (1964) *Democracy and excellence in american secondary education.* Chicago: Rand McNally.

Buchler, J. (1961) *The concept of method.* New York: Columbia University Press.

Buchmann, M. (1980) *Practitioners' concepts: An inquiry into the wisdom of practice* (Occasional Paper 29, Institute for Research on Teaching, Michigan State University). East Lansing, MI: Michigan State University.

Calderhead, J. (Ed.). (1988). *Teachers' professional learning*. Basingstoke: Falmer Press.

Clark, C. M. (1986, October) *Asking the right questions about teacher preparation: Contributions of research on teacher thinking*. ISATT Conference Paper.

Elliott, J. (1991) *Action research for educational change*. Buckingham: Open University Press.

Eraut, M. (1982) What is learned in in-service education and how? A knowledge use perspective. *British Journal of In-Service Education, 9* (1), 6–14.

Eraut, M. Goad, L., & Smith, G. (1975), *The analysis of curriculum materials* (Occasional Paper 2, University of Sussex Education Area). Brighton, UK: University of Sussex.

Fuller, F. (1970). *Personalized education for teachers: An introduction for teacher educators*. Austin: R&D Center for Teacher Education, University of Texas.

Grumet, M. R. (1989). Generations: reconceptualist curriculum theory and teacher education. *Journal of Teacher Education, 40* (1), 13–17.

Harris, I. B. (1982, March). *Communications for guiding teachers: The impact of different conceptions of teaching and educational practice*. AERA Conference Paper.

Hirst, P. H. (1979). Professional studies in initial teacher education: Some conceptual issues. In R. J. Alexander & E. Wormald (Eds.), *Professional studies for teaching*. Guildford, UK: Society for Research in Higher Education.

Hirst, P. H. (1985). Educational studies and the PGCE course. *British Journal of Educational Studies, 33* (3), 211.

Jackson, P. W. (1971). The way teachers think. In G. S. Lesser (Ed.), *Psychology and educational practice*. Chicago: Scott Foresman.

Korthagen, F. A. J. (1988). The influence of learning orientations on the development of reflective teaching. In J. Calderhead (Ed.), *Teachers' professional learning*. Basingstoke: Falmer Press.

Kuhn, T. (1974) Second thoughts on paradigms. In F. Suppes (Ed.), *The structure of scientific theories*. Urbana: University of Illinois Press.

Lanier, J. (1983). Tensions in teaching teachers the skills of pedagogy. In G. Griffin (Ed.), *staff development* (NSSE Yearbook 1983, Part II). Chicago: University of Chicago Press.

Lortie, D. C. (1975). *Schoolteacher: A sociological study*. Chicago: University of Chicago Press

McIntyre, D. (1980). The contributions of research to quality in teacher education, In E. Hoyle & J. Megarry (Eds.), *Professional development of teachers* (World Yearbook of Education). London: Kogan Page.

McNamara, D., & Desforges, C. (1979). Professional studies as a source of theory, In R. J. Alexander & E. Wormald (Eds.), *Professional studies for teaching*. Guildford, UK: Society for Research in Higher Education.

Nisbett, R. E., & Ross, L. (1980). *Human inference: Strategies and shortcomings of social judgement*. Englewood Cliffs, NJ: Prentice-Hall.

Oakeshott, M. (1962) *Rationalism in politics: And other essays*. London: Methuen.

Petrie, H. G. (1981). *The dilemma of enquiry and learning*. Chicago: University of Chicago Press.

Reddy, M. J. (1979). The conduit metaphor—a case of frame conflict in our language about language. In A. Ortony (Ed.), *Metaphor and thought*. Cambridge, UK: Cambridge University Press

Ross, L. (1977). The intuitive psychologist and his shortcomings. In L. Berkowitz (Ed.), *Advances in experimental social psychology* (Vol. 10). New York: Academic Press.

Russell, T. (1988), From pre-service teacher education to first year of teaching: A study of theory and practice. In J. Calderhead (Ed.), *Teachers professional learning*. Basingstoke: Falmer Press.

Schon, D. A. (1983). *The reflective practitioner: How professionals think in action*. New York: Basic Books.

Schon, D. A. (1987). *Educating the reflective practitioner: Towards a new design for teaching and learning in the professions.* San Francisco: Jossey-Bass.

Tom, A (1980), The reform of teacher education through research: A futile quest. *Teachers College Record, 82* (1), 15–29.

Tversky, A., & Kahnemann, D. (1973). Availability: A heuristic for judging frequency and probability. *Cognitive Psychology, 5,* 207–232.

White, P., & White, J. (1984, June). *Practical reasoning and educational theory.* Paper for University of London Institute of Education Conference on Educational Theory.

Zeichner, K. M., & Lipson, D. P. (1987). Teaching student teachers to reflect. *Harvard Educational Review, 57* (1), 23–48.

CHAPTER 6

Student Teachers' Access to the Practical Classroom Knowledge of Experienced Teachers*

Sally Brown
Department of Education
University of Stirling
Scotland

Underlying the study described in this chapter is a conception of teacher education that builds on the complementary but different kinds of knowledge and criteria that different groups bring to the development of, and judgments about, the practice of teaching. In the context of the Oxford internship scheme, McIntyre (1990) described the implications of this for the preservice education of teachers as involving a "dialogue" that

> embodies a respect for, and a questioning of, both the craft knowledge and the practical wisdom of practising teachers and also the more systematised and abstract knowledge of university tutors. It is through this process of questioning dialogue and attempted synthesis that the model seeks to overcome the problems of discontinuity between university and school components. (p. 31)

A program of teacher education planned on this basis would capitalize on the complementary perspectives and encourage student teachers to view ideas, from whatever source, as requiring testing against a variety of criteria. The criteria arising from the school context might concentrate on the practicalities of resources, skills, and time available, while those from the university/college context might include consistency with research

---

*This chapter is based on work carried out with three colleagues in two institutions and rests heavily on their ideas and the research report by McAlpine, Brown, McIntyre, and Hagger (1988).

evidence and implicit educational values. An essential feature of the program would be the opportunity for student teachers to gain access to the practical classroom knowledge of teachers and test that knowledge for themselves against the different criteria. That done, and where appropriate, they could assimilate that knowledge into their own teaching.

It is with how student teachers can gain access to the practical classroom (or professional craft) knowledge of experienced teachers that this chapter is concerned. As such, it is only a part of the thinking and research which is necessary to establish a program of this kind. For example, the research reported here did not extend to a study of how student teachers could take the next step of assimilating the craft knowledge of experienced teachers into their own teaching. In the concluding section, however, there is some discussion of this point based on the experience of the Oxford scheme.

It has long been acknowledged by teacher educators that student teachers have much to learn from observing the "good practice" of experienced teachers, that is, from observing the kinds of ordinary, everyday things which teachers do routinely and more or less spontaneously in the classroom. But *what* they should learn and *how* that learning should be accomplished have been left vague. In addition, and this is confirmed by our earlier research (Brown & McIntyre, 1988), it is apparent that the more skillful the teaching, the easier everything looks, and the more difficult it is to understand how success is achieved. Indeed, it is our experience that the observer seldom understands all that is going on in a classroom, and may, in fact, *misunderstand* it if he or she is not thinking about the class and the teaching in the same way as the teacher.

For a start, there are substantial differences between the perceptions of student and experienced teachers. What can seem ordinary, everyday, familiar, routine aspects of teaching to the teacher with several years in the classroom, may be a source of considerable anxiety to the beginning teacher. Many a student has had an opportunity to watch a teacher with a class of interested, hard-working, well-behaved pupils, and on the following day has charge of the same group, who turn out to be disruptive, bad-tempered, idle, and showing signs of extreme boredom. It is usually difficult to explain how the experienced teacher achieved success with the class, and it is rare for the initial training of teachers to provide students with the means of unravelling these mysteries. Trial and error, and reinvention of the wheel, by the beginning teacher as he or she is launched into a career in the classroom is often the approach. Such unguided and nonanalytic means do little to explicate teaching for the student teacher or lead to measured development of his or her own competence and critical analysis of alternative practices.

This chapter describes an experimental study that explored the possibilities of helping student teachers to create the conditions to enhance what they get out of their observation of experienced teachers. It built on findings from our earlier research that had suggested that one way to achieve a fuller understanding of the teacher's actions is for the observer to discuss with the teacher his or her teaching as soon as possible after the lesson. This is more difficult than it sounds: the routine nature of everyday teaching, together with the way these routines have developed from the teachers' experiences of teaching, does not make it easy for them to articulate what they do in their teaching, and to give an account of how what they do contributes to what they are trying to achieve. However, an initiative was taken by the Department of Educational Studies at the University of Oxford to develop, on the basis of the procedures used in the earlier work, a simple procedure that student teachers could use to gain access to the craft knowledge of individual experienced teachers. The context for this approach in schools was not altogether promising. It was described by McIntyre (1990):

> Little value is generally attached to the observation of experienced teachers, with apparently little learning resulting from such observation. It is abundantly clear that the craft of teaching is highly complex and subtle, and that the majority of experienced teachers have developed this craft to a much higher level than would be apparent from their generalised talk about it. Yet student-teachers' observation of experienced teachers at work tends to be concentrated at the early stages of their school experience, when their own understanding of the task of teaching is so limited that they do not know what to note or to ask questions about. Too soon both they and their supervising teachers tend to believe that it is time to concentrate instead on 'the real task' of learning to teach from experience. Very little of the knowledge that is implicit in the teaching of experienced teachers is passed on to beginners. (pp. 20–21)

The procedure that was adopted was the basically simple one of observing a lesson and then asking the teacher questions about what had happened in that lesson.

As with the earlier research emphasis was put on the *strengths* of the observed teaching, on the events of the *particular observed lesson*, and on the *teacher's own perspective* on these events. In the earlier studies, teachers' discussions of their lessons revealed a richness in their pedagogical knowledge that could not have been inferred from observation alone and which pleased and excited them.

The development of guidelines for student teachers and training them to follow these proved not to be easy. The guidelines emphasized that the conversation required for the postlesson interviews was distinctive, and that, although there were other kinds of conversation with experienced teachers that could be useful, the value of this interview depended on restricting oneself to this particular kind. Student teachers were encouraged to ask about the *specific* lesson by formulating all questions in the simple past tense; the student teachers, however, were inclined to seek *generalized* answers to the problems of teaching. They also found it difficult to accept that experienced teachers might think about teaching in ways different from their own and, therefore, to avoid closed questions (like "Had you planned to do that?"). They could easily put teachers on the defensive by asking questions such as "Why didn't you . . . ?"; a ban on questions of this kind was introduced, and the student teachers were urged to seek ways of *encouraging* experienced teachers to articulate the knowledge underlying their teaching. Finally, they were urged not to accept teachers' initial answers to questions as the whole truth; it was often only when teachers were pressed to elaborate on these initial answers that the insights underlying their teaching became apparent, and so *probing* for elaboration was emphasized.

As well as written guidelines, a videotape was made in which student teacher actors and an experienced teacher demonstrated positive and negative models of postlesson interviewing. This provided an opportunity to see in advance the effects of a supportive approach on the sharing of such craft knowledge in comparison with a more critical and unsupportive stance. A commentary on the portrayal of the two students interviewing the teacher about the same observed lesson pointed up the recommendations from the guidelines.

The adequacy and usefulness of these guidelines had to be tested and this was the focus of the study carried out in Scotland and reported here. In particular, it asked:

- Would student teachers, given a brief introduction to this procedure, recognize its purpose as valuable, be persuaded of the need for it as prescribed, and be able to use it in practice?
- Insofar as the student teachers made use of the proposed procedures, would the hypothesized relationships be apparent between the extent of this use and the teachers' provision of useful information about what they had done and why they had done what they had done?
- Would teachers find the procedures acceptable, feasible, and valuable?

THE SAMPLES OF STUDENTS AND TEACHERS

Three small samples of student teachers and experienced teachers in Scotland were involved. Two of these came from the Jordanhill College

PGCE in the West of Scotland; neither students nor experienced teachers had previous association with the research, and no attempt was made to integrate the research approach to the college courses. The college tutors had no active involvement in the work, although we had substantial discussions with them about the research. In other words, the research exercise was an independent "add-on" to the students' preservice program. One of the samples comprised eight student-teachers in four subject areas, and their supervising teachers; these students were at an early stage in their training and undergoing their first induction period of school experience. The second sample was four in number, all science specialists, and in their second period of school practice toward the end of their first term.

The third sample of students, following their PGCE in the east of Scotland at Moray House College, was working with four of the teachers who had been involved in the earlier stages of the research and so were used to giving researchers the same kinds of information which the students were seeking. However, like the west of Scotland student teachers, and unlike those at Oxford, this sample did not have the backing of the approach being built into their college courses.

PREPARING THE STUDENTS AND EXPERIENCED TEACHERS

The guidelines and video offered ideas on interviewing techniques. It was suggested that the focus of the interviews should be on making sense of the *teaching actually observed* and not with finding out about such things as the school's or regional policies, the teacher's background or beliefs about teaching, curriculum or lesson planning, or departmental organization. (The latter are not unimportant concerns for students, but the interviews were not intended as vehicles for their clarification.) Furthermore, if the aim was to find out about the teaching observed, it was important that the questions should not be framed to invite generalized answers. So, for example, an appropriate framing would use the past tense:

What did you do to encourage these pupils to work?

rather than the present:

What do you do to encourage pupils to work?

The emphasis of the interviews was to be on *what went well* with the teaching, either in the teacher's eyes or the student's. Having identified positive aspects of the teaching, the questions should focus on what *actions* the teachers took to achieve them, and what led them to choose these actions. When a teacher was asked why a particular action was taken, the purpose was not to elicit a defensive rationalization (based perhaps on some educational theory), but rather an account of how they judged this to be such-and-such a situation, this to be such-and-such a group of pupils and that action to be appropriate. In other words, how did the teachers' practical experience lead them to make the immediate on-the-spot judgments which characterised their classroom teaching? For example:

> I was interested in the way you dealt with John's problems. What was it exactly that you did? Why did you do it that way?

Given that the purpose of the interviews was to try to understand the teachers' perspective of the events of the lesson, students were advised to ask their questions in a way which would encourage the teacher to offer expansive answers. This was more likely to be achieved if the questions were open in their framing; that is, they should neither invite a "yes/no" reply, nor suggest a possible answer, that is, a preference for:

> What was it you did to make the changeover of activities go smoothly?

rather than:

> Did you have a strategy for making the changeover of activities go smoothly? (invites yes/no)

or:

> Was asking the pupils to help with the equipment intended to make the changeover of activities go smoothly? (yes/no invitation, and a suggested answer)

It was further suggested that the students be *supportive* of the teachers, at all times be ready to *accept* what the teacher was telling them, allow the teacher *time to reply* (not be anxious to fill up pauses) and be prepared to *probe* the teacher's answer. The last of these might imply a question such as:

> You said you made your explanation as simple as you could. Would you tell me what it was you did to make it simple?

Meetings were held with the experienced teachers to familiarise them with the research, allay their fears, answer their questions, and set up the administrative arrangements. Two important aims of this meeting were:

1. To provide a general picture of the information it was intended the students should try to elicit from the teachers.
2. To make clear to teachers that it was the specifics, the ordinary things of teaching, that were important and helpful for students. Also to let them know that we realized how difficult it can be to talk about what one does routinely and habitually, but to ask them not to underestimate what they had to offer.

COLLECTION OF DATA AND THE RESEARCH QUESTIONS

The students conducted two interviews, each with a teacher whose teaching they had observed, but not necessarily the same teacher on both occasions. During the observation the student identified aspects of the lesson to figure as topics for discussion in the interview. The interview took place as soon as possible after the lesson, always on the same day. The interview, but not the lesson, was tape-recorded.

Within 24 hours the student and researcher met to listen to, and discuss, the earlier taped interview with the teacher. The researcher undertook the role of college tutor, and the student was given the opportunity to talk about his or her reactions to the interview with the teacher. The concern was with the contribution of the interview to the student's understanding of the lesson, the extent to which the student considered any understanding gained as of likely use in his or her own teaching, any problems encountered in the interviews and suggestions for improving the second interview. When it was clear that the student had no more to say on the topic, and in the light of what he or she said, the researcher suggested possible improvements that were based on the evidence of the first teacher interview and reflected the general recommendations of the project on interviewing techniques.

Our primary sources of data, therefore, were the recordings of:

- The students' two interviews with teachers, following observations of lessons and separated by a discussion with a researcher;
- The discussions between the student and the researcher following each of the interviews with the teachers.

The analysis of these data was designed to explore the following questions:

- To what extent did the student/teacher interviews help the student to gain a fuller understanding of the teaching observed?
- To what extent did the students recognize any value for their own teaching in speaking with the teachers about the teaching observed?
- To what extent did the students experience problems in arranging or conducting the interviews?
- To what extent did the students do what was asked of them? Did they ask questions in the recommended ways?
- To what extent do the recommended questions elicit the desired information?
- What were the teachers' reactions to the student/teacher interviews?

RESEARCH FINDINGS

Student teacher Reactions

No obvious differences among the samples' reactions were apparent except that the group that had only recently started its course seemed to have a generally higher level of anxiety about the school practice and encountered more practical problems with the recording equipment.

Most found their interviews with the teachers helpful:

Yes, definitely . . . there was no way I would have known why [the teacher] was [choosing particular pupils to answer]. I thought it was random, but when I spoke to him he did have a system.

and identified information from the interview that would not have been available from observation alone:

It seemed to me the . . . class he was teaching would have had the lesson explained to them better if he'd taken it step-by-step on the blackboard rather than presenting them with a prepared overhead. But when he explained it was in relation to the class he knew was very badly behaved if he turned his back on them, I can now see why he did that.

One student expressed amazement at finding out during the interview that an experienced teacher never produced detailed lesson plans of the kind required of the student teachers.

Despite their recognition of what was to be learned from interviews, however, only a few student teachers were explicit about how, in their own teaching, they might make use of the information.

A minority of students did not recognize any real value in discussing a lesson afterwards with the teacher.

> A lot of the teachers' replies were self-evident . . . you could have gleaned that information just watching the lesson itself. It [the interview] helped perhaps to confirm conclusions.

These students "knew" from observation alone what was happening in the teaching, and why; in their actions, as well as their words, they regarded any subsequent interview simply as a means of confirming their assumptions. For example, two of the students separately interviewed a teacher in relation to the teaching of the same lesson.

Both queried her decision to move a pupil to the back of the room. "A" asked why that pupil had been chosen to move rather than one of her companions. This drew from the teacher a history about that pupil and the others, and the teacher's reasons for singling her out to move. The student learned a substantial amount about the teacher's strategy for establishing classroom order and the variety of knowledge about pupils on which this was based. "B" (the student who considered observation of a lesson was sufficient to gain understanding of the teaching) simply asked, "Did you move Linda because she was talking?" The teacher concurred and the topic was closed. When asked by the researcher whether more could have been elicited from the teacher, "B" was firm that there was nothing more to be said: she "knew" from observation that the girl was moved because she was talking, the teacher confirmed this, and that was that.

There were some doubts about the formality of the interview although the majority of the student teachers recognized its advantages. It was seen as:

- Improving their concentration on the lesson and making their observations more purposeful and useful
- Giving a status to their questions that they would not otherwise have had
- Enabling them to have extended, in-depth conversations with teachers (apparently a rare event) without being cut short
- Facilitating a good relationship with the teacher, and making it easier subsequently to approach the experienced professionals with questions about their teaching.

These perceived benefits, together with the gains in students' understanding, suggested that the interviews had offered a worthwhile contribution to their school practice experience. They also went some way to allaying our initial concern that the students might appear critical in their interviewing and damage their relationships with the teachers. There were only two disadvantages the student teachers mentioned explicitly:

- Their fears that the formality of the interview would be threatening to the teachers
- That in classes where individualized teaching was prevalent, it was not sensible to delay asking questions until the interview after the lesson; where pupils' work was self-paced, teachers had the opportunity to discuss their teaching *during* the lesson and often found it difficult to recall individual actions in the later interviews.

Although the second of these is understandable, it seemed to us unlikely that circumstances in which the teacher was constantly attending to individual pupils with frequent interruptions would be conducive to detailed discussion about aspects of the teaching.

Several aspects of the interviewing task itself presented difficulties for the student teachers. They reported problems in

- finding useful questions to ask
- articulating questions clearly
- formulating probing questions while listening to what the teacher was saying
- avoiding leading questions
- giving teachers enough time to answer.

Their problems seemed to arise because the teaching was so heavily structured that there was little to ask about; or the relevant questions had been asked before; or questions were easy to find only with the more competent teachers; or (in contrast) experienced teachers resolved each problem before the student was aware of its existence; or there was concern that the teacher would think the question posed demonstrated the student's ignorance.

One student reported having too little time to prepare his questions, because the interview took place straight after the lesson. He was one of only three in this position, and two of them made a poor showing at implementing recommendations. Since the remaining students had the time to prepare their questions and generally gained the information in the detail wanted, perhaps students should have some time for preparation between the lesson and the interview. There is a risk, however, of students preparing overelaborate or generalized questions. Another problem, experienced by one student, of fitting the interview into a full timetable is not easily met. If the experiment was incorporated into preservice teacher-training courses, the students' and the teachers' time-tables would have to take account in some way of the need for time.

STUDENT TEACHERS' BEHAVIOR: HOW DID THE STUDENTS' BEHAVIOR CORRESPOND TO WHAT THEY HAD BEEN ENCOURAGED TO DO?

Here we must distinguish from the others those who were working with the teachers with whom we had earlier worked ourselves. Whether for that reason or some other, these student teachers tended much more than others to do what they had been asked: They concentrated firmly on teachers' strengths; they asked about what had happened in the lesson and why and how teachers had done what they did; and they asked open questions:

"When you were doing the examples, you went back to the same ones several times. Why did you do that?"

They did not, however, probe very well.

Results were less satisfactory for the other student-teachers. Again, however, they concentrated almost without exception on the teachers' strengths and based their questions on the lessons they had observed. But the great majority of questions were in a *generalized* form: "What do you do about . . .?" "Why do you . . .?" "How do you . . .?" In addition, most of the questions were also closed: "Do you do that because . . .?" and "Did you plan to do that or was it spontaneous?" Very few attempted to probe the teacher's answers, though these frequently lacked detail and begged questions.

Student: [with reference to pupils leaving the room]. It's always an organized kind of thing?

Teacher: Yes, oh yes. That's important, to have an organized start and an organized end to the day.

Student: Well, that's all. Thank you very much.

Most students, however, had at least one example of a question focusing on the actual events of the lesson, but overwhelmingly these implied the student knew *what* had happened, he or she only required to understand *why*:

You spent some time with Jane. Did she have a specific problem?

On a number of occasions a student identified the area of teaching he or she wanted to discuss, but did not actually ask a question:

I noticed that John was a bit excitable today. I understand they'd just come from a chemistry lesson.

Because the students had *two* opportunities to interview teachers, the majority improved second time around in the appropriateness of the questions they asked. The improvement in most cases, however, was modest.

RELATIONSHIP BETWEEN QUESTION APPROPRIATENESS AND SOUGHT-AFTER TALK

One advantage of the variation in student performance was it allowed us to test the hypothesis that questions of the kind we recommended were necessary and sufficient to generate teacher talk of the kind we are looking for.

We considered the questions asked about the particular events observed, and what consequences such questions had. At first sight it appeared that focused questions led frequently to generalized answers. A more careful analysis showed, however, that the typical answer to "What did you do?" "How did you do it?" or "Why did you do it?" did provide an initial explanation of what had been done, but then spontaneously launched into a more generalized discussion of "If it had been a different pupil, or topic, or time of day, then I would have . . ." We should be very pleased if all questions and answers were like that.

All the questions were then categorized as "appropriate" or "inappropriate," and the answers as "successful" or "unsuccessful." Because the match between our recommendations and the students' questions was less than we hoped, the following criteria for an "appropriate" question were less stringent than they might have been. "Appropriate" questions should:

- Indicate a positive, or at least neutral attitude to the topic
- Be phrased in open terms
- Be focused on the events of the particular lesson in the sense of asking what the teacher did or why, or what the teacher does or why, or any combination of these.

In judging teachers' responses, any particular or generalized indication of their actions, or of why they act in this way, or any combination of these, was judged a "successful" answer; this was the case whether or not the answer was preceded by an "appropriate" question. All other answers were coded "unsuccessful." An additional criterion was that the teacher had to be judged to have answered the question posed.

The four combinations of student question followed by teacher answer were:

1. "Appropriate" questions and 'successful' answers, e.g.,
   Question: How did you ensure your instructions were clearly understood?
   Answer: The workcard helps ... Even in the workcard, that doesn't cover all the possibilities. I'll use some of the time tomorrow for tying up what we covered today. I ... would go through a very idealistic example on the board with them just to make sure that if anyone is in doubt they can take that one down in their jotters.

2. "Appropriate" questions and "unsuccessful" answers, for example:
   Question: I noticed a pupil sitting ... obviously finished. What do you do in that situation?
   Answer: What happened there was a second-year child must have had the book in his folder. As we go on with the SMP, we will have more materials, and that type of thing shouldn't happen.

3. "Inappropriate" questions and "unsuccessful" answers, for example:
   Question: How many times have you taught that lesson before?
   Answer: 15 years. ... At least once a year for 15 years.

4. "Inappropriate" questions and "successful" answers, for example:
   Question: You use the right mixture of authority and humour. It went down very well, but obviously there is a danger of being too humorous. Do you do this consciously, or is it instinct?
   Answer: I don't want to appear totally didactic ... I want the pupils to do the work, and I want them to do it in a relaxed atmosphere, and if to get the atmosphere more relaxed I throw in a couple of silly jokes ... it makes them laugh, it breaks any tension, and it gets them to work. It's a combination of didactic teaching and liberal teaching. I don't think a concentration on any one suits my ... style, so I do a combination of both.

The relationship was very clear (see later). Appropriate questions, with rare exceptions, produced "successful" answers; but "inappropriate" questions produced "successful" nearly as often as "unsuccessful" answers. Closer examination, however, suggested that six teachers, including the four with whom we had worked previously, were largely responsible for the "successful" answers to the "inappropriate" questions. Some teachers, it seems, do not need "appropriate" questions; but others, unless they have been prepared at length, will give the kind of answers we aimed for only if they are asked "appropriate" questions.

	Successful Answer	Unsuccessful Answer
"Appropriate" Question	118	6
"Inappropriate" Question	83	100

TEACHERS' REACTIONS

All the teachers involved asserted that the exercise had been valuable for the student teachers.

Absolutely . . . Sometimes it's not obvious to the student why you're doing something, because it's based on experience with a particular class over time. . . . In that respect you would explain the background . . . the history.

Only three of them, however, thought that the more formal interview was in itself an advantage, but six thought that the effect of the expected interview on the observation was a considerable advantage.

The formality of the interview gave the questions an importance. . . . It wasn't just a staffroom thing where you were [cut short]. The question took on an added importance . . . you were taking your time and considering your answer.

I [the teacher as a student] just blankly watched and then went into a classroom and did my own thing . . . [the interview] made them more aware of the teaching . . . made them look for things to discuss.

Almost half of the teachers admitted to having been surprised and informed by questions the student teachers had (or had not) asked:

[The students] certainly asked me one or two things . . . I didn't expect, but thinking back to when I was a student they are the kinds of things you would want to know anyway . . . Trivial things like 'How should I write something on the board?'

Yes, because some of the questions seemed to be on things that I didn't regard as very important. It made me realize there must have been a point where [for example] you don't know how to set something up.

A similar number admitted to having had some difficulty in explaining aspects of their teaching that had become routine:

> It's automatic [answering pupils' questions with another question] . . . and when I thought about it . . . I thought "Well, why do I do it?" . . . I suppose it's to try and get them to use their brains.

There were no common criticisms of the student teachers' questioning. Although only two readily admitted having time problems in fitting in the interviews, most of the teachers revealed under questioning that they had had to use their lunch breaks to to cancel meetings or some such thing:

> I have very few free periods, and when I do I am usually travelling between schools [the school annex is at some distance]. It's almost impossible to find the time. Even lunchtime . . . Two days I have a class at lunchtime.

CONCLUSION

In focusing on how students can gain access to teachers' professional craft knowledge, this study addressed only a limited aspect of the overarching conception of teacher education. The results were encouraging in their confirmation of the effectiveness of the procedure, when used, and in the suggestion they offered of an alternative route. That alternative arises from the finding that teachers who really understood the possibilities and value of articulating their craft knowledge were not dependent on the student teachers' questions for doing so. We were sufficiently encouraged to maintain our view of the approach as a valuable one but, at the same time, to accept that we need to reexamine several aspects of the procedures, particularly the preparation of both students and teachers.

The least satisfactory aspects of the results were the student teachers' modest levels of success in implementing the recommended procedure, and the limited extent to which some of them were impressed by the distinctive possibilities it offered. Some of this could be accounted for by the study being an isolated "experiment" and not integrated into the students' program. There was no requirement of, or commitment by, the colleges involved to include in their courses any structured support of our approach or encouragement of students to seek what we regarded as valuable classroom knowledge. Especially in the case of those students in the early part of their course, we were conscious of the relatively firm ideas they already had about teaching and, if those ideas are to be challenged or sustained, of the need for time and encouragement of students to test the merits of their assumptions.

If this kind of approach were made use of in an actual program of teacher education, the development would include the trio of groups: student teachers, teacher mentors, and university/college tutors. Because the researchers acted as (scant) tutors, and most of the school teachers had not been socialized into our approach, our evidence was narrowly focused on specific matters. Also, a student activity of this kind requires substantial administrative arrangements and negotiation. This was carried out by the researchers, but is not a task to be underestimated, either for teachers or tutors, if the scheme were to be institutionalized. Despite these caveats, we are optimistic about the value of the approach and have four messages for its institutionalization in the light of our experience:

- Because it seems that teachers who have a good idea of what the procedure aims to achieve can overcome inadequate questioning and reveal their professional classroom knowledge, more emphasis should be placed on the role and induction of the teacher mentors.
- The procedures should become integrated with the curriculum jointly planned by university tutors and teacher mentors. Our experience suggests that once the procedures have been effectively used, both mentors and student teachers will be sufficiently motivated to continue with them.
- The school-based element of the work should be complemented by a more generalized, university-based element, providing a framework to help students assimilate the professional classroom knowledge they acquire and go on to test its usefulness in their own teaching.
- We should experiment with less formal procedures but avoid abandoning any of their essential features.

Such an approach has the potential to enhance not only what student teachers learn from experienced teachers but also our understanding of how they learn to become fluent classroom teachers.

REFERENCES

Brown, S. R., & McIntyre, D. (1988). The professional craft knowledge of teachers. *Scottish Educational Review* (special issue entitled *The Quality of Teaching*, edited by W. A. Gatherer) pp. 39–47.

McAlpine, A., Brown, S., McIntyre, D., & Hagger, H. (1988). *Student teachers learning From experienced teachers* (SCRE Project Reports). Edinburgh: SCRE.

McIntyre, D. (1990). Ideas and principles guiding the internship scheme. In P. Benton (Ed.), *The Oxford internship scheme: Integration + partnership in initial teacher education.* London: Calouste Gulbenkian Foundation.

CHAPTER 7

The Acquisition of Professional Activity in Teaching

Richard Vincent Dunne
School of Education
University of Exeter

INTRODUCTION

Myth abounds in teaching. In teacher education the myth of the primacy of school-based work has secured a viselike grip on practitioners and administrators alike. This general prejudice about the rightness and inevitability of learning from experience has perhaps gone beyond myth. Myths invite examination and attention to their origins. "Myths are metaphoric, hence ambiguous and open to interpretation" (Buchmann, 1981, p. 339). Yet the insistence on the centrality of school experience has sloganlike qualities rather than mythlike qualities.

There is ample evidence (see, for instance, Duffy, 1987) that student teachers perceive school-based work as the most valuable part of their course. Although such evidence is interesting, it ought not to be interpreted as an imperative for increasing or even maintaining the current emphasis on this experience. There are two reasons for this. Firstly, the ability to distinguish "value" from, say, "enjoyment" demands considerable powers in self-evaluation, which, arguably, is a legitimate *long-term* aim of teacher education rather than a simple and always-available quality. Secondly, although it is undeniable that student teachers usually do improve in some sense with classroom experience (notably, in the management of tasks), the nature of that improvement, rather than creating a "base" for subsequent development, can militate against improvement in more subtle aspects of the teachers' work. The precise nature of the contribution of classroom experience, or teaching practice, to the initial training of teachers is too often taken to be unproblematic, and relatively little attention has been given to the techniques and conditions that enable students effectively to learn from this work. Furthermore, the very notion of what it means for beginning teachers to learn "effectively" is one which, although not neglected, has been treated largely in the process–product research paradigm. Such "black-box" methods typically explore one of two phenomena: either the extent to which teachers who receive a particular training subsequently show evidence of this in their work, or the relationship between particular teaching behaviors and pupils' learning outcomes. Neither of these has any great potential for informing the design of course programs and materials; consequently, our aspiration is to develop "white-box" methods and focus on student teachers' cognitive processes during and about school-based work.

Although we contend that a concentration on cognitive processes is crucial, there are important pointers that can be derived from process-product methods. A substantial amount is known, for instance, about the influence of the host teacher on student teachers, particularly that there is a tendency for students to conform to the prevailing methods and attitudes, and that this can derive from a desire for a favorable evaluation (Barrows, 1979). Such is the strength of this influence that Zeichner and Tabachnick (1981) found this tendency to conformity even when the emphasis of the training establishment was markedly different from that of the host teacher. However, Leslie (1969) reported some innovation among student teachers when they were placed with teachers whose beliefs were not completely congruent with their own. Following this, Hollingsworth and Goodman (1988) suggested that it may be possible to promote competence in student teachers by deliberately placing them with teachers who, in their practice, provide cognitive dissonance.

Although this tactic is an understandable response to such a finding, it is, in our view, inappropriate. At the practical level, it is unwieldy in that it demands a prior analysis of the beliefs of all participants and a pairing that exhibits "appropriate" but not total disagreement. At the personal level, it elevates manipulation above professionalism. But, more importantly, it ignores the cognitive nature of dissonance and attempts to replicate only its superficial features.

Our concern about reliance on student evaluation of the value of experience is based on a desire for initial training to go beyond the existing practice in certain clearly defined respects; but this does not mean that we are critical of that practice, nor that we expect student teachers to rapidly become more accomplished than their hosts in performance terms. It means, rather, that time in schools should make a contribution to the emerging disposition and ability to evaluate and innovate as part of the day-to-day work. Additionally, we believe that, even in those classrooms that are not exemplary in this respect, the actions of the teacher carry important craft knowledge that can provide an accessible starting point for relevant learning for student teachers. Crucially, we do not believe that such development is inevitable; it is promoted by deliberate attention, the conditions and techniques for which are the subject of this and the following chapter.

The importance of craft knowledge has not gone without recognition. It is implicit, if naively interpreted, in the assumption that learning to teach is adequately achieved by working alongside experienced teachers. There are two major problems with this assumption that have not been given adequate recognition; firstly, the difficulty of discerning by observation what it is that underpins a seemingly effortless performance; secondly, the difficulty the accomplished practitioner experiences in identifying and describing the constituent parts of a routinised activity.

These problems have been confronted in a limited sense by McAlpine, Brown, McIntyre, and Hagger (1988), who trained student teachers in basic interviewing techniques so that they might elicit from the observed teacher the reasons for, and assumptions about, her actions. The evidence cited indicates that the students achieved "modest levels of success in implementing the recommended [interviewing] procedures" (p. 46). Although all the teachers involved asserted, with varying degrees of enthusiasm, that the exercise had been "a valuable one for the student teachers" (p. 46), the problem remains of how this work would affect classroom practice. Although, we support the idea of the centrality of a conference between teacher and student teacher, we are not convinced that eliciting descriptions from teachers, in itself, is necessarily likely to lead to the growth of competence.

The nature of discourse in supervisory conferences is clearly an important area of study and has been characterized by a variety of category systems (see, for instance, Zeichner & Liston, 1985). There has been a tendency to concentrate attention on, for example, changes in attitudes or in observable teaching behaviors (e.g., Popkewitz, Tabachnick, & Zeichner, 1979) rather than on the cognitive processes consequent upon such conferences.

Calderhead (1987, p. 276), in a study of 10 student primary teachers, identified "three typical phases" in field experience: "fitting into the school and the teacher's routines . . . tuning into those behaviors that signalled competence and the supervising teacher's approval . . . experimentation with different types of lesson, alternative classroom organisation and new subject matter." Crucially, this third phase was characterized by minimal supervision, and the experimentation was not accompanied by any substantial analysis by the students themselves. Although these findings, if typical, might be considered encouraging in that there is some experimentation, it is clear that there is a distinct need for mentor support in making that experimentation purposeful. Nevertheless, we accept that the three phases are likely to be typical, and will propose an approach to the supervision of teaching practice that is intended to tune in to these rather than to regret them.

A DELIBERATE APPROACH TO LEARNING TO TEACH

A scheme we developed and piloted with intending primary school teachers takes seriously the need to be explicit about the learning and thinking processes which are involved in experiential learning. A discussion of the theoretical background to this work follows an outline of the methodology, techniques, and instruments we employ.

Teaching is a complex activity. To help people learn how to teach we have identified nine dimensions of teaching, listed in Figure 7.1.

Each dimension is summarized in (usually) eight criterial levels. An example is provided in Figure 7.2.

The category system of the nine dimensions, together with their associated criterial statements, are known as the *Teaching Practice Criteria*. There are a number of important points about this category and criterial system. Firstly, the nine dimensions provide a mode of analysis designed

dimension 0 - Ethos

dimension 1 - Direct instruction

dimension 2 - Management of materials

dimension 3 - Guided practice

dimension 4 - Structured conversation

dimension 5 - Monitoring

dimension 6 - Management of order

dimension 7 - Planning and preparation

dimension 8 - Written evaluation

Figure 7.1. The nine dimensions of teaching.

STRUCTURED CONVERSATION

Learning begins with uncertain understandings which need refining. The mature learner can test that emergent understanding by, e.g., posing alternatives, testing against experience, and seeking elegance. Children need experience of these processes and a model of them in use. The beginning teacher needs to develop the ability to elicit children's perspectives, enable them to listen to each other, draw attention to conflicting ideas, provide conflicting ideas, ask for examples, support children in their attempts to report their thinking, and remove the stigma generally associated with making a mistake. This complex set of skills we summarize as STRUCTURED CONVERSATIONS. It is not expected that the entire range of activities under this heading be brought into play every time structured conversation is attempted, but the beginning teacher should be aware of the variety of useful strategies. This dimension of teaching, STRUCTURED CONVERSATION, is summarized below. The first four levels illustrate the fundamental requirements of using this approach; the remaining levels indicate that structured conversation, drawing on the range of strategies, should be attempted in increasingly complex settings. It is this development — deliberate use of certain aspects, followed by the selection of appropriate aspects in more demanding contexts — which we expect you to undertake.

1. Listen carefully to what children are saying and respond supportively.
2. Attempt to elicit children's responses; recognize and attempt to analyze difficulties.
3. Use planned and unplanned opportunities to hold conversations with children in order to establish their perspectives; be sensitive to problems of teacher intrusion.
4. Focus on challenging children's ideas by drawing attention to and providing conflicting ideas; by asking for examples and supporting children in reporting their thinking.
5. Experiment with planned conversational teaching on particular aspects of the curriculum.
6. Experiment with small scale and limited duration conversational teaching as an occasional feature of the classroom work.
7. Plan for, and experiment with, conversational teaching in many curriculum areas, by maintaining the children's engagement in exploring a variety of directions raised through conversational teaching.
8. Adopt a chairperson's role in fostering thoughtful consideration of appropriate concepts and issues.

Figure 7.2. The criterial statements for the dimension 'Structured conversation'.

to promote learning; they are not intended as a mutually exclusive set of teaching behaviors. Secondly, the language of the criterial statements is deliberately problematic, because, as discussed later, it provides the basis for negotiated understanding of classroom events. Thirdly, although the criteria can be (and are) used for making assessments of student-teachers' classroom work, it is our view that they are adequate for this purpose only when used in the context of our deliberate approach to learning.

Our scheme involves the student teacher in working with three mentors during school-based work: the class teacher, the teacher tutor (a member of the school's teaching staff trained to undertake supervisory work different from that of the class teacher), and the university supervisor. The division of roles is planned, not merely to reduce the workload, but as a central feature of a scheme that focuses on the development of cognitive processes.

The initial problem for a novice faced with making sense of a complex activity is how to gain access to the craft knowledge of the skilled practitioner. In our scheme, this entry to craft knowledge is gained by modeling the class teacher: The student teacher observes the class teacher at work during a short episode (say, distributing materials, assigning tasks, supervising group work, or telling a story) and attempts a similar episode. What is clear from our work is that, in such situations, the novice cannot immediately perceive which aspects of the teacher's performance are essential and which are idiosyncratic, nor is the teacher typically able to recall, distinguish, and communicate this information. We designed certain techniques that facilitate this process.

It is crucial for our purposes that the class teacher observes the student practicing a variety of similar episodes and discusses each one soon afterwards; in this way both participants refine their perceptions of the pivotal events. When they are confident that the student teacher can produce a good performance of this type, they nominate a time when this will be undertaken and closely observed. However, this more formal episode is preceded by the student and class teacher, in a supervisory conference, collaborating on producing a written outline of the content and sequence of the proposed episode. This item, on one side of a sheet of paper, is known as the *agenda* for that teaching episode. Its importance lies in its being a representation of a complex event which is already well known in performance terms by both people. There is one further aspect of the agenda: during this conference, when the content and sequence are agreed, a note is made of a dimension (see Figure 7.1) to which the class teacher will attend during the observation.

While observing the episode the class teacher annotates the agenda with points, relevant to the selected dimension, about the student teacher's and the pupils' actions and responses. The intention is to avoid evaluative statements and to concentrate on observable features, including both those that are present and those that are absent. The agenda receives further annotation during a conference after the episode, when both people recall the significant features. The annotated agenda is known as the *validated account* of that episode (*validated* in the sense that it is valid as the basis for further learning).

The validated account is an accessible representation of a classroom episode which itself contains craft knowledge that the student, in terms of performance, has appropriated from the class teacher. Later conference work (with other mentors) will raise to consciousness certain aspects of this craft knowledge and thereby render it available for modification and deployment in related circumstances. Consequently, the validated account is an important feature of the deliberate approach to learning to teach. Modeling is employed for each new aspect of classroom work which, for that student, is distant from current personal practice. However, the production of validated accounts does not always proceed on the basis of modeling. There are three methods available: modeling; inductive planning, and theoretical planning.

There will be certain aspects of the classroom work that, different in sequence, subject matter, and duration, say, from the modeled episodes, are nonetheless sufficiently similar for the student to construct an agenda by working inductively from current accomplishments. These episodes can be practiced and treated in the same way as previously, with the class teacher making annotations during a closely observed session. These, with appropriate conferences, generate the validated accounts that derive from inductive planning.

However, the accounts produced from theoretical planning derive specifically from conferences with the teacher tutor, and it is necessary to describe some aspects of such conferences to illustrate how these validated accounts are developed.

The student teacher's work with the class teacher, represented in the validated accounts, comprises the evidence used in a conference with the teacher tutor. This mentor, not being the class teacher, has not observed the episodes that will be discussed. Working from a particular representation (the validated account) the student teacher has the responsibility of describing the purposes and detail for the teacher tutor. It is the outcome of this that enables the student teacher to engage in theoretical planning and later, with the class teacher, to generate validated accounts on the basis of such planning.

Although the conduct of the conference deserves detailed discussion (see Harvard, this volume), we can summarize it here in three phases: (a) What? (b) So What? (c) Now what?

This shorthand reflects the requirement for the student:

1. to describe, by reference to the validated account, what happened in the episode;
2. To locate the several events during the episode in the criterial statements of the nominated dimension, and then to explore how the same event can be located in other dimensions;
3. To suggest, describe, and agree on what kinds of performance would be necessary to justify description in a higher level criterial statement, or in yet another dimension.

The outcome of the conference is an agreed, written statement that outlines the student's intentions in future, observed episodes. This statement is known as the *zone of development*.

It is the zone of development, with its requirement to plan on the basis of as yet unrehearsed criterial statements, that is the basis of the theoretical planning for further validated accounts.

There is a further purpose for the zones of development: They are used, together with the contributory evidence of the validated accounts, for the supervisory conference conducted by the university supervisor. This mentoring role has the specific function of promoting the student teacher's consciousness of how learning is taking place. It must be emphasized that this is not a single postpractice conference, but occurs at points during the practice. This means that the complex symbiosis of the various aspects of learning are given expression in the methodological detail of the scheme.

Of course, learning and thinking about learning are not separate psychic events; nor are they exclusively the domain of separate conferences. The purpose of making a distinction between the various conferences is in fact to point to their indivisibility, and this is an aspect the university supervisor will discuss in an appropriate conference. The separation, as with the delineation of the separate categories of the dimensions, is made precisely because it promotes analysis, not because it is assumed to be a reality.

THE PROBLEM OF EXPERIENTIAL LEARNING

We attempted to address a central problem of experiential learning of the relationship between cognition and physical activities: How are practice and thinking about practice related? How do they affect each other? It is this difficulty, of conceptualizing any mechanism that convincingly explains the mutual transformation of experience into cognition and cognition into enhanced performance, that has promoted a black-box orientation in teacher education.

We have been persuaded by Ryle's (1949) argument that "thinking" and "doing" are not separate, and that to so consider them is a category mistake. Following Ryle, this position is not unusual, although we are not convinced that the implications of adopting this point of view have been sufficiently intensively explored. Ryle's (1949) contention from a philosophical analysis is mirrored by the central principles of Soviet psychology that have guided work in this area since Vygotsky established them as: (a) the integral unity of external activities and the psyche, and (b) an approach to the psyche as a phenomenon that by its nature is social.

These principles, which have been extensively developed, deny the dualism of "doing" and "thinking" and, in insisting that human mental acts are socially determined, locate their origins in the process of adult–child interaction. Although the theory, occurrence, and practice of this has been explored by some English-speaking writers (Wertsch, 1981, 1985) and the ideas given some recognition in teacher-training courses (Tharp & Gallimore, 1988), there has on the whole been an emphasis on the orientation adopted by Vygotsky and little attention has been given to the markedly different line of research followed by later Soviet scientists (but see Broeckmans, 1986).

The main direction Vygotsky's work took was in an explanation of the role of language as a mediating tool in the development of concepts. Where this has been taken up, together with the idea of the *zone of proximal development*, there have been important contributions made to the understanding and promotion of learning. What has been missed, however, is the subsequent development of Soviet psychology. It is this later work we find persuasive, because it provides a closer explanatory link between experience and cognition.

It is clear from Vygotsky's work that, in their most characteristic form, meanings are represented by words, and it is the manner in which words acquire their meanings that epitomizes the link between practice and cognition. Yet, in asserting that "the meaning of every word is a generalization or a concept. And since generalizations or concepts are undeniably acts of thought, we may regard them as a phenomenon of thinking," Vygotsky (1962, p. 120) made no distinction between meanings and concepts. Consequently, he concentrated on how concepts develop as the key to the development of consciousness. So it seems that, in Vygotsky's work, the level of development of concepts determines the specific characteristics of the manner in which people understand the world. In this way, an emphasis was placed on communication as the significant factor in the development of cognition at the expense of a consideration of the development of meaning through a person's practical relations with reality. So it was, then, that despite enunciating the unity, Vygotsky perpetuated the category mistake (Ryle, 1949, p. 17) of the dualism of mind and physical activity.

This is not to discount a significant role for language in the development of cognition: rather, it is to avoid the separation of this mediating instrument from real activities and to intensively explore the implications of an insistence on the unity of external activities and the psyche, as Vygotsky originally intended.

It must be emphasized that this discussion should not be interpreted as a justification for an oversimplified view that advocates "relevance" or "meaning residing in real activity" as an unproblematic key to learning. On the contrary, we want to show that, all too often, the missing element is that of appropriate attention to the problem of how to represent knowledge, how to sequence it, and how to embody it in a form appropriate to the learner.

The emphasis on communication, and specifically conversations, in the development of concepts find expression in teacher education in the persistent use of the supervisory conference. The conference does, of course, occupy a central position in our own scheme, but, as shown later, its genesis is somewhat different.

Arievich (1988) showed how the essential features of the post-Vygotsky development can be appreciated by reference to a mental act's *outsidedness*, meaning its reference to the outer world, its object-relatedness. This is an important idea, because it emphasises how English-speaking researchers, impressed by Vygotsky's view of the social nature of cognition, have unwittingly compounded the mistake of over emphasizing verbal interaction rather than specifically developing its role in the context of purposeful activity.

Arievich (1988, p. 2) emphasized that "those forms of activity which later on become the forms of human consciousness primarily have an objective or object-directed (as opposed to inward-directed) character." This is a significant statement that receives intensive interpretation in our scheme; it is the more significant when we move to giving a specific, technical meaning to "activity" beyond its everyday implication.

The persistent dualism of external practical activities and the psyche was resolved for the purposes of Soviet psychology by Leont'ev. He identified the substance of their unity by conceiving the psyche, not as some addition to activities, but as a form of activity, so that human consciousness exhibits the characteristics of the activity structures governed by the social relations of real activities.

The conception of the "unity" of the psyche and external practical activities is not to be taken simply to imply that whenever we are "doing something" we are *ipso facto* thinking about it; nor that "thinking" cannot take place in the absence of "doing." Equally importantly, Talyzina (1981, p. 32) emphasized that the subject engages in both external, practical acts and in psychic acts, but "the psyche is not merely an image of the world and a system of representations." The problem to which we are seeking a solution is that of the development, in practical acts, of consciousness, as Vygotsky (1962, p. 91) put it: "awareness of the activity of the mind." The "outsidedness" or "object-relatedness" in the development of mental activity insures, under appropriate circumstances in a stage-by-stage approach, that mental acts always have an exterior referrent, an object toward which both exterior acts and mental acts are directed. It is this feature that facilitates a white-box approach to learning to teach. In order to clarify this, we need to summarize the distinction made by Leont'ev, as explained and developed by Talyzina (1981), between *activities* and *actions*.

An *activity* is a process that carries out the living, active relations on the part of the subject with respect to reality, being characterized by a coincidence of objective and motive: It is motivated by the particular objective to the achievement of which it is directed. A person's activities are always responses to a corresponding need and are directed toward objects that are able to satisfy that need. The learning that can be observed in indigenous societies, and that is often cited as exemplary by Western educators, is conducted at the level of activity, this being possible because those things that need to be learned are sufficiently limited to serve as the objective of and motivation for learning.

In cases when students do not have such a need, they will either not be engaged in learning or they will be learning in order to satisfy some other need. In this latter case, when learning serves an intermediary objective, it ceases to be an activity and instead is known as an action. Complex learning is achieved through a sequence of actions. It is in the concept of an *action* that the approach is most detailed and most productive. Although an acceptance of the specifically social nature of learning has promoted an emphasis on *talk* and on an examination of the teaching-in-context of indigenous societies, this has signally failed to address the more symbolic, more abstract, more verbal form of knowledge which is an essential mode of transmission in a technical society.

In an advanced technological society any knowledge achievable by the individual is one part of a complex whole. Attempts to engage the learner in the appropriate *activity* will be too demanding, because any activity is the outcome of lengthy sociohistorical development. Attempts to initiate the learner into an arbitrarily assigned part of it will not insure that the complexity of the whole will be represented. It is in this latter case that the question of identification of the *central concepts* and of *transfer* becomes an issue, and in which *transfer* is destined for failure. This is the reason for our criticism of the apparently self-justifying notion of *authentic activity*: If it is genuinely *activity* in the technical sense, then, for much of schooling, it is too complex; if it is the "kinds of things people actually do" then it is not appropriate for induction into the activity of which it is a part, because it omits important features. The resolution of this difficulty lies in the idea of an *action*.

The notion of an *action* as a part of an activity is not simply that it is a "section" of it, an arbitrary compartmentalization. Its importance is that it carries the essential features of the activity, although the motivation of the activity, residing in its objective, is absent from the action. It is the understanding and identification of what constitutes that *essence* which is a significant feature of our deliberate approach to learning to teach.

The developments in Soviet psychology, following Leont'ev, have substantially informed our work with students in initial training for teaching.

The following section indicates how we have adopted and adapted many of the important principles for our scheme. In so doing, we drew extensively on Talyzina (1981).

THE DEVELOPMENT OF THE DELIBERATE APPROACH TO LEARNING TO TEACH

Teaching is a complex activity. It is an *activity* in the technical sense discussed earlier: The objective of the activity, of promoting learning, is also the motivation for the activity. This *activity* of teaching has features that appear only in advanced technological societies, notably in the mode, content, and site of its delivery systems.

Teaching includes the need to deal with larger groups than those of indigenous apprenticeship modes, deals with abstractions remote from their point of creation (school math is always different from the work of mathematicians), and is not undertaken in the workplace. Each of these could serve as the focus for much regret and handwringing, with a consequent determination to recapture the "authenticity" of learning. This is a misplaced traditionalism; the fact is, in societies in which it appears, school learning *is* authentic. This is not to say that it is effective, uniquely appropriate, or insusceptible to modification; but it is not less so simply because it is different from those apprenticeship modes of indigenous peoples. Schooling is necessary because it focuses on abstraction, generality, and transferability in favor of embeddedness.

The task of teaching is to represent, sequence, and embody knowledge in ways accessible to learners; the task for teacher education is to represent that complex activity to students. The *activity* of teaching, including curriculum design, test technology, and detailed planning, as well as specifically interactive aspects, requires the contributions of a variety of different agencies and individuals on a series of different occasions; it is not possible to "capture" this activity at any one site or at a given time. Nor it is possible to engage students in initial training in this range of processes; quite apart from their extensiveness, some of them are dependent on previous competence in the others. It may seem to follow from this that the question of course design for teacher education can be characterized as a problem of "breadth versus depth"; yet it is precisely this oversimplification that is denied by the concepts of *activity* and *action*. The activity of teaching includes its methods, modes of analysis, organization, social relations, and content. This complex activity is comprised of a large number of *actions*, each more limited in scope than the activity itself yet retaining its essential features. The problem of course design becomes one of representing, say, interactive classroom work in ways in which the *essence* of teaching is retained, notably its uncertainty and its need for deliberation on the basis of inconclusive evidence. If, in doing this, we take seriously the contention that the psyche and external practical activity should be viewed as a unity, then the question of generalization or transfer need no longer be conceived as the problem of extracting knowledge from one context in order to apply it somewhere else; it becomes part of the problem of developing actions that contain the essential features of the given system of knowledge and will provide for its application within predetermined limits. If we can develop in our students *actions* with these qualities, then the problem of learning to teach need no longer retain its current dominant feature of induction from a large number of events. Furthermore, the element of training in our scheme is no longer suscep-tible to criticism of its being merely *skill training*; it can be seen in its true light of being training in this wider sense.

An *action* should be understood, not simply as the physical, observable performance on a given occasion (there may be none), but as an integral psychophysical unity that contains all the basic elements of mental activity in relation to interactions with the external world. The difficulty of comprehending this as a definition finds resolution in the following discus-sion of the nature of an action.

Following Talyzina (1981), our use of the idea of an *action* as an elementary unit of learning activity requires an analysis in terms of the three components of an action: an orienting component, an executive component and a control component. Furthermore, an action is always directed at some object (which may be in material, materialized, or ideational form).

This is summarized in Figure 7.3 and described below.

The Orienting Component. The orienting component of the action is comprised of a number of stages through which the learner passes in order that the action becomes "mental, generalized, condensed, and assimilat-ed." These stages are:

1. an outline of the orienting basis of the action
2. the development of the action in material form
3. the development of the action in materialized form
4. the development of the action in external speech
5. the development of the action in internal speech
6. the full development of mental action.

The first stage requires "an outline of the orienting basis"; this reflects the fact that, in order to do something, the learner needs some perception of what is to be done. It is an "outline" in recognition of the novice not being

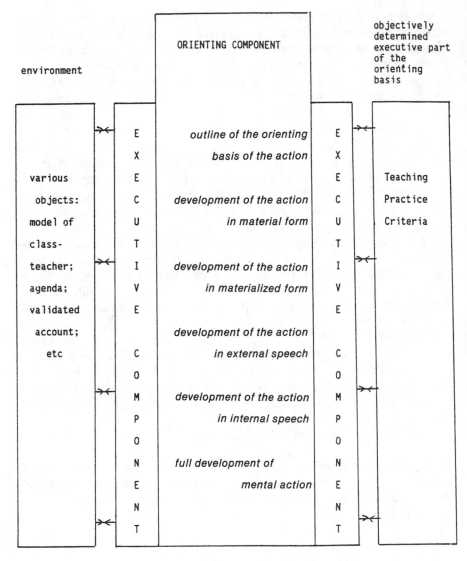

Figure 7.3.   The development of actions.

able to achieve an immediate, fully developed view of what is necessary; it is an "orienting basis" in that it "points" to what is necessary, and this "pointing" will continue to be developed beyond the initial outline. The specific feature of this detail in the context of an *action* is that the "pointing" is so designed as to engage the learner in processes which possess *the same structure as the associated activity.* It is not sufficient for the learner merely to "do" something and then, on the basis of a number of similar experiences, to induce the useful features of it, as seems to be the dominant assumption in most experiential learning. On the other hand, because it is essential that these processes do in every respect retain the essence of the activity, the use of this "pointing" must in itself recognize and utilize the social nature of learning to engage the student in deliberation in uncertain, practical tasks.

The orienting basis, of which an outline is required, consists of the object towards which the action is directed *and* a pattern that guides the way the subject acts. Before considering the remaining components of an action, it will be useful to relate this to the scheme for learning to teach outlined earlier.

At points in the course, students are asked to observe the host teacher, practice similar episodes, and attempt to narrow the gap between their own performance and that which was observed. The performance of the host teacher is an object in material form; agendas are objects in materialized form. These and other objects, together with the pattern for classroom work that constitutes the teaching practice criteria, comprise the orienting basis of the action. The student teacher does not perceive all that is available in the orienting basis: the *outline* of the orienting basis is the student's current perception. The subsequent development in the various stages of the orienting component (see Figure 7.3) is made on the basis of the various objects in the context of the external referent (the category and criterial system) and vice versa.

The "pattern" to which we have referred, being the category system of the dimensions and the criterial statements of each, serves to illustrate what constitutes appropriate action in teaching. Its very style is one that, rather than attempting to prescribe the detail of teaching in preestablished form, reflects the *activity* of teaching in that its complex and sometimes competing aspirations require interpretation and resolution in the context of a specific classroom. This pattern has not been empirically derived. It is the objectively determined executive part of the orienting basis.

The availability and determined use of the objectively determined executive part of the orienting basis promotes the *development* of the action in its several forms. It is not assumed that the orienting component exists as an established ontological reality, successfully assimilated and available for some kind of reflective inspection; nor is it assumed that the "pattern" can be assimilated from its written form. It is the successive deliberate attempts at *execution* that make another contribution.

The Executive Component of the Action.   The development of action requires that the subject "does something," but the nature, timing, purpose, and consequence of what is done are not random or accidental. Our deliberate approach to learning to teach recognizes that observing the class teacher, modelling that teacher, planning teaching episodes on the basis of working with the teacher, undertaking teaching, planning episodes on the basis of earlier ones, and planning episodes by working from the criterial statements are aspects of the executive component of the action that are all treated in the same way. Each aspect is an object amenable to the several stages in the orienting component of the action. We do not suggest that this will happen instinctively: It requires a deliberate approach to regulate it, and this is the *control* component of the action.

The Control Component of the Action.   Each *object* in the environment is tested against the emergent understanding of the "pattern," so that each is gradually modified in the action of the student; that is, both practical activity and understanding of the "pattern" are changed to reduce the gap between the two. This overt modification or accommodation is exercised and is apparent in the various processes of the stages in the orienting component. The initial modeling of the class teacher represents a narrowing of the gap in physical action; the same process is undertaken in external speech in supervisory conferences with the teacher tutor; the progress and process of learning, including the consideration of how "internal speech" can be seen to follow the same course as the overt aspects of the action, are examined in conferences with the university tutor and in written evaluation. It is this deliberate examination at each stage that constitutes the control component of the action.

REFLECTION AND THE DELIBERATE APPROACH TO LEARNING TO TEACH

The experienced teacher has achieved the stage of mental action in which the performance and thought about that performance are integrated. This automaticity of action is obviously an essential attribute of the professional teacher, but, under certain circumstances, this can be a disadvantage. The essence of what others call *reflection*, and what we refer to as *intelligent practice* (see Harvard, this volume), is the ability deliberately to examine the predicates, likely consequences, and alternatives to personal teaching moves. This is facilitated by being able, at will, to examine an appropriate object at any of the different stages of the orienting component of the action. This is the function of the control component of the action.

Talyzina (1981) suggested, and our studies are beginning to confirm this, that the manner in which actions are developed is a crucial determinant of whether "revisiting" is possible. Specifically, the flexibility of selection is not available to those students who have either omitted one of the stages in the orienting component of the action or have prematurely routinized a stage. However, it should not be assumed that Figure 7.3 suggests that the stages are sequential; they are identified as "stages" because they are distinct and recognizable features, but their actual development proceeds in complex combinations and sequences.

FURTHER ANALYSIS

This analysis illustrated how "activity theory" has contributed to the design of a scheme for a deliberate approach to learning to teach. This has been productive, particularly in its notion of the "outsidedness" of mental action, which has precipitated an emphasis on the "object-relatedness" of each aspect of the work with student teachers. It is the necessity of working with appropriate objects, in material, materialized, or ideational form, which prompted us to design specific techniques to sponsor the acquisition of professional activity.

It is our view, however, that our analysis in terms of *activity* and *action* is important because it is productive, not because it describes the world "as it is." We found it equally productive to review the scheme with a different unit of analysis, specifically, in terms of mental representations. In order to do this, we adopted and adapted Kolb's (1984) model. This resulted in a concentration on the conditions associated with effective learning about teaching. A detailed analysis of this is (in part) the subject of the next chapter, but it is useful to summarize here the deliberate approach to learning to teach in diagrammatic form. However, this description (Figure 7.4) is not simply a summary of the earlier description. The diagram emphasizes, not the methodological chronology of the scheme, but the conceptual relationship of the different aspects. So it is, then, that although a class teacher conference in fact takes place between the modelling by the class teacher (A1) and the demonstration of mastery by the student teacher (A2), in Figure 7.4 a direct relationship is implied between A1 and A2. This is because there is a direct relationship conceptually. It is this conceptual model that is explored in the next chapter.

CONCLUSION

We developed a deliberate approach to learning to teach that utilizes a variety of objects and techniques (and promotes associated conditions), that not only allows the learning process to be examined in detail but

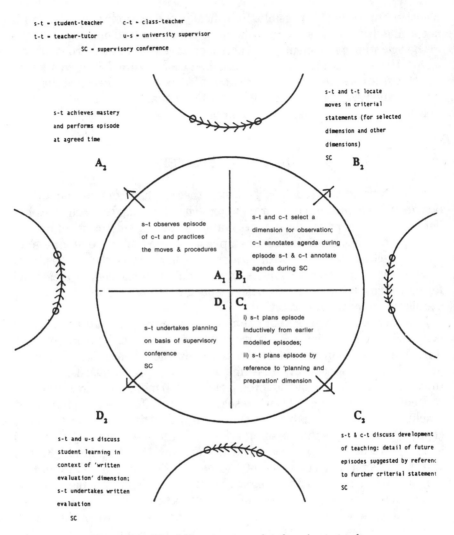

s-t = student-teacher   c-t = class-teacher

t-t = teacher-tutor   u-s = university supervisor

SC = supervisory conference

s-t and t-t locate moves in criterial statements (for selected dimension and other dimensions)

SC

B_2

s-t achieves mastery and performs episode at agreed time

A_2

s-t observes episode of c-t and practices the moves & procedures

s-t and c-t select a dimension for observation; c-t annotates agenda during episode s-t & c-t annotate agenda during SC

A_1 B_1

D_1 C_1

s-t undertakes planning on basis of supervisory conference

SC

i) s-t plans episode inductively from earlier modelled episodes;
ii) s-t plans episode by reference to 'planning and preparation' dimension

D_2

C_2

s-t and u-s discuss student learning in context of 'written evaluation' dimension; s-t undertakes written evaluation

SC

s-t & c-t discuss development of teaching: detail of future episodes suggested by reference to further criterial statement

SC

Figure 7.4. The deliberate approach to learning to teach.

incorporates this examination into its methods. Consequently, the data generated by the scheme for its very operation are precisely those which allow progress and impediments to progress to be traced. It is in this sense that we characterize the scheme as contributing to a white-box orientation to research in teaching.

When a scheme such as this is implemented, it is not surprising that many of its subjects adopt its techniques and show evidence of working in ways the scheme is designed to develop. What is more interesting is that there are student teachers who do not do so. It is in this area that a great deal of work needs to be done. White-box methods allow this kind of detail to be addressed.

Our current work suggests that the aspect that receives least attention from the students and their cooperating teachers is the development of the action in materialized form: the agendas. We are experimenting with providing surrogate experience for students with videodisc material accessed with a bar-code reader (Harvard, 1990; Harvard, Day, & Dunne, 1991) in ways that are consistent with the model outlined here. We suspect that this work with materialized forms is difficult to get adopted in classrooms because of the dominant practice, associated with school-based work, of encouraging student teachers to plan with reference to "aims and objectives"–as if this were unproblematic. In fact, it is this type of planning that exhibits the style of "inner speech," being abbreviated and condensed, and is suggestive of premature routinization that precludes further examination.

What, then, of the myth of the primacy of school-based work? We believe it needs examination. It may well be that shorter periods in school, carefully focused to generate appropriate representations and intensively analyzed, would be more productive.

REFERENCES

Arievich, I. (1988, September). *From Vygotsky to Galperin: Development of an idea of a mental act's "outsidedness."* Paper presented at I.V. Cheiron conference, Budapest.

Barrows, L. (1979, April). *Power relationships in the student teaching triad.* Paper presented at the Annual Meeting of the American Educational Research Association, San Francico.

Broeckmans, J. (1986). Short-term developments in student teachers' lesson plans. *Teaching and Teacher Education, 3,* 215–228.

Buchmann, M. (1981). Can traditional lore guide right choice in teaching? *Journal of Curriculum Studies, 14* (4), 339–348.

Calderhead, J. (1987). The quality of reflection in student teachers' professional learning. *European Journal of Teacher Education, 10* (3), 269–278.

Duffy, P. (1987). Student perceptions of tutor expectations for school-based teaching practice. *European Journal of Teacher Education, 10* (3), 261–268.

Harvard, G. R. (1990). Some exploratory uses of interactive video in teacher education: Designing and presenting interactive video sequences to primary student teachers. *Educational and Training Technology International, 7* (2), 155–173.

Harvard, G., Day, M., & Dunne, R. (1991). Studying students' schemas of typical primary classroom practice using interactive learning techniques and videodisc materials prior to beginning a teacher education course. *Interactive Learning International, 7,* 101–118.

Hollingsworth, S., & Goodman, S. (1988, April). *Looking at pre-service teacher - university supervisor relationships: Factors that facilitate growth.* Paper presented at the Annual Meeting of the American Educational Research Association, New Orleans.

Kolb, D. A. (1984). *Experiential learning.* Englewood Cliffs, NJ: Prentice-Hall.

Leslie, L. L. (1969). *Improving the student teaching experience through selective placements of students* (Final Report of Grant no. OEG-8-9-540015-2019 (058)). Washington, DC: U.S. Department of Health, Education and Welfare.

McAlpine, A., Brown, S., McIntyre, D., & Hagger, H. (1988). *Student teachers learning from experience*. Edinburgh: Scottish Council for Research in Education.

Popkewitz, T. S., Tabachnick, B. R., & Zeichner, K. M. (1979). Dulling the senses: research in teacher education. *Journal of Teacher Education, 30* (5), 52–61.

Ryle, G. (1949). *The concept of mind*. Harmondsworth, UK: Penguin.

Talyzina, N. (1981). *The psychology of learning*. Moscow: Progress Publishers.

Tharp, R. G., & Gallimore, R. (1988). *Rousing minds to life*. Cambridge, UK: Cambridge University Press.

Vygotsky, L. S. (1962). *Thought and language*. Cambridge, MA: MIT Press.

Wertsch, J. V. (Ed.). (1981). *The concept of activity in Soviet psychology*. Armonk, NY: Sharpe.

Wertsch, J. V. (Ed.). (1985). *Culture, communication and cognition: Vygotskian perspectives*. Cambridge, UK: Cambridge University Press.

Zeichner, K. M., & Liston, D. (1985). Varieties of discourse in supervisory conferences. *Teaching and Teacher Education, 1*, 155–174.

Zeichner, K. M., & Tabachnick, B. R. (1981). Are the effects of university teacher education 'washed out' by teaching experience? *Journal of Teacher Education, 37*, 7–11.

CHAPTER 8

An Integrated Model of How Student Teachers Learn How To Teach, And Its Implications For Mentors

Gareth Rees Harvard
School of Education
University of Exeter

INTRODUCTION

The description in Chapter 7 of a deliberate approach to learning to teach has outlined a number of instruments and techniques and examined the conditions which contribute to the development of competence in primary student teachers in initial training. A central aspect of this deliberate approach is the nature and purpose of the supervisory conference, in which student and mentor engage with specifically prepared "objects" that are accessible as learnable representations of professionally relevant knowledge in the form of annotated agendas or validated accounts of teaching episodes and a category system of teaching dimensions and criteria. It is the detail of how these techniques and conditions promote students' professional learning that are described in this chapter.

It will be shown how in the context of a conference the process of mentoring focuses on and examines the integration of material actions, practiced with and modeled by the class teacher, and their representation as professionally relevant knowledge. The dimensions and criteria provide the basis of a principled understanding of teaching. The necessary conditions for student learning consist of the modeling of strategic teacher actions and, crucially in the conferences, techniques for thinking about teaching. We discuss how these techniques and strategies are used to develop the idea of a mentor's supportive role when working with student teachers.

Learning is prompted and sustained through communicative activities that highlight the need for structured discourse, practical reasoning, and argumentation on selected aspects of teaching that go beyond general conversation about teaching events. Green (1976) and Fenstermacher (1990) refer to this as *practical rationality*. Consequently, each supervisory conference has a purpose very different from mere encouragement or criticism and eschews any kind of deficit model of students in initial training.

In particular, this detailed analysis of mentoring in conferences will illustrate how the most essential features of our program to encourage students to learn how to teach are precisely those that underpin the notion of self-assessment as a form of appraisal. In this sense, appraisals form an important part of the learning cycle. We also discuss ways in which various formative assessment processes are used to monitor how professional knowledge is organized and how it is progressively structured over time. In this scheme students' self-assessment is an inevitable and carefully developed aspect of their professional competence. The program also highlights the essential nature of collaboration between student teachers and mentors, requiring reflective monitoring of existing practices and their origins, as well as systematic analyses and testing of theories of teaching and their conscious production.

It is for the main purpose of developing student teacher competence and a professionally relevant knowledge base for teaching, that we create the opportunity for different kinds of mentors to use particular "instruments" – as models of thought and action – to examine, understand, and change teaching practices. Our research is helping us to produce a general model of learning how to teach which links experience to the thinking and learning processes by which student teachers acquire and develop professionally relevant knowledge. This type of developmental research is providing a deeper understanding of how to integrate teacher training and the development of teaching practices into a teacher development framework. But it also presupposes a more elaborate notion of competence.

THE NOTION OF COMPETENCE

Any examination of the extent to which supervisory conferences can contribute to the growth and development of competence presupposes some clear idea of what constitutes competence. Clearly, our category system, and the criterial statements discussed by Dunne in Chapter 7, make some contribution to an understanding of the performance features of "competence," yet what needs elaborating here is how these "instruments" are linked to particular learning processes to provide models of thought and action for examining existing practices and changing them.

A guiding principle in our model of learning how to teach derives from Ryle's (1949) important notion of *intelligent practice* as a more elaborate explanation of competence, and understanding as a part of knowing how in which competence, knowledge, and understanding are interdependent. Competence, in this scheme, characterizes professional development in three related areas: intellectual processes, performance, and a learner's organization of past experiences (for which we use the term *schema*) and their development as professionally relevant knowledge structures.

Thus stated, it is all too easy to agree that these are important features of competence, and even to consider it unremarkable that these aspects should feature in the definition; but this would be to miss the intended emphasis on their relatedness. It is their relatedness that will provide a clearer understanding of how people are enabled to think effectively about current practice and examine their previous knowledge to change practices. If we treat performance, intellectual processes, and schemas separately, then the well-known problems of experiential learning are perpetuated. How then, can we direct attention to their connectedness rather than accidentally reify their separateness?

Although the notion of *reflection* is often advanced to summarize the qualities of thinking we seek to develop in teachers, we find it to be insufficiently focused to use heuristically. We prefer Ryle's concept of *intelligent practice*, which he contrasted with *habitual practice*. Habitual practices repeat previous performance, but intelligent practices modify performance by what has gone on before, so that "the agent is still learning" (1949, p. 42). Furthermore, Ryle insisted—and we adopted this as a guiding principle in our deliberate approach to developing competence—that the knowledge required for understanding intelligent performance is some degree of competence in performance of that kind. It is in starting with competent performance that we are able to develop understanding as a part of knowing how.

Ryle (1949) argued that the notion of understanding as a part of knowing how means that the capacity to appreciate a performance is one in type with the capacity to do it. In this scheme we explore some of the practical implications for mentors of this and another of Ryle's important distinctions: that the capacity to perform and to appreciate a performance does not necessarily involve the ability to formulate criticisms, or that the ability to appreciate a performance does not involve the same degree of competence as the ability to do it.

Similarly, we explore in our analysis of the procedures used with class teachers the difference between witnessing a performance and understanding what is witnessed. In each conference mentors develop the student teachers' ability to relate competent performance to knowledge and understanding: the hallmark of intelligent practice.

Basically, the students learn how to judge whether someone's performance is or is not intelligent. This requires going beyond the performance itself. In doing so we consider the abilities, skills, capacities, and habits of which the performance is an expression. These abilities and dispositions can be expressed in various ways to signify students' meaningful acquisition of professionally relevant or strategic knowledge. The capacity for intelligent practice is not a single disposition.

The various techniques of coaching, modeling, structured conference discourse, and the instruments of dimensions and criteria are used to provide data for judgment or strategic knowing. Informed judgments involve comparing, contrasting, and analyzing specific cases and principles of teaching. These principles are based on a theory of stage-by-stage formation of mental activity described by Dunne.

This chapter describes the main practical aim of this approach: to find out and to describe the system of conditions that provide the necessary features for such activity formation. It is in this sense, and in this way, that students learn how at various levels of orientation, in observing, planning, and reconstructing teaching episodes with the class teacher, and in being more persistently provoked in the various conferences to elaborate on their understanding of selected aspects of teaching. Students' knowledge of how is exercised primarily in what they do or demonstrate and in their understanding of how professionally relevant knowledge is selected and organized. The conferences are chiefly concerned with analyzing and reconstructing such knowledge as material actions and their materialized forms.

The conferences support student teachers in revisiting and reorganizing actions and their representation as an internal loop of constant reconstruction. On each occasion the student teacher perceives things differently, so that the respective and changing roles of subject and object in that reconstruction process can be monitored. In this way, we can see how schemas and intellectual processes become powerful mediators of experience and determinants of action. These processes and schema can be modified. Therefore, learning, in this study, consists of the progressive development of schemas and processes, that is, students' emerging capacities to process and organize professionally relevant knowledge and to use this strategically in designing, enacting, and evaluating their professional practice.

What should be stressed here is that the orientation scheme for the professional activity of teaching should be accessible for student teachers in its entirety and in its parts. It needs to be made clear to student teachers how different elements of the scheme are connected and how these can be related to specific learning outcomes. It is because we cannot deduce from performance that a student teacher is also capable of formulating criteria to judge intelligent performance that we allocate specific roles and responsibilities to the class teacher, teacher-tutor, and university tutor. All three engage in specific training strategies that, although they consist of some repetition and practice for mastery of particular skills and classroom manoeuvres, also critically involve the "stimulation by criticism and example" (Ryle, 1949, p. 42) of the students' own judgments. This is the chief function of the school-based teacher tutor and the university supervisor.

Our main emphasis is on how students learn how to teach. Our procedures enable us to monitor the growth and development of all aspects of competence. This involves students in a constant analysis and reconstruction of classroom experiences by using and working with carefully chosen representations of pedagogical knowledge that are richer and more robust than mere descriptions of events. The learning process stresses deliberation on actions when working with the class teacher, making informed judgments about how to represent those actions as relevant and strategic pedagogical knowledge so that a coherent account, consisting of practical reasoning about actions, can be presented to the teacher tutor and university tutor, respectively.

In this way, professionally relevant knowledge is being continually reconstructed at successive layers of interpretation, that is, by developing an understanding of the process by which we link material and mental actions. The mediating step in the course of student teachers' internalization of the orientation scheme for teaching is the quality and purpose of conference discourse. We consider it necessary to create these different levels of orientation and of specially created learning activities, each of which is aimed at the formation of mental orientation at a given level, that is, actions, representations, and re-representations, to allow mentors and student teachers to monitor the acquisition and development of professionally relevant knowledge and their professional learning.

A MODEL OF STUDENTS' PROFESSIONAL LEARNING

The mentoring program described here is school based and involves three types of mentors: two teachers in each school, one of whom is a class teacher, and another who is specially trained as a teacher tutor. Both work alongside a university supervisor. All three mentors are responsible for conducting supervisory conferences with students, and although each conference is undertaken for a quite specific purpose, they are designed to complement one other. The different mentoring roles emphasize that the task of mentoring is probably more complex than effective teaching. This complementarity secures appropriate conditions for movement toward competence in the specific sense required by our scheme, specifically, mental orientation.

The notion of appropriate conditions is best explored through the vocabulary and some ideas offered by Kolb (1984). Its most sophisticated features resemble a model of "cognitive apprenticeship" proposed by Collins, Brown, and Newman (1989) that sees learning embedded in activity and makes deliberate use of the social and physical context. Their theory of situated cognition suggests that activity and perception are importantly and epistemologically prior to conceptualization, and that it is on them that more attention needs to be focused. But we extended this notion to accommodate Galperin's stage-by-stage theory of activity formation described in Chapter 7.

Similarly, we adapted and elaborated Kolb's (1984) learning cycle involving four adaptive learning modes—concrete experience, reflective observation, abstract conceptualization and active experimentation. But we have focused upon the nature of movement within and between these phases of learning as a means of monitoring student teachers' conceptual change. This is summarized in Figure 8.1, in which the four stages are labeled A1, B1, C1, and D1, together with the methodological description of our scheme, reprinted from the previous chapter.

Although Kolb pursued these ideas to explain the distinctive features of different learning styles, we prefer to show how this cycle can be used to plan for a succession of learning experiences for each student, showing how it helps us to focus on and monitor changes in students' pedagogical knowledge and understanding of themselves as teachers. This involves them in understanding how component skills, or the parts of the orientation scheme, are organized into viable systems of molar competence, for which our category system provides a framework. We agree with Boekaerts (1991) that we need to make reference to student teachers' "subjective feelings of competence" (p. 1).

We provide opportunities for deliberate movement through the four levels of representation so that we can promote the use of the specific intellectual processes of analysis and reconstruction. We refer to these as cognitive activity procedures that select from and organize experience in constructing professionally relevant knowledge representations. Each representation, A1, B1, C1, and D1, is associated directly with specific actions and events and, indirectly, with more abstract and personalized re-representations of those actions, which can then be tested by noting student teachers' ability to make appropriate pedagogical choices in planning for and enacting teaching. Effectively, students have to revisit and

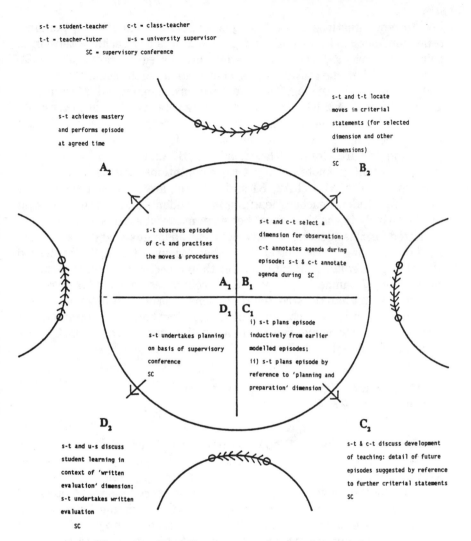

s-t = student-teacher   c-t = class-teacher
t-t = teacher-tutor   u-s = university supervisor
SC = supervisory conference

s-t and t-t locate
moves in criterial
statements (for selected
dimension and other
dimensions)

s-t achieves mastery
and performs episode
at agreed time

A_2

SC

B_2

s-t observes episode
of c-t and practises
the moves & procedures

s-t and c-t select a
dimension for observation;
c-t annotates agenda during
episode; s-t & c-t annotate
agenda during SC

A_1 B_1

D_1 C_1

s-t undertakes planning
on basis of supervisory
conference
SC

i) s-t plans episode
inductively from earlier
modelled episodes;
ii) s-t plans episode by
reference to 'planning and
preparation' dimension

D_2

C_2

s-t and u-s discuss
student learning in
context of 'written
evaluation' dimension;
s-t undertakes written
evaluation
SC

s-t & c-t discuss development
of teaching: detail of future
episodes suggested by reference
to further criterial statements
SC

Figure 8.1.   The deliberate approach to learning to teach.

rewrite specific events to capture in schematic form the most salient features of their teaching. Hence the importance of an agenda and its annotations.

These processes of analysis and reconstruction takes student teachers beyond performance to the nature and development of the underlying capacities, skills, abilities, and dispositions of which the performance was an actualization. We refer to these successive levels of orientation that are deliberately designed to examine how student teachers adjust and readjust to new situations and challenges as personal experience, personal reflection, personal meaning, and personal action. Specific attention is paid to different aspects of orientation, namely equilibrium, disorientation, exploration, and reorientation. They emphasize the students' increasingly autonomous learning. These features are summarized in Figure 8.1 and are labeled, A2, B2, C2, and D2. The whole cycle is not necessarily linear: students and mentors can choose to start from the most appropriate point, depending on the purpose and context for learning.

A1 and A2 are closely related, as are B1 and B2, and so on. The techniques that promote the eight representations, and the crucial relationship between A1 and A2, B1 and B2, etc., are discussed below. The context for student teachers' learning is of students and mentors working collaboratively in the "interface" between material actions and their materialized form as agendas, to develop a shared language and to construct an understanding of teaching. This is what Arievitch (1989, 1991) referred to as the *outsidedness* of mental acts, or their *object-relatedness*, discussed more fully by Dunne in Chapter 7. It comprises relevant professional knowledge built into the structure of actions. It is not just helping student teachers learn how to teach, but also helping them how to reason about and learn from their teaching. We continue by discussing how A2, B2, C2, and D2 are interrelated.

(1) *A1: Concrete Experience* promotes *A2: Personal Experience*

We described in Chapter 7 how the student teacher observes the class teacher, practices various strategic actions and procedures, and demonstrates them in appropriate contexts. Incidentally, exemplar activities provided by the university curriculum courses serve a similar purpose. The observation contributes to an outline of the orienting basis for the action in a material form—the actions—which evolves into a materialized form as the student practices how to integrate the various actions. These combined actions, summarized as concrete experience, have an associated cognitive representation that we denote as A1. This representation, being associated with a specific event, is at a low level of generality. As the student practices the moves and acquires mastery in a variety of events, the largely kinesthetic representation A1, with its low level of generality, is re-represented as A2. Here the student teacher and the class teacher work on an articulate linguistic or spatial-graphic representation of what's been practiced.

This is based on a personal, emergent analytic vocabulary. This is the representation denoted by A2, which we call *personal experience*, being mindfully derived from concrete experience by focusing on, sharing, and testing whether and to what extent these various descriptions of their shared activity capture the salient features of the teaching events.

(2) *B1: Reflective Observation* Promotes *B2: Personal Reflection*

As part of our deliberate approach to learning how to teach, we require student teachers to create opportunities for concrete experience as part of their developing professional competence. The next series of deliberate actions occurs when, in a supervisory conference, the student and the class teacher, together, identify which dimension or dimensions of teaching will be the focus of particular attention in a future teaching episode. They draw up an agenda that sets out the content and sequence of that episode, with the selected dimension noted at appropriate points. These actions, of identifying dimensions and creating an agenda, we summarize as *reflective observation*, this being a joint observation of specific episodes which both the student and the teacher have undertaken. Associated with these actions is a cognitive representation that we denote as B1, this being the materialized form of a shared, specific language and set of categories to think about teaching. They test the use of these categories by annotating an agenda.

It is at this point that the deliberate approach of our scheme most clearly resembles Collins, Brown, and Newman's (1989) model of *cognitive apprenticeship*. Cognitive apprenticeship seeks to enculturate students into authentic practices through activity and social interaction. The teacher's modeling, observations, and annotations of particular teaching episodes reveals in a more explicit form how professionally relevant or strategic knowledge is selected and organized. The class teacher conferences focus on the reasons for those actions, and the judgments that govern what is noted as being present and as being absent. In this sense, the criterial statements offer some guidelines for determining professionally relevant decisions. This strategic knowledge is made accessible to the student when the agendas are annotated or when new ones are constructed. This is a crucial step towards practicing the cognitive activity procedures of analysis and reconstruction.

These activities help teachers to codify relevant professional practicefor student teachers. Teacher knowledge is being elicited and explicitly and powerfully reproduced in the agendas, but because experienced teachers' actions are so automatic and much of their professional knowledge implicit, we need to press the teacher into a further activity that engages them in the explicit process of articulating and showing student teachers how they construct and reconstruct learnable representations of that knowledge, and of those actions and demonstrations. This is achieved in two ways: by collaborating with the student teacher in constructing and annotating agendas and in interpreting the language and categories of our scheme.

Both procedures involve the participants in analysis and reconstruction. The student is involved in reproducing, and learning how to analyze and reconstruct, relevant professional knowledge-in-actions in the appropriate representational format of agendas and their annotations.

This is an important transition stage from practical to more verbal, theoretical activity, but it is perception and activity that regulates it. The teacher merely points, using indexical terms, to the selected dimension, that then provides an essential structure for discourse in supervisory conferences, simultaneously capturing the salient features of a teaching activity. The annotations provide a validated account – an authenticated record of what took place – that the teacher tutor uses to help the student identify particular generic descriptions in the teaching practice criteria.

It is this process of asking students to identify, recall, and interpret classroom events through detailed and thorough documentation, and then to locate them in deliberately problematic, generic descriptions of classroom practice, which ensures that they construct a learnable cognitive representation, which we call *personal reflection* and denote by B2. This represents a more sophisticated level of thinking than the assimilative mode of personal experience, and serves to familiarize students and teachers with the conventions of a system of representations and mental actions to describe and explain teacher competence.

In this sense, appraisal is a process of continual comparisons, influencing established and more recent cognitions and feelings. Self-assessment is a form of appraisal that involves a comparison between actual performance and internal and external criteria. We believe that students' skill to assess their performance in this way is a major aspect of any professional competence category.

(3) *C1: Abstract Conceptualization* Promotes *C2: Personal Meaning*

Eventually, students' planning of teaching episodes does not begin from modeling, although this technique is available if needed, but depends rather on specific attention to the variety of dimensions of teaching and their criteria. This is not, as traditionally conceived in many teaching practice programs, a simple move from objects of action – watching what the teacher does – to a plan of action, but is, more systematic in plotting the successive moves from objects of action to models for action to a plan of action, referred to as the *zone of development*.

Interposed between observing what experienced practioners do and students doing it for themselves is a set of external guidelines in the form of models of thought for action: They consist of annotations, criterial statements, exemplars, and modelled processes of analysis and planning. These are negotiated and adapted for use with class teachers and teacher tutors to suit particular conditions and contexts. Student teachers now begin to appropriate relevant modes of thinking about teaching, by identifying available choices, judging which to select, and examining stipulative claims for choosing particular actions. It is these informed judgments that are being continually practiced in planning episodes inductively from earlier modeled episodes. More ambitiously, student teachers plan teaching episodes from the criteria for planning and preparation.

Learning is conducted as narratives and conversations within a framework of structured discourse that highlights the problematic nature of classrooms against external criteria that help to determine the relative difficulty of various aspects of performance. The practical result of such discourse and appraisal is the plan of action. On a first practice these plans arise chiefly from working alongside the class teacher and then representing their meaning to the teacher tutor. On a final practice the plan of action starts from the generic statements of the "planning and preparation" dimension. This is a demanding test of the robustness of students' pedagogical content knowledge, requiring more complex expressions of competence: Students have to specify, from general principles, the specific necessary and sufficient conditions and procedures for a successful teaching program. It is this process, started during on-site university courses and used specifically in schools, that promotes the representation C1 – abstract conceptualization.

In the supervisory conferences with the teacher-tutor, predicated on the basis of validated accounts of teaching, the students discuss their progress using the various levels of criteria. They specifically assess the closeness between intended and actual achievements, and judge how best to frame plans for possible classroom practice that exemplifies improvement as represented in higher, adjacent levels of competence. It is this action of collective problem solving and of making informed judgments, framing practical actions that exemplify the theoretical but professionally relevant descriptions of improvement, that promotes the re-representation of C2 – personal meaning.

(4) *D1: Active experimentation* promotes *D2: personal action.*

The emergent, flexible representation C2 is the basis of the next deliberate action: how to indicate the nature of improved performance. This is a critical stage in students' professional learning: to judge what is meant by an adequate performance and point to the criteria for judging adequacy. The previous activities and conferences have focused on ways of acquiring appropriate criteria for judging what constitutes success and using these as "building blocks for generating internal standards" (Boekaerts, 1991, p. 13). In this sense, self-assessment consists of clear indications of future levels of performance and signals a developmental change in the student teachers' capacity to make realistic professional judgments using internal and external criteria for assessing their performance. The tutor must press students on how they are using and framing these internalized standards by monitoring what important information they are selecting about past learning experiences. An internal standard of performance is developed as a personal judgment. Our instruments and techniques help to make these judgments more informed, more conscious, habitual, and deliberate.

Our external criteria are provided to help students and teachers codify professional knowledge. "Once teachers' vernacular pedagogical knowledge enters the realm of codified knowledge there is the potential to develop a corpus of systematic pedagogical knowledge" (McNamara, 1991, p. 307). The criteria also safeguard against student teachers overaccentuating particular dimensions of performance and, often unwittingly, practicing inadequate techniques and strategies. Our procedures also demonstrate with students how to generate internal standards of performance by collecting and constantly working on sufficient information about task features that represent particular competence categories.

Moreover, they also provide necessary practice in applying inferential rules to experiences and their accompanying documentation. It is the tutor's role to help students form realistic appraisals of the relative difficulty of tasks and their own ability to accomplish them, so as to set themselves manageable goals for learning. Once again, the external criteria can be used heuristically to gauge what improvement might look like, and to offer sufficient information about teaching activity representative of the various competence categories or dimensions.

The planning of a new teaching episode promotes the cognitive representation we call *active experimentation*, denoted by D1. It is characterized by its high level of generality and comprehensiveness. A follow-up on the teaching of this episode in a supervisory conference provides for a transformation of experience to the representation we call personal action – D2. This is characterized by the enhanced properties of reasonableness of action and resilience across contexts. This tests the student teachers' ability to consider and evaluate their actions, to qualitatively evaluate a practical situation, and to consider all existing conditions in order to accomplish a task or solve a problem.

It is the responsibility of all three mentors to continually monitor, at their various levels of orientation in actions and representations, how students develop the ability (a) to clearly understand what they have already accomplished with a correspondingly clear idea of what counts as improvement, that is, their future level of performance; (b) to detect bias in their appraisals, especially in their definitions of adequacy and the criteria by which they judge success; (c) to detect any discrepancy between specific task demands and their resources to meet those demands; and (d) to judge the reasonableness of actions in terms of the benefits or extra effort required for different courses of action. Eventually, this is articulated further in a written evaluation.

Our description of the various instruments, techniques, and roles and responsibilities of the students and mentors provide some insight into how students can act on the circumstances of particular classrooms to create opportunities to assess their competencies. Such procedures are intended to improve students' understanding of assessment systems by promoting and sustaining constructive self-explanation. In this sense, they become increasingly knowledgeable about their capacity to generate internal standards, judge how to relate existing abilities to future performance, and make informed judgments about the probability of success in various competence categories. Our conditions and techniques promote movement between the representation of personal experience, personal reflection, personal meaning, and personal action, as a means of generating internal standards of performance.

This sequence provides another layer of interpretation, characterized by increasing student teacher autonomy and self-assessment. But above all, it involves the university tutor discussing student teachers' learning in terms of their mental orientation to the professional activity of teaching. This form of self-assessment is mediated in the form of summary sheets of various levels of criteria and written evaluation. It is in these conferences that the tutor and student teacher examine the beliefs that students hold about their capacity to appraise their actions, select from and organize their experiences and professional knowledge, and understand the meaning of the assessment system. In all of this the self-activity of the student teacher is of paramount importance.

(5) Certain Conditions Promote Movement Between the Representation *A2: Personal Experience; B2: Personal Reflection; C2: Personal Meaning; D2: Personal Action*

As described earlier, and summarized in Figure 8.1, the successive deliberate techniques of our scheme are designed to provide for specific primary cognitive representations (e.g., A1) and then associated secondary representations (in this case A2). There are further aspects inherent in our work that provide the *conditions* for movement along the chain A2, B2, C2, D2 of secondary representations.

The representation A2–personal experience–is achieved during the acquisition of mastery of specific teaching actions. It is this procedural success, the practical demonstration of being able to do something, that provides the motivation for the student to find a cognitive interest in the action. The condition of equilibrium summarizes the motivation encouraged by increasing mastery in performance and the cognitive interest associated with motivation that contributes to personal reflection. It coincides with the deliberate promotion of the generic descriptions in the criterial statements for codifying pedagogical knowledge, so that practical mastery, knowledge, and understanding are seen to be interdependent.

The recognition of a demand for improved practice is signalled in the class teachers' annotations. They alert the student to specify actions in terms of the criterial statements. "On the basis of direct and vicarious experiences of a specific competence category, students are expected to build up a database in which actions are causally related to effects" (Boekaerts, 1991, p. 13). This induces a condition of disorientation in the form of a developmental challenge, which is appropriate at this level of abstraction. Performance can now be related to an ability to ask which actions are linked with positive or negative results, to judge the relative difficulty of tasks, and one's competence to tackle various tasks and the probability of success.

This, in turn, provides the condition of exploration in which, at a practical level, the students attempt to plan realistically for improved performance, and at a cognitive level promotes the movement from personal meaning to personal action, by using criteria, defining tasks, and assessing the difficulty of tasks and their capacity to harness sufficient time, effort, and mental resources to meet those demands.

An important feature of our scheme in helping students to learn how to teach is the emphasis we put on the validity of revisiting and reinterpreting actions and experiences at different levels of representation, each of which reorients the student-teachers to a further understanding of how they think about teaching. These correspond with the three types of conferences. We start from new actions that are a further aspect of concrete experience. We do not assume that successful adaptive performance in one aspect immediately transfers to other aspects. Consequently, it is the condition of reorientation that makes possible the adoption of a new starting point, which is conceived in our model as informing the successive versions of A2–D2 and then, from D2–A2, rather than a setting aside of D2 in order to start the cycle again.

This model of students' professional learning is deliberately linked to appraisal as an important feature of the learning cycle. In order to be able to assess teaching performance realistically, the student must have access to internal standards of performance. It is by generating these internal standards that the student will acquire self-regulatory control in critical areas of professional competence along with domain specific knowledge and skills.

The conference discourse focuses on procedures for examining how practical reasoning is used and developed. Recently, Fenstermacher (1990) produced a working definition for practical rationality as "the capacity of a person to reason in some relatively coherent and logical fashion from action to the grounds for that action and back again" (p. 10). But it is too easily assumed that there is an easy transition from one state of knowing and doing to another. Fenstermacher's analysis of what should be included in a practical argument—robust accounts of situation, stipulation of central ideas governing children's learning and curriculum development, empirical claims or contentions about what does or does not work and moral and ethical grounds—requires deliberate mentoring in the form of structured discourse.

MENTORING STRATEGIES USED IN CONFERENCES

There are three specific mentoring strategies used in the conferences to promote and develop students' professional learning and prompt specific movement from one stage of the learning cycle to another. The mentoring strategies control the process of self-assessment and monitor the growth and organisation of students' professionally relevant knowledge. The strategies are eliciting, elaborating, and challenging student teachers' professional knowledge. Here is a brief description of how these mentoring strategies are used in conferences with the school-based teacher tutor and university mentors. They are all equally important and it is necessary for student teachers to use them in all aspects of their teaching, planning, and evaluation.

One of the strategies is to elicit students' feelings and judgments about their capabilities as teachers and the criteria they use in appraising them. The mentor also elicits descriptions of their actions and perceived capabilities on certain tasks and domain-specific knowledge and skills. Students' categories for self-appraisal invariably include statements of self-doubt and confidence and positive and negative feelings about particular situations and tasks. The categories they use to represent the difficulty of tasks and their ability to accomplish them are matched with the scheme's dimensions and criteria to gauge what realistic self-assessment looks like.

Learning is further enhanced by inviting student teachers to elaborate the essential features of teaching activity by comparing and contrasting specific teaching events for relevant details, identifying recognizable patterns of teaching procedures, and using the language and categories of the dimensions and criteria within more general descriptive accounts of classroom events. They are being asked to elaborate the meanings of those activities and demonstrate how relevant features of professional knowledge are being recognized and understood. This provides students and mentors with a firm basis for conceptualizing the growth of professionally relevant knowledge, how they select from and apply this in their planning, and how they develop an understanding of how to set and achieve future levels of competent performance.

Having described the significance of teaching events, they then have to explore their implications for subsequent thinking and planning. The purpose of this particular strategy is to challenge students' professionally relevant knowledge as domain-specific knowledge and skills, and the reasons for their choices and actions, that is, how they make professionally relevant judgments. The criteria help to identify what would count as improvement. Student teachers are asked to identify what they consider to be salient, to justify selections of content and pedagogy, and to make personal judgments about how the provided criteria influence their own subjective competence. It is crucial to explore a range of practical options to determine how they are influenced by the context in which the student teachers work.

The combined efforts and the complementary roles of the two school-based mentors (the class teacher and the teacher tutor) serve as models for student teachers on how to use a range of teaching and learning strategies for monitoring competent performance and evaluating their experiences. Both mentors are constantly eliciting, elaborating, and challenging students' schemas or professional knowledge at different levels of activity and representation. This knowledge is being continually tested, amended, and refined through practice and in discourse. These successive layers of continual appraisal through experimentation and interpretation, in both classroom actions and conference discourse, are designed to provide the necessary conditions for generating internal standards of performance and realistic self-assessment.

An Example of Mentoring Focusing on a Selected Aspect of Teaching

Here is an example of how student teachers and mentors focus their thinking on a selected aspect of teaching. This particular conference is conducted by the school-based teacher tutor. The extracts are taken from two conferences, the first of which can be located on our learning cycle as movements within and between reflective observation and abstract conceptualization, and shows how the student copes with disorientation. The second judges the success of the exploration stage in which new techniques are being tried out. The mentor monitors how the student teacher assesses her ability to progress in a specific competence category and how she realistically appraises the difficulty of the tasks she sets herself.

The conference discourse focuses upon the practical implications of adopting this particular dimension to work on and how to plan to make informed judgments of its appropriateness. *Appropriateness* refers to the particular features of the classroom context, the type of curriculum activity, and how these influence the perceived difficulty of improving in this competence category. The emphasis on realistic self-assessment is crucial. The student teacher is learning how to assess past performance realistically and frame realistic aspirations for future action. Eventually, the student teachers will generate internal standards by which to judge their capability to tackle specific tasks to achieve a high probability of success.

The selected aspect of teaching chosen for this example is one of the nine teaching dimensions, referred to as *structured conversation* (see Chapter 7, Figure 7.2). The description of this dimension and its criteria are used alongside classroom exemplars to help students make finer differentiations in their teaching, planning, and evaluation.

Each dimension provides descriptions of simple levels of performance and more complex levels and expressions of competence. These criteria are intended to provide a structure for students' self-evaluation and planning for improvement. At this level of discourse the mentor focuses on how students use the language and categories of this dimension and its criteria to think about this aspect of their work. The criteria are problematic. In this instance the student had already observed the class teacher discussing a topic with the class and felt that this was an important skill and pedagogical strategy to develop.

But in eliciting her descriptions and explanations of what she perceived to be happening in these episodes, the student teacher represented events in general terms, such as "the teacher asked many questions and provided many explanations" or "the teacher talked frequently with the pupils." To orient the student to a more specific way of differentiating "teacher and classroom talk," the complex set of skills summarized as structured conversations were introduced. The outline description accompanying this dimension was used to orient the student to some of the important pedagogical features of classroom talk in which the purpose and function of talk, and the respective roles and responsibilities of the teacher and the pupils, feature prominently.

The following brief descriptions and conference extracts illustrate how one can use the mentoring strategies of elicitation and elaboration to modify what has been seen or practiced on a selected aspect of teaching. Selecting a particular dimension is agreed between the class teacher, student teacher, and teacher mentor to insure that no one aspect or dimension of teaching is being overaccentuated, or that inadequate techniques and strategies are being used without the student teacher realizing it. In this case, they have chosen *structured conversation*.

It is not expected that the entire range of activities under this heading be brought into play every time structured conversation is attempted, but the beginning teacher should be aware of its differentiated nature. In this way there is some structure for deciding on appropriate teaching and learning strategies. The teacher-tutor mentor asked the student teacher to refer to, and elaborate on, specific exemplars of this dimension experienced in working with the class teacher.

The annotated agendas were used to refer to specific events and actions. At first the student crudely categorized a whole range of different exemplars of the teachers' exchanges with the children from various curriculum tasks and activities. The mentor and student decided to share and elaborate their knowledge and understanding of such events by emphasizing the multifaceted nature of classroom talk by focusing on the nature and purpose of frequent exchanges between the pupils and the teacher as a means of managing children and monitoring their learning. This is an important aspect of the mentor's role: to practice using, testing, and extending the language and categories of the dimension to avoid undifferentiated and ambiguous references to teacher–pupil exchanges as "classroom talk" or "finding out what the children know."

The mentor asked the student teacher to describe the context in which conversation had occurred, and to explain its purpose and refer to how the children reacted to it. Next the mentor examined these descriptions and showed how they related to some of the more differentiated elements of structured conversation in the outline description. This enabled them to focus on what aspects of this dimension could be changed. So already they had agreed on the basis for further differentiation of classroom talk. They went on to discuss how talk is transformed in various subtle ways, so that talk in classrooms is not seen as a homogeneous event. Remember that the training aspect of mentoring is to stimulate, by criticism and example, the students' own judgment. In this way, the criticism consisted of questioning the limited use of the student teachers' general description of classroom events. In recognizing the nature and purpose of talk, they were able to consider other examples of how talk can be used in classrooms.

The mentor continued to elicit and develop these understandings of the nature and purpose of "talk" by elaborating students' schema of this aspect of teaching. The student teacher was asked to compare and contrast the exemplars provided by the class teachers or more generally observed, with the language and categories of the dimension, to determine the necessary conditions for structured conversation. For example, in her descriptions the student teacher concentrated solely on teacher performance. The mentor then agreed with the student teacher to discuss how these actions illustrated and exemplified a basic necessary condition expressed in the first set of criteria – "Listen carefully to what children are saying and respond supportively." – and to judge and explain whether and how it was accomplished.

The mentoring strategy focused on the specific actions and procedures being used by the teacher, and tested whether the student could stipulate the necessary conditions for this aspect of structured conversation to occur. It is when the student teacher talks convincingly about how actions and criteria can help in strategic planning that it can be agreed with the mentor which specific criteria can be used to set a realistic target for improvement. The mentor and student teacher may decide to concentrate on various ways of "responding supportively" for different types of tasks, either in a particular curriculum area or in different ones. Alternatively, they may decide to incorporate into their planning the more advanced teaching strategy, which was not evident in the student teachers' general descriptions, as suggested in the next set of criteria, namely, a more specific purpose for structured conversation – "Attempt to elicit children's responses; recognise and attempt to analyse difficulties."

Once again, the mentor elicited from the student teacher descriptions of teachers' actions that exemplified these criteria before asking the student teacher to elaborate on how they might be used to prompt and sustain structured conversation. It still remains problematic how these strategies can best be planned for and used: This is the nature of the challenge. The criterial statements have to be interrogated so that there is some agreement on what the student might be involved in when attempting to "elicit children's responses." The mentor and student teacher have to decide on suitable strategies and procedures to meet these criteria. This requires an accurate knowledge of a variety of classroom factors that will influence its successful accomplishment. In this way discourse is either structured around and focused on a number of validated accounts of teaching in which the student has practiced various strategies for sustaining structured conversation, or by starting from the criteria as a way of framing plans for action, that is, strategic planning.

Here is an extract from that part of the conference discussion in which the teacher tutor persists in trying to elaborate the student teachers' personal judgments of professional adequacy on aspects of this dimension. The tutor also begins to challenge the student-teachers' skill to assess her own performance and set realistic goals for further improvement on selected aspects of this dimension. In this sense, appraisal is a major aspect of a more general professional competence category, and one that goes beyond competence in particular teaching skills. The student has already presented a number of examples of what she classifies as "talk and discussion with the pupils" from her own teaching and that of her class teacher. She has presented the evidence in her validated accounts – her agendas and their annotations – and she is already beginning to elaborate her knowledge of this aspect of teaching in more detail and with clearer categories that refer to its nature and purpose. The mentor now challenges the student to elaborate on her use and understanding of this aspect of her teaching by stating how she judges her capacity to improve on it. In this way, she is becoming increasingly less dependent on feedback from the mentor.

Student: I have already spoken to the class teacher about this and observed her discussing ideas with children. I have tried to address the criteria at levels one and two. They focused my thinking about problems of teaching children, so that I've been trying hard to try not to influence what a child says; to keep my ideas to myself. I was conscious of it because on a previous experience if someone just didn't understand something I'd tend to just tell them, so that they could get on with it. But now, I've really tried not to directly influence what they say.

Tutor: I can see how your ideas are changing on this aspect of teaching but tell me more about how it is affecting what you actually do in the classroom?

Student: I'm listening more carefully to what they say and trying to encourage them to say more. I'm consciously thinking about it this time "Keep your views to yourself."

Tutor: How is this affecting the way in which you are learning how to teach?

Student: First, I wouldn't have thought of it myself. That's what I like about this system, you have some guidelines so that you can really think before you go into a lesson, right, now I'm going to do this and you go in there with that in mind, and you make sure that you do it which is really nice. Otherwise, you just get wishy-washy about what you've done or achieved. Also the teacher in the class doesn't really know what to comment on but now they've got something specific to comment on."

Tutor: How are you learning how to teach?

Student: I've learned how to focus my thinking about my teaching and become more confident in judging whether what I do is reasonable. Otherwise there are so many things that you could say about what goes in classrooms which could leave it all over the place. Whereas the criteria helps to focus your attention on specific things. It's been more directed learning for us. I'm beginning to know how to assess my competence to do certain tasks.

This extract shows how the student teacher has amended or elaborated her "schema" of classroom talk in practical and conceptual terms. It shows how she is using appraisal as an important feature of the learning cycle to include aspects of subjective feelings of competence. This is being done by determining whether, and how much of, a discrepancy exists between the tasks she sets herself and the necessary resources required to meet them.

The rest of the conference concentrated on her zone of development. This consisted largely of an attempt to move attention from the acquisition of new knowledge and skills to their sustained use in new situations. This would involve the student teacher in negotiating appropriate planning with, and observation of, the teacher in which she might consider how to adapt structure conversation for the specific purpose of analysing children's difficulties.

In analyzing or planning for further improvement on this dimension, the mentor refers to the criterial statements at a simple level of performance to focus the student's thinking on specific teaching strategies and their pedagogical content. The mentor now challenges the student on how the criteria can be used to categories and plan for specific teaching events. But the main thrust of the conference is to elaborate and challenge students' understanding of selected aspects of professional knowledge, especially, how activities can be designed to promote children's learning.

Different aspects of structured conversation are examined to show how differences about talk and their purposes can be divided up for use in different curriculum areas, how these purposes are entangled with one another, how they govern and are governed by one another. This is a structure within and around which student teachers learn to differentiate their knowledge about an important aspect of teaching. Student teachers also practice their strategic knowing by analyzing, comparing, and contrasting events to judge whether there is a discrepancy between what they intend to do and the material resources and competence needed to accomplish it, as well as the relative benefits and disadvantages of different courses of action.

In a later conference the same student began to assess her understanding of, and progress in, various teaching episodes incorporating this dimension of teaching: It shows clear evidence of reorientation. She begins to differentiate her ability in various competence categories. She examines the practical implications for planning and improving her teaching. She also show how her professional knowledge is becoming more strategic by testing, amending, and extending particular cases of teaching against more principled understanding of teaching.

> Student: I feel that this is so much improved. I now draw out their views and understandings through questions, although there is not much listening to each other; some are working in pairs, therefore, helping each other. I didn't actually encourage this enough. But I did draw their attention to conflicting ideas and provided them with some as well, in the form of questions and ideas from the results of their work. I greatly supported them in their attempts to to report their thinking, this I believe to be a very important aspect both orally and in their writing. I never made the point of being wrong. I asked them to look at what was written and to decide what they were needing to look at, for example, the way they had linked two or more ideas together or interpreted a result. They were not told that it was wrong. I asked them if it was right.
>
> I listened carefully to what they were saying although I had problems when more than one child wanted help. I had to tell them to wait for a minute or two. I also needed to respond supportively in various ways with different children. They needed more guidance in plotting their progress through a task, I think that's where I can prompt them. I suppose that comes under eliciting their responses and the other aspect is in analysing difficulties.

The student is expected to take responsibility for using the criteria as a learning aid. In focusing on a selected aspect of teaching, the student teachers also have to consider some of the necessary conditions for improving on it. Frequently, student teachers follow through the implications of improving on selected dimensions by considering other key dimensions such as management of materials and direct instruction. They also judge what degree of freedom there is to test these different combinations of dimensions and criteria at increasingly complex level in similar and different contexts. The teacher tutor's conference deliberately steps back from but also feeds back into the class teachers' system of mentoring by extending the way in which complex teaching activity can be systematically and strategically planned and conducted. It is the teacher tutor's role to insure that student-teachers are beginning to perceive patterns in the changing forms of their performance and professional knowledge, and a specific use of the categories and language of the dimensions in describing and explaining their actions. Both the mentor and the student teacher constantly monitor how these are being used as the necessary condition for judging adequate performance.

The following extract is taken from a later conference with the same student, who had decided to persist with this dimension of structured conversation. She begins to show increasing evidence of some internalization of this aspect of teaching activity. This is shown in how she is organizing an increasingly complete orientation of acquired activity and the acquisition of a whole pattern of activity rather than separate, discrete skills.

Developing student teachers' competence in appraisal consisted, initially, of testing the properties of this dimension in its relatively uncomplicated form. This student teacher's learning is being developed further by testing the characteristics of this dimension to discover how internal contradictions and oppositions may exist when trying to apply this teaching dimension in different situations. The dimension is not homogeneous but combines a number of elements. She is showing an increasingly sophisticated capacity to reorientation by adapting her knowledge to specific instances.

Tutor: How are you testing the usefulness of this dimension in other contexts?

Student: I combined aspects of monitoring with structured conversation: the two seemed to be naturally linked and dependent on each other. I worked systematically with each group in craft, design and technology lesson. I posed questions to elicit their views but this also required them to listen to each other. Some children found this quite difficult. I kept emphasizing that this was important. There were a number of conflicting ideas which I asked for and even provided some myself. But the groups need more experience in working together to handle and process these ideas. I had to show them a strategy for working them out but I didn't want to help them too much.

Increasingly, the student teacher judges which specific criteria to use, deciding whether and how the lessons of single principles contradict one another or the precedents of particular cases are incompatible. So there are varying degrees of constructing professionally relevant knowledge that alternate between analyzing, comparing, and contrasting specific cases or teaching episodes in similar contexts, and analyzing, comparing, and contrasting cases and principles on different dimensions and more challenging criteria in both similar and different contexts.

Here is another account of how mentoring can be used to challenge student teachers' learning by focusing on a range of more complex issues. This is a typical example of the general strategy for using the various combinations of dimensions and criteria to develop more sophisticated forms of self-assessment and teaching strategies. The student has agreed with the tutor in her zone of development to plan to use the dimension of *monitoring* in her next lesson, having already achieved some success in fulfilling the basic criteria for this dimension – "observing children working and intervening to sustain the momentum of the work and in checking that children can follow and complete the work set." (See Figure 8.2.)

This is a complex dimension, and although we are focusing on it separately, its successful use presupposes some competence in some of the other dimensions, and in doing so illustrates movement from exploration to reorientation in the learning cycle. The mentor and student teacher

MONITORING

Our view of successful teaching is one which emphasizes the actively thoughtful role of the teacher in collecting information about children on a moment-by-moment basis, sensitively interpreting this information, and using it to guide action. This action must be directed towards maintaining an orderly working environment and developing understanding. This process involves observing and listening to children; creating hypotheses to make sense of their reactions; and testing these hunches by altering teaching, tasks, and interventions accordingly. It requires good management of time, alertness and rapid response.

This dimension, MONITORING, is outlined below.

1. Observe children working and intervene to sustain the momentum of the work.
2. Check children can follow and complete the work set.
3. Monitor in order to sustain order and momentum of work; give appropriate feedback; keep simple records of evaluation.
4. Monitor flow of work to sustain availability of resources and ensure efficient transitions; monitor use of time; detect problems of order early; keep thorough records of attainment.
5. Explore children's understanding of work set; make appropriate observations and attempt hunches to explain children's responses; keep records of evaluation.
6. Use monitoring to create hypotheses about children's difficulties; attempt to analyze and test hunches; use monitoring to inform larger scale adjustments of teaching.
7. Create time for and attempt deeper diagnosis of children's responses to tasks.
8. Sustain a broad program of diagnostic teaching.

Figure 8.2.

discuss the nature and quality of the judgments needed to specify some of the necessary conditions that will determine or guarantee success on this selected aspect of teaching. Increasingly, the student teacher is engaged in making and testing the quality of her professional judgments. She decided to test the interdependence of monitoring, management of materials and structured conversation and their specific criteria for a lesson in environmental science that included map reading. She commented that:

> I should have spent more time on giving instructions. This is an aspect of direct instruction that I thought I had mastered but there are different levels and types of instructions. I felt more able to discuss with the children how to read references; they tried to draw out what they knew from each other and discussed their own ideas. The activity did allow them to listen to each other and check each other's responses. They were better on this occasion in listening to each other and supporting each other in their thinking. When they offered me answers I always asked for an alternative but some found that unhelpful. This time I tried to use unplanned opportunities for conversation and felt much more confident. I spoke to groups rather than individuals but I was aware of others too. I soon discovered those with problems in understanding the purpose of the activity and those who needed support in working with examples. Teacher intrusion is difficult to balance, in that some welcomed you to check their work but there were problems which meant stopping the whole class which can sometimes disrupt those who are working, although some continued to work and didn't give me their attention.

The level of discourse in the conference involves an explanation of how to relate comment to action. These judgments are part of the quality of thinking required when working with the dimensions. The tutor and student are constantly engaged in the processes of analysis and reconstruction by comparing and contrasting specific events and principles. They involve the mentor and the student teacher in working more persistently on available choices, judging which choices can be made for improving on a separate dimension so that mentoring becomes a means of modelling ways of thinking about teaching.

In this example the student teacher chose to set herself a more demanding task in monitoring: to monitor pupils' work and give appropriate feedback for the purpose of keeping simple records of evaluation. The mentor and student teacher then focussed on a relevant portion of the monitoring dimension that refers to a purpose for records of evaluation, to "collect information about children, sensitively interpreting this information and using it to guide action." They agreed to ask the class teacher for exemplars of how this process involves the precondition of "observing and listening to children; creating hypotheses to make sense of their reactions."

The class teacher, teacher tutor, and student teacher work on a plan of action that attends deliberately to the student teacher's subjective competence in tackling this task by elaborating what these criteria might mean in terms of material resources, time allocation and teaching procedures. Next, they have to deliberate on how these are to be incorporated into specific teaching episodes. It is in discussing the prospect of improving on this crucial dimension of teaching that other dimensions have to be considered as necessary conditions for judging the probability of success. In this sense, the teacher tutor continually supports the student teacher in grasping the meaning of the assessment system. Mentoring consists primarily of monitoring students' criteria for self-assessment and in generating internal standards for performance by adapting these for particular situations.

The mentor then refers the student to the other dimensions to judge what the necessary conditions are for developing more competent performance in monitoring and to think out how these are to be used as part of an integrated teaching episode. The mentor elicited from the student teacher what features of the classroom's physical and social context had to be reviewed or changed to accommodate such practices, and what constraints might prevent them from being implemented. In this way specific actions progressively develop into more purposefully planned and strategic teaching activity.

The teaching dimensions include some of the more basic teaching and management competence categories, and also these three more complex dimensions: planning and preparation, ethos, and written evaluation. These provide the overarching concepts that presuppose competence in all other dimensions. These dimensions and their criteria show how component teaching skills are organized into viable systems of broader professional competence. The criteria are used to extend and challenge student teachers' professionally relevant knowledge as a series of developmental challenges. Asking student teachers to justify their choice of selected dimensions and their criteria, and testing them in practice, signifies increasing self-monitoring of professional learning. It is a necessary precursor to self-guidance and the construction of self-explanation.

The Role of the University Tutor

Finally, the university tutor mentors are involved in conferences along similar lines to those of the teacher-tutor mentor, and, where necessary, can decide to validate students' accounts of teaching by observing relevant practices, but essentially they have a more specific role: to conduct an overall evaluation of students' progress in terms of competent performance, professionally relevant knowledge, and understanding. The summary sheets are used as a structure within and around which specific judgments are made on what the student teachers have accomplished. Their developmental progress is evaluated in two such conferences on a first practice, and in three on a final practice. It is also the university mentor's responsibility to hold a postteaching practice conference with students back at the university, sharing the responsibility for writing an evaluation of the whole practice.

The student teachers have had ample rehearsal and practice in articulating and defining their progress in previous conferences with the class-teacher and teacher-tutor mentor. The purpose of the university mentor conference is to develop students' capacity to map out and articulate their progress in teaching competence and to reason how professional their knowledge is becoming. Student teachers' appraisals consist of the zones of development agreed and acted upon in the teacher-tutor conferences. The university mentor challenges student teachers on the criteria used for self-appraisal and how they have created opportunities to assess their overall professional competence.

Guidelines for conducting this summative appraisal are provided in the full set of criteria for each dimension of teaching at each level. These are the summary sheets. They are used to map out the integrated nature of student teachers' developing professional competence. They show how students' knowledge and understanding of intelligent practice has derived from competent performance. Their use focuses on understanding as a part of knowing how. Again, this is elicited, elaborated, and challenged by annotating relevant parts or the whole of a single or combined summary sheets. Once again, the exercise is designed to generate more data and apply inferential rules to that data about students' capacity to appraise themselves (Figure 8.3).

For example, after a few weeks' practice mentors are advised to annotate selected summary sheets with students to show them how improvement on specific dimensions is being consolidated so that the student teachers can see progress in terms of a professional profile. The learning process involves students in self-evaluation at increasingly complex levels. The tutor and the student use the overall structure of the summary sheets to (a) get a real sense of progress, (b) set themselves a set of realistic aspirations, and (c) structure a way in which students can continue to monitor their professional understanding in further professional and academic studies.

More specifically, at the end of a practice students and tutors annotate these summary sheets across levels, so that a professional profile emerges that can be analyzed in terms of the knowledge gaps they perceive in their capacity to act professionally. Such knowledge gaps can continue to be addressed in their university curriculum courses.

SUMMARY OF LEVEL 1	**SUMMARY OF LEVEL 2**
Attract children's initial interest; maintain appropriate sequence using supplied material for demonstrations and description.	For demonstrations and descriptions, organize suitable seating arrangements, introduce material well, use appropriate visual aids, sustain children's interest
Provide and manage materials for an exemplar activity.	For an exemplar activity, check availability and accessibility of required materials; insure proper use of those materials; manage appropriate use, including sharing and subsequent collection.
Distribute provided material; check children's responses.	Manage provided material; make time to respond to children during work period; check children's work for accuracy.
Listen carefully to what children are saying, and respond supportively.	Attempt to elicit children's responses; recognize and attempt to analyze difficulties.
Observe children working, and intervene to sustain the momentum of the work.	Check children can follow and complete the work set.
Attempt to operate some procedures for orderly activity.	Attempt to operate an established framework of rules and procedures.
Plan basic resources for children working on a given activity.	Plan with a clear purpose; indicate materials for teacher and children; recognize practicalities, including resources, time and safety; select content to meet purposes.
Give some account of own performance.	Provide valid descriptions of own performance and children's reactions to tasks. Offer tentative, justifiable analyses, especially with respect to appropriate use of resources and materials.

Figure 8.3.

On a final teaching practice the students should be learning, not only how to progress on the dimensions, but also, more generally, how to monitor and develop their own aspirations and express how their strategic knowledge is helping them to formulate plans of action. Students engage in more self-evaluation and goal setting. But the goal setting refers both to teaching performance and their own mindful learning of how to teach.

The criteria are not to be reified, but they do help students gain a sense of progress over a period of time by judging how their experiences have contributed to their overall professional development: Development that shows how their professionally relevant knowledge is organized by moving from relatively straightforward dimensions to more subtle and complex ones, from few to many dimensions, and from simple levels of performance to more complex levels and expressions of competence. The focus is on how student teachers learn how to teach, with its emphasis upon self-assessment as a specific competence category. The process of learning is sustained by the direct use of explicit mentoring strategies that enable student teachers to become conscious agents in their pedagogy (Britzman, 1989).

There is a further learning strategy that elaborates and challenges student teachers' capacity for self-assessment They are expected to revisit their accumulated data and reexamine it to meet certain criteria for a written self-evaluation. This, in turn, is used as a basis for further professional learning and theorizing about educational issues back in the university. This is the first time that we ask them to engage in dialectical processes in writing, similar to but not the same as those practiced in conversation and conference discourse (Figure 8.4).

The criteria for this dimension test how well student teachers have assimilated professionally relevant knowledge and have developed the ability to theorize within their practical experiences. Written evaluation has close links with the "monitoring" dimension: Both stress the importance of the collection and interpretation of data and the development of constructive, practical consequences, from analysis. There is a need, therefore, to show thoughtfulness in the context of the other dimensions, including, of course, monitoring and ethos. The outline of the written evaluation dimension explains to students how we expect them to make progress in becoming deliberately reflective about their teaching.

Student teachers are expected to meet the written evaluation criteria by demonstrating their ability to engage in *practical rationality*. The criteria are organized so that students are required to begin with description, and then move into analysis and justification. The criteria offer them a framework on how to construct self-explanation and engage in self-guidance. Written evaluation tests the quality of their strategic knowledge and strategic knowing or judgment. The purpose is to develop their capacity for deliberate and contemplative thought and action, seeing a close congruence between the two. These processes and procedures also provide the mentors with evidence of students' misunderstandings. Ryle (1949) contended that misunderstanding is a by-product of knowing how. We can often misinterpret what we are looking at, but not always so, "for we could not even learn to misconstrue save in learning to construe, a learning process which involves learning not to misconstrue" (p. 59).

We find that, given the support of a structured, collaborative mentoring scheme, the student teachers can and do realistically cope with more

WRITTEN EVALUATION

This dimension has close links with the 'monitoring' dimension: both stress the importance of the collection and interpretation of data and the development of constructive, practical consequences, from analysis. There will be a need, therefore, to show thoughtfulness in the context of the other dimensions, including, of course monitoring. The outline of the EVALUATION dimension, below, shows how we expect you to make progress in becoming deliberately reflective about your work.

1. Give some account of own performance.
2. Provide valid descriptions of own performance and children's reactions to tasks. Offer tentative, justifiable analyses, especially with respect to appropriate use of resources and materials.
3. Provide broader ranging but concise descriptions of own performance and children's reactions including reference to knowledge, skills, and attitudes.
4. Offer alternative analyses especially with respect to appropriate use of resources and materials. Evaluate, albeit selectively, across whole class.
5. Offer justifiable explanations of children's responses to work; use explanations in practicable ways to plan the next phase of work; show understanding of diversity of pupils' attainments.
6. Systematically evaluate aspects of class work using a broad range of data to check out explanations and challenge assumptions about specific children.
7. Relate evaluations to broader curriculum planning seeing, for example, the necessity for replanning schemes.
8. Reflect on evaluations to reconceptualize personal model of teaching; challenge own assumptions about subjects, curriculum, organization.

Figure 8.4.

intellectually demanding accounts of their teaching, first, by providing valid and broader ranging but concise descriptions of their performance; then with tentative, justifiable analyses of the appropriate use of resources and materials, and of the children's reactions, with some reference to skills, knowledge, and attitudes, until, more ambitiously, some are able to offer alternative analyses of the appropriateness of resources, materials, and activities across a whole class. But we consider this to be too demanding for students on a final practice, at least when it is done thoroughly.

Sharing the process of mentoring among a class teacher, a specially trained school-based teacher tutor and a university mentor may seem to be cumbersome, but it has helped to clarify the complex process of mentoring, by recognizing the need for student teachers to constantly appraise, reconstruct, and rerepresent their professional knowledge at different levels of reasoning and thinking. It seems logical, therefore, to identify the necessary conditions for such professional learning to occur and to differentiate the roles of each mentor, so that student teachers' professional learning goes beyond the limitations of experiential in-context practice. It also guarantees that the appraisal system is openly shared with student teachers and demonstrates how they can become empowered in using it. These features correspond to the capacities and skills that Ryle referred to as *intelligent practice.*

The way in which this model of mentoring influences student teachers' professional learning illustrates some of the necessary conditions that Ryle (1949) identified for intelligent performance: that we learn how by practice, informed by example and criticism; becoming increasingly competent requires that one performance is being modified by its predecessors; training in learning how to teach includes rehearsal and practice but also involves provoking, through example and criticism, the students' own judgment; and competence must entail looking beyond performance itself to the capacities and skills of which the actions are exercises. It is also necessary in Ryle's thesis to understand that "the capacity to perform and to appreciate a performance does not necessarily involve the ability to formulate criticisms or lessons," or that "the ability to appreciate performance does not involve the same degree of competence as the ability to execute it" (p. 55). This scheme is primarily concerned with developing these capacities and abilities.

CONCLUSIONS

The implications of this model of learning how to teach and the attempt to reconceptualize the notions of competence and mentoring as crucial learning processes for appraisal and self-assessment, are that teachers and teacher educators need to have a shared agenda for research into the nature of professional learning and development. It should try to establish an understanding, not only of the development of classroom performances, but also of the intellectual processes and structures that mediate these. There is a need for a general model of learning that links experiences to the thinking and learning processes by which student teachers (a) select from and interpret professional experiences as actions and activity, and (b) acquire appropriate pedagogical knowledge.

Such a model must be able to describe and explain sufficiently the nature of teaching competence and the processes of its acquisition and development in initial teacher education. The perspective being proposed here emphasizes the development of student teachers' professional learning and their emerging capacities to process and organize professionally relevant knowledge in specific mental acts that have their origins in object-related activity and social interaction.

We believe that insufficient attention has been given in research studies on teaching to the activity theory of Soviet psychology (Arievitch, 1991) to explain student teachers' learning as the progressive modification of mental actions. "By incorporating tool mediation, broadly conceived, activity theorists bring human intelligence into the action itself, rather than leaving it back in the head as a controller of the action" (Bereiter, 1990, p. 610). Incidentally, this is the core of activity theory in Vygotsky's methodology – the idea of *outsidedness* of consciousness in opposition to the methodology of solipsism with its central idea of inward directedness, the "inner" nature of mental processes (Arievitch, 1991).

More specifically, such a model of learning how to teach is mutually beneficial to student teachers, experienced teachers, and teacher educators. The division of labor associated with this scheme of mentoring is organized on a collaborative basis, so that all participants aim at continuing professional development. Moreover, the conference with a school-based trained mentor provides an important layer of interpretation aimed at analyzing existing and producing new pedagogical practices. The new pedagogical practices necessarily mean that all participants need to develop new pedagogical instruments for models of planning, implementation, and evaluation of teaching and learning.

But ultimately, such developmental work must enable student teachers to use a system of appraisal for self-assessment that they can take away with them. The language and categories of the teaching dimensions, and their criteria, encourage student teachers to extend their understanding of professionally relevant practices by having some professionally relevant concepts and ideas with which to think.

These approaches set out to provide learning opportunities for student teachers to acquire robust and professionally relevant knowledge, and become increasingly capable of providing equally robust accounts of their own learning. In this sense, professional learning consists of the progressive modification of students' schemas and intellectual processes. One student commented recently,

> There is a need for a framework. It does help because you really do think, right, here is something I have to learn but what have I got to do now to develop further. It's necessary to plan for the children but I think it takes them further with you in knowing how you are developing your own abilities too.

REFERENCES

Arievich, I. M. (1989). *The psychological conditions of the meaningful (comprehensive) acquisition of professional activity.* Moscow: Lomonosov University, Department of Psychology.

Arievich, I. M. (1991). *Galperin's stage-by-stage theory* (Research Seminar). Moscow: Lomonosov University, Department of Psychology.

Bereiter, C. (1990). Aspects of an educational learning theory. *Review of Educational Research, 60* (4), 603-625.

Boekaerts, M. (1991). Subjective competence, appraisals and self-Assessment. *Learning and Instruction, 1* (1), 1-17.

Britzman, D. P. (1989). Who has the floor? Curriculum, teaching, and the English student teacher's struggle for voice. *Curriculum Inquiry, 19* (2), 143-162.

Collins, A., Brown, J. S., & Newman, S. E. (1989). Cognitive apprenticeship: Teaching the craft of reading, writing and mathematics. In L. B. Resnick (Ed.), *Knowing, learning and instruction: Essays in honour of Robert Glaser.* Hillsdale, NJ: Erlbaum.

Fenstermacher, G. D. (1990, September). *The concepts of method and manner in pedagogy.* Paper presented at an International Symposium: Research on Effective and Responsible Teaching. Fribourg, Switzerland.

Green, T. F. (1976). Teacher competence as practical rationality. *Educational Theory, 26,* 249-258.

Kolb, D. A. (1984). *Experiential learning: Experience as the source of learning and development.* Englewood Cliffs, NJ: Prentice-Hall.

McNamara, D. (1991). Vernacular pedagogy. *British Journal of Educational Studies, XXXIX* (3), 297-309.

Ryle, G. (1949). *The concept of mind.* Harmondsworth, UK: Penguin.

CHAPTER 9

Working in Classrooms With Teachers

Linda Thomas
EcATT
Institute of Education London

John Bowden
EQARD
Royal Melbourne Institute of Technology
Melbourne Australia

BACKGROUND

The context for this chapter is provided by the work of members of the Economic Awareness Teacher Training Program (EcATT). The program, established in 1986, aims to promote economic awareness within the entitlement curriculum for all young people, and, in particular, to support curriculum and teacher development activities involved in its achievement. A core team of 10 people, together with teachers and advisers from over 80 local education authorities in England, Wales, Scotland, and Northern Ireland, contribute to a network of activities that involves all sectors of education and all areas of the curriculum.

The designation of economic awareness as a cross-curricular theme in the National Curriculum[1] is an indication of the need to root activities designed to promote its development within core and foundation

---

[1]The Education Reform Act, 1988, established a National Curriculum that makes statutory provision for an entitlement curriculum for all pupils between the ages of 5 and 16. Statutory orders, including specifications for attainment targets and programs of study, were published for core and foundation subjects. Areas of interest and issues such as education for equal opportunities, special educational needs, and personal and social education are designated as cross curricular dimensions; economic awareness, health education, careers, environmental education, and education for citizenship are defined as cross-curricular themes. Statutory provision does not extend to these dimensions and themes but schools are expected to establish cross-curricular procedures to insure that such issues permeate the curriculum.

subjects.[2] The implication is that knowledge gained within English, history, science, and so on, is crucial to an understanding of economic activity. Coincidentally, the published orders for such subjects assert that knowledge of mathematics, geography, and so on, should incorporate the capacity to bring that knowledge to bear on the economic, political, social, environmental, and technological issues, problems and activities of the adult world. By these means, National Curriculum documents give the impression that the decision to entrust the development of economic awareness to science, mathematics, and so on, is unproblematic. EcATT's role is to question this assumption, to raise rather than ignore the many issues involved in attempting to define and explore the relationship between National Curriculum subjects and economic awareness, to consider what is involved if subject teachers are to discharge their responsibility for securing its development and to map the effects of institutional and organizational variables on progress toward its achievement as an entitlement for all.

Essentially, the learning tasks in economic awareness programs within any subject or context involve students in looking at phenomena from both a subject and an economic perspective. The aim is to help them to gain some insight into the economic issues inherent in the phenomena, and to do so in such a way that they become aware of the existence of multiple perspectives that may be brought to bear in any situation, and, in particular, in those adult-world situations involving economic activity.

By implication, what is involved in teacher development terms is for teachers to see their subject and their teaching role differently. Science teachers, for example, need to understand that what may seem to them to be exclusively scientific phenomena are not as easily differentiated when encountered outside the science classroom. Nor is a purely scientific perspective sufficient for their comprehension, which often depends on the ability to see things from an economic perspective (among others). In consequence, they need to discover ways of teaching that reflect the existence of multiple perspectives.

Because teachers work under the constraints of an educational system, it is also important that school management and educational authorities understand the changes that teachers are making and encourage their members to provide the support mechanisms that will assist teachers and students to capitalize on the opportunities created for development.

This chapter is specifically concerned with the teacher education approaches adopted by EcATT to help teachers gain a fuller understanding

---

[2]The core subjects in the National Curriculum are English, mathematics and science. Foundation subjects include technology, geography, history, a modern foreign language, art, music, and P. E.

of their role and their contribution to the development of students' economic awareness. The first section of the chapter provides an account of the theoretical foundations for the characteristic features of EcATT's teacher education programme–the emphasis on active reflection and collaborative problem solving. In the second section, some of the practical and theoretical problems with which this program must contend are identified and explored. The third section examines the ways in which EcATT's programme is designed to address these issues and problems. Two case studies are used to illustrate successes and difficulties. The final section draws conclusions about ways of working with experienced teachers, within the context of a general model of teacher education.

THEORETICAL FOUNDATIONS

Conceptual Change

The underlying learning theory in economic awareness programs involves a conceptual change notion (Marton, 1981)–their basic purpose is for students to understand how various subject perspectives (including the economic) can be applied to a range of real-world situations. It also underlies EcATT's teacher education program, on the assumption that activities designed to help teachers develop a fuller understanding of their teaching role and their contribution to the development of students' economic awareness are learning activities in themselves (Bowden, 1989). This is the crux of the argument–that to change the ways in which they see their teaching role is as much a learning task for teachers as learning subject matter is for their students. It should be approached from the same theoretical base that we argue should underpin the teaching of any subject. The theories of learning that drive our approaches to teaching students are equally relevant to teacher education.

So what is conceptual change learning? Marton (1988) referred to the various terms which are used to describe the different ways in which students think about phenomena in their studies – *conceptions, conceptual frameworks, constructs, misconceptions, alternative frameworks, minitheories, ideas, notions, beliefs, schemata, scripts, frames, phenomenological primitives, mental models, mental representations, understandings,* and *ways of seeing*. He quotes reviews of the field to suggest that, in the ever growing number of studies conducted since the 1970s, the *same* kind of differences, although variously labeled, have been identified by people working from a range of theoretical standpoints:

> It has been found again and again that students have their own ways of thinking about the things they are gong to learn about. And on the whole,

these ways of thinking differ distinctively from the ways of thinking presupposed by the content taught in school. . . . Furthermore – and this is perhaps the most striking kind of result obtained from such studies – educational experiences seem to bring about only very limited changes in this respect . . . I want to argue that there is a competency, simply labelled "understanding", which is different from and more fundamental than the two other kinds of competencies, commonly referred to as skills and knowledge. . . . According to this line of reasoning, mastery is less a question of applying knowledge and procedures to a certain class of phenomena, but of seeing phenomena belonging to that class in certain particular ways. (pp. 2–5)

Marton's argument is that "learning for understanding" (which involves a different way of seeing or thinking about the world) is superior to learning that simply increases the store of knowledge, the accumulation of information and skills. Without the former, the latter, however, sophisticated, is meaningless. Conceptual change learning, therefore, is about a process – searching for meaning, developing understanding, and relating that understanding to the world around. As a consequence, the world is seen differently, conceptions change, and conventions, skills, and knowledge gain meaning and are more easily remembered (Marton & Saljo, 1984) – so conceptual change is also about outcomes. Student approaches to learning, and their learning outcomes, are linked. An approach involving a search for meaning is a necessary but not sufficient condition for achieving understanding or conceptual change as a learning outcome.

In terms of teacher development, the implication of adopting this theory is that there is no point in merely informing teachers of general principles they should adopt or in providing opportunities for them to practice skills and techniques. The theory suggests that teachers can best develop their "understanding," of what it means to develop students' economic awareness within a subject context, if they engage in a process of active reflection, a search for meaning in the world to which it applies, the world of student learning. The purpose of EcATT's plan/teach/review model is to engage teachers in this process and to promote a fundamental change in their views and attitudes toward both their teaching role and their contribution to the development of students' economic awareness.

Collaborative Planning, Teaching, and Reviewing

The first stage in EcATT's teacher development program involves a collaborative planning exercise. Teachers are asked to consider how students would develop an appreciation for the multiple perspective analysis that is necessary if any planned activities are to be an effective form of economic awareness education. They are then invited to develop course materials, teaching strategies, and assessment instruments within the relevant subject context. The primary objective is conceptual change. The focus is on the nature of that change and the ways in which "learning for understanding" might best be achieved, given the context. Theoretical issues are addressed as they arise in planning.

The second stage involves collaborative teaching. It is always the case that teachers exercise judgment and make choices at every stage in their interaction with their students. Any particular pattern of decision making and consequent action cannot be prescribed. Each teaching episode is unique and requires active diagnosis and problem solving by the teacher. This stage enables teachers to gather data for later use in discussions about the quality of their intervention.

The third stage involves collaborative review, which aims to provide insights into students' understanding. The data provided in the teaching stage is used as a basis for study and as evidence of the occurrence and possible cause of any conceptual change. Results are then available to guide future planning.

Helping Teachers Develop

The aim of encouraging teachers to become involved in this process of active reflection and collaborative problem solving is to help them to focus their attention on developing their students' *understanding* (in Marton's terms) in the context of economic awareness. This is the first outcome— their role in the world of student learning is seen differently by teachers. The second, related outcome is that teachers' developing practical and theoretical knowledge and skills—for example, teaching strategies (e.g., role play), practical classroom skills (e.g., those involved in effective classroom intervention), and theory (e.g., about economic awareness, learning for conceptual change, or about what it means to view phenomena from different perspectives)—are harnessed to this changed perspective, gaining meaning from and contributing to its further development.

PROBLEMS

Paradoxically, some of the main problems in affecting such change in teachers' views arise from the success of the economic awareness movement. The effects of developments originating from a speech by the then Prime Minister, James Callaghan, at Ruskin College, Oxford, which linked economic prosperity with a "relevant" curriculum, were becoming clear by the middle years of the 1980s. Many teachers, convinced of the need for relevance, were exploring the use of the issues, problems, and activities of the modern world as contexts for learning. As a result, opportunities were increasingly provided for pupils to gain experience of industrial and commercial undertakings, to take part in problem solving and decision-making exercises concerned with local or national issues, and to simulate various aspects of economic activity through games, minienterprises, and other projects.

The opportunities for the development of students' economic awareness were, therefore, potentially very significant. But the results of research studies involving classroom observation of pupils' responses and scrutiny of the learning outcomes of such activities raised some important questions. Riley (1987) was interested in the use of role play as a means of helping pupils to experience both the conflict that can exist within the economic system and the ways in which it is often resolved. Over a 3-day period he shared his classroom with teachers of drama and observed, recorded, and analyzed the processes and outcomes of the work of 13-year-old pupils from an 11–18 comprehensive school. He was encouraged by some aspects of the experience but was unsure about the effects of such learning opportunities and insights on pupils' long-term perceptions and economic understanding. The role-play experience seemed to achieve greater success in reinforcing existing beliefs than in developing economic understanding.

> Should I worry about the student who, having expressed highly critical views of trade unions in previous lessons, enthusiastically took on the role of shop steward, achieved a great deal within the parameters of the role play but played the part as an uncompromising, pedantic bully and maintained the stance throughout the role play and the review? . . . Just how good was the lesson? Good for what, imaginative thinking, decision-making, using their knowledge and understanding, exhibitionism? (p. 21)

Solomon (1988) reviewed the growth of the science, technology, and society education (STS) movement. She argued that for this to be effective, it was not sufficient merely to raise social and economic issues within science lessons, even if this did secure students' interest.

> It seemed that the affective and value laden attitudes provoked by the social context made the skills of applying knowledge or logical processes more difficult. (p. 275)

and that

> it does highlight the difficulties that education in STS faces. When an issue has already been met and has raised affective judgements, the commonplace

or life-world system of thinking, which uses value claims and typifications in place of logical argument and application of knowledge, may become paramount. (p. 275)

These illustrate the growing body of theoretical and empirical knowledge on the nature of economic understanding (Thomas & Hodkinson, 1991) that cast doubt on the effectiveness of some of the efforts of the "relevance" movement to provide experiences of various economic contexts within the curriculum (e.g., work experience, industrial visits, minienterprise). Nevertheless, the designation of economic awareness as a cross-curricular theme in the National Curriculum, referred to earlier, is an indication of the need to root any activities in the core and foundation subjects.

This presents teachers with considerable problems. On the one hand, evidence suggests that experience of economic contexts and issues does not guarantee the development of students' understanding and may lead to the reinforcement of existing stereotypes. On the other hand, as is argued by Marton (1988), the accumulation of information, knowledge, and skills may not provide a meaningful alternative. A theoretical solution to these problems is provided by phenomenography (Marton, 1981), on which the theories of learning (Marton, 1988) and teacher development (Bowden, 1989) described above are based. This is a research approach which studies the different ways in which individuals understand or conceptualize a particular phenomenon. It makes it possible to differentiate between surface differences (for example, in vocabulary or images used) and "qualitative" differences which describe fundamental differences in the ways in which the phenomenon may be understood. Marton (1988) argued that qualitative differences are educationally critical because they are effective tools, capable of informing decisions about which teaching strategies are appropriate in helping students to develop any educationally preferred understanding.

For example, in a study of undergraduates' understanding of the relation between force and movement, Johansson, Marton, and Svensson (1955) showed that the qualitative difference between two fundamentally different ways in which such a problem may be understood is that, in one way, force is related to the speed at which a body is moving, whereas in the other, force is related to movement itself, that is, simply whether the body is moving or not. And there was evidence of both forms of understanding in existence among the undergraduates, despite the fact that they were all highly skilled and knowledgeable. Sixth-grade students, on the other hand, who were taught by means of teaching strategies that required them to focus on force in relation to speed or velocity rather then in relation to motion had a far greater understanding "after two months . . . in comparison with high school physics students, five years older, who had been taught about force and motion using traditional methods" (Marton, 1988, p. 22).

There is a message here for subject teachers who wish to promote economic awareness. Marton's work suggests that teachers should help students to change the focus of their attention, to look beyond the surface features of their experience and to search for its meaning in relation to a range of subject perspectives. Only through such a search for meaning can the desired conceptual development occur. The *teacher development* problem is that this theory has very little meaning unless it is embedded in a particular view of the world of student learning. Unless teachers see that world and their role in it in a certain way, theoretical insights such as Marton's or practical experience of classrooms are not effective (*according to that same theory*). The teacher education challenge is to provide the means for teachers to change the focus of *their* attention. The two case studies that follow illustrate, in particular contexts, how this challenge was met by the teachers concerned, in collaboration with EcATT.

ADDRESSING THE PROBLEMS

Developing a Business Dimension in a Primary School

Thompson and Pattison (BBC, 1988) wished to develop a business dimension to their project work in an Enfield primary school. They chose two projects, the first focusing on health through a local fitness center, and the second on the lack of interesting games to play when the weather kept pupils indoors during play time. They chose to start with the gym. They took their pupils to visit a center, observed the gym in action, and let them try the equipment, talk to employees, and discuss health matters in general. Classroom work involved science investigations into levers and pulleys. However, discussion with others in the local authority's economic awareness network raised doubts. They were not sure that their intention to locate the activity in a real business had had any effect on pupils' perceptions of business. In conjunction with a secondary teacher seconded to EcATT, they decided to change the focus in order to bring business more sharply to the attention of pupils. Material published for the 14–16 age range was modified in order to allow pupils to explore the potential problems facing a small hairdresser. The pupils became engrossed in the idea of solving someone's problems as was recorded by the teachers (BBC, 1988, p. 9): "The work which was stimulated was extraordinary and the childrens' enthusiasm encouraged us to develop a similar problem in relation to the gym."

Groups of children were given information about a fictitious gym and asked to identify any potential problem. They then set about solving it by developing their own plan of action for the gym. The teachers felt that this approach had had more effect than the original activity on pupils' understanding of the gym as a business. They therefore decided to adopt the same strategy for a wet games project.

There were six stages in the work. A questionnaire was developed, trialed, and used to obtain responses from 12 classes. The results were analyzed to reveal the features affecting the popularity of the games (e.g., the fact that pieces go missing). These were used to develop a game from the consumer's angle. The next stage was to consider the matter from the manufacturer's point of view. A simulation of the process of production of a game was used to spotlight the factors a manufacturer would need to consider, for example, the costs involved, how best to deploy the workforce, the cost to the public. These factors were used by the pupils to prepare for a detailed exploration of the manufacture of games during a visit to the Spears factory in North London. They identified two different areas of investigation: the process of production, and differences in the priorities and functions of different management teams. They agreed to examine the process of production by talking to production workers, trying out the jobs, describing the machinery, listing the resources needed, obtaining a view of the factory itself, and working out who was involved. They tackled the second area by interviewing in some depth the production manager, a member of the development team, and the marketing manager. After the visit the pupils attempted to combine the considerations raised by the manufacturer with the consumer's considerations. This led them to question some decisions, for example, the price increase and the decision not to include spare parts in the game.

The whole process was recorded on video and formed part of the first program in the BBC's Teacher Education Project on Economic Awareness. Pupils' verbal and written contributions were thus available as evidence that they were aware of the importance of asking the question: Who is Spears serving? They brought moral and social concepts to bear when, for example, they considered the danger in packing small pieces in a children's game. They related their own ideas and those of management by the use of critical questions that challenged managerial statements. They also listened carefully to the views of the mainly female workers on the production line who expressed a feeling of commitment to the production team and pride in the provision of a quality product. The teachers felt that the pupils had been given an opportunity to develop a new perspective about industry, because the challenges with which they had been faced had required them to pay serious attention to and understand the views of people other than consumers. Pattison (BBC, 1988, p. 12) commented during the review stage of the work that

> they're able to think about profits and loss and they're able to put themselves in positions where they can see a stand point as a manager of a factory but then they as consumers have a very strong feeling for what they want and they're very adept in putting forward that point.

Science and Technology Work for 12-Year-Old Pupils

Within the National Curriculum, Design and Technology provides a framework that encourages pupils to consider the design process as a whole. Nigel Heslop and Duncan Gregg, teachers in Surrey, wanted to use the local playground as a context for work with 12-year-olds. They decided to adapt a unit originally designed by the Science and Technology in Society project (SATIS, 1988) for 14–16-year-old pupils which raised the issues of risks and safety, issues crucial to the design and technology problems raised by playgrounds. The teachers felt that they could use the opportunity for some scientific work on energy, forces and friction, etc. They also felt that pupils would be capable of understanding the safety aspects of the design problem and of appreciating the effects of cost constraints on the designer's decisions.

The first stage of the activity took place in two local playgrounds. Pupils observed and recorded and the results became the focus for follow-up lessons in the classroom. Initially, teachers and pupils talked about safety in general, exchanging views about various preventative measures such as the provision of wood-chipping flooring. The teachers then switched to the scientific aspects and found themselves using the playground experiences in a rather labored way as a backcloth to concept teaching. They referred to the following extract of classroom discussion (Surrey, 1990) to show that their concern that pupils were merely engaging in the teachers' game was justified.

> T: Do we know what sort of energy we've got when we're moving? We had it on our sheets. Have a look at our sheets. What sort of energy have we got when we're moving?
>
> P: Can't read it
>
> T: That's the one
>
> P: Kinetic
>
> T: Does it look like kinetic to you?
>
> P: Kinetic energy

T: So we can accept the word kinetic. What sort of energy do you have when you're moving down a slide?

P: Heat

T: No, what sort of energy when we're moving? It's that one there, kinetic. Because you're moving it's kinetic energy. What about when you're standing at the top of the slide?

P (reading from the sheet): Potential

T: Potential energy (p. 12)

The teachers were also disturbed by their inability to utilize the pupil's comment about heat. But they felt that they had been more alert to possibilities in the lesson as it progressed and that, as a result, the quality of interaction improved. This is illustrated in the following extract of later discussion:

T: Do you keep your feet down all the time just to be safe:

P: Yes

T: If you lifted your feet up what would have happened?

P: Gone faster

T: What do you think you'd have gone faster?

P: Because your feet slow you down, they're like brakes

T: Describe how it slows you down

P: The rubber scrapes along like that.

P: The grip of your soles go onto the slide

T: So something actually stops you going down?

P: It grips on the side of the slide.

T: What else could you describe that as?

P: It's like a brake

P: Friction

T: If you wanted to speed up and reduce the friction on the slide?

P: Take your feet up

T: Can anyone think of other ways?

P: Go on your tummy

T: Why would that be different?

P: Your back's got bumps in it (p. 13)

During review, the teachers concluded that as the lesson progressed, both they and their pupils began to realize the complex nature of many features of concepts they had always taken for granted. Analysis of the data led them to correct their original prediction that safety was a relatively straightforward issue for designers. Designers have to attend to safety (and meet the needs of parents, for example) while taking into account the need in children for risk taking and an ability to circumvent safety features (for example, by going down slides on their fronts to reduce the effect of friction). They concluded that, if pupils were to understand and explore this further, they would be required to do more than view safety in playgrounds from a science perspective. Relating scientific knowledge to such aspects of their experiences as movement, speed, and the effect of forces would lead them to view the solution to the design problem in terms of the imposition of mechanical constraints, for example, on the height of swings. Viewing safety in playgrounds from an economic/ social perspective would focus attention on the different needs of children, parents, and designers and allow pupils to use their science to consider the safety implications of childrens' need for excitement and their ability to circumvent the safety limitations imposed as a result of application of a purely scientific perspective. In this way their scientific understanding would be secured and their economic awareness enhanced.

Commentary

The two case studies illustrate many of the issues raised above. In the first case study, information about the gym as a business and their science work had not required pupils to see the gym as a business and to bring the different subject perspectives to bear. Neither the experience nor the scientific knowledge had formed a challenge for their consumer-based opinions, which remained intact. The teachers became aware of this, because members of the local teacher group were not content with a descriptive account (and passive reflection) of what they considered to be "surface" features of the lessons. Instead, they asked questions about pupils' responses, questions that forced the two teachers to reconsider matters which they had taken for granted. Once this happened, they could see that it was necessary to change the activities. Pupils' language, mathematical, and design activities were anchored to the need to solve a production problem, and they were thus required to focus on the producer as well as the consumer, and to develop their ideas about the nature of the relationship between consumers and producers.

In the second case study, pupils were also offered a mix of experience and theoretical principles. But the evidence on which the group focused during the review of the lesson brought to the teachers' attention the fact that the experience, scientific work, and consideration of safety issues were treated as separate entities. Furthermore, *this* was what pupils learned from the lesson. They continued to view safety issues in terms of the prevention of accidents. Their solutions referred, for example, to supervision by park keepers and the provision of soft floors, despite the fact they were perfectly aware of the risks they took in using the equipment in certain ways. The review provided the teachers with a new "understanding" of a familiar lesson and, at the same time, pointed the way forward. They recognized the need to reorganize the lesson's activities by making children's risk-taking behavior the focus of pupils' experiences and science work.

GENERAL STRATEGIES

On the basis of particular examples such as those described in detail here, it has been possible for EcATT to identify and describe some of the strategies which are used within its teacher education programs.

Collaborative planning exercises such as those described in the case studies allow teachers to work out, for themselves, the implications of accepting responsibility for promoting economic awareness. Discussion is recorded as fully as possible; intentions are specified as precisely as possible. This strategy imposes discipline and a benchmark for review.

Because of teachers' recognition of the importance of providing evidence of student understanding, a set of classroom activity indicators has been developed and communicated through another of EcATT's strategies, the network described below. Through common use they have been refined and adapted. They provide evidence useful in answering questions asked during review. They relate to practical classroom work and thus represent a realistic focus for teachers' concerns and their professional discussions. They also form a useful framework for writing detailed accounts of lessons. They include the following:

- evidence of the ways in which students deal with the situation with which they are faced
- evidence of the various ways in which students make use of subject-based knowledge
- evidence that students relate their ideas to the content and procedures of the subject of study
- a list of the various methods used by teachers to assist students to become aware of the nature of their ideas and their ways of dealing with the situation
- a description of incidents illustrating the methods used by teachers to help students to understand the basis for different ways of dealing with the situation

- a list of methods used by teachers to encourage students to identify the characteristics of preferred responses and to relate these to the content and procedures of the subject of study
- evidence that students appreciate the need to share ideas
- illustrations showing the ways in which students articulate their ideas, giving reasoned explanations where necessary
- evidence of students relating their ideas to others' contributions through critical questioning
- evidence that students are actively and genuinely involved

Wherever possible, those involved in planning, teaching, and the review of classroom activities are encouraged to provide as detailed a record as possible of every aspect of the work. These records become the data for further review and reflection by others, and a great deal of importance is attached to the need to make them available and accessible to a wider audience. Finally, the results of this secondary process of review are made available for publication.

The importance of networking to extend the process of review and research is recognized. The network exists for two reasons. First, the teacher development model places a great deal of responsibility on teachers. The benefits accruing to an alternative approach—the provision, for adoption by teachers, of prescriptive objectives, lesson plans, resources, and organizational suggestions—are unavailable in this case. Second, none of the tasks involved are easy to fulfill. For example, subject teachers must accommodate the challenging economic contexts of the adult world within statements of intent, normal lesson plans, and schemes of work in a nontrivial way without sacrificing the validity and rigor of the subject. Intentions must be reviewed in the light of evidence of their success in influencing perceptions. These are research task that make demands on the most experienced subject teacher. The network is intended to contribute by providing support in the form of subject expertise and by acting as a research community.

WHAT CONCLUSIONS MAY BE DRAWN ABOUT TEACHER EDUCATION?

The features of EcATT's work illustrated here include an emphasis on a particular view of learning and the use of the collaborative plan/teach/review strategy to organize development activities within classrooms, schools, and LEAs, and to produce accounts for further reflection by a whole network of people.

To the extent that the National Curriculum's emphasis on cross-curricular dimensions, skills, and themes, and on innovations such as technology, is treated seriously by teachers and schools, they will need to consider undertaking or contributing to curriculum development programs such as the one described here. In this case, it is vitally important that the link between the quality of the teacher development strategy and the achievement of the curriculum development objectives established by EcATT is recognized and understood. The implications of this and other features of EcATT's work will need to be considered, especially in the context of teacher education.

The first is that teacher education that aims to promote in student and experienced teachers the capacity to contribute to curriculum development should recognize the importance of a thorough understanding of specialist subject matter and of the interaction of subject matter with whatever learning theory is used to inform predictions about pupils' classroom responses.

The second is that the development of learning experiences and curriculum materials that reflect multiple perspectives necessarily requires expert contributions from each perspective. Collaboration is thus an inherent requirement. Furthermore, in practical terms, new perspectives on familiar material do not develop as a result of a passive process of reflection in which the focus is on surface features. Once again, collaborative procedures that are securely bound to classroom experience seem to help teachers to generate new ways of thinking.

Third, it is probably important that teacher educators in higher education model this behavior both within their own classrooms and by setting up collaborative networks in local schools. Obviously, in a curriculum development program there is a formal requirement and a reason for this particular emphasis. But perhaps the curriculum development/teacher development link should be given more prominence, generally. The pace of change in education is increasing. When events move so quickly, new challenges that require curriculum development in the sense of the adaptation of the content/learning mix are always appearing. It may, therefore, be an appropriate time for higher education to state clearly that the induction of teachers into collaborative teacher/curriculum development networks is an essential part of teacher education.

REFERENCES

Bowden, J. A. (1989, November). *Curriculum development for conceptual change learning: A phenomenographic pedagogy.* Paper presented to the Sixth Annual Conference of the Hong Kong Educational Research Association.

BBC. (1988). *Notes for teachers and course leaders in support of two television programmes in the BBC's Teacher Education Project on Economic Awareness.* London: BBC Education.

Johansson, B., Marton, F., & Svensson, L. (1985). An approach to describing learning as a change between qualitatively different conceptions. In L. H. T. West & A. L. Pines (Eds.), *Cognitive structure and conceptual change.* New York: Academic Press.

Marton, F. (1981). Phenomenography – describing conceptions of the world aroung us. *Instructional Science, 10,* 177–200.

Marton, F. (1988, April). *Phenomenography and "The art of teaching all things to all men."* Paper (revised) presented at the annual meeting of the American Educational Research Association.

Marton, F., & Saljo, R. (1984). Approaches to learning. In F. Marton, D. Hounsell, & N. Entwistle (Eds.), *The experience of learning.* Edinburgh: Scottish Academic Press.

Riley, C. (1987). Economic awareness through drama. *Economic Awareness, 1* (1), 21–26.

Satis, (1988). *Physics in playgrounds* (Science and Technology in Society: Unit 705). Hatfield, England: Association of Science Education.

Solomon, J. (1988). The dilemma of science, technology and society education. In P. Fensham (Ed.), *Development and dilemmas in science education.* London: The Falmer Press.

Surrey Local Education Authority. (1990). *Notes for teachers and course leaders in support of a video program on Economic Awareness.* London: EcATT. Institute of Education.

Thomas, L., & Hodkinson, S. (1991). Economics education for all. In D. Dyer & D. Whitehead (Eds.), *New developments in economics and business education: Institute handbook for teachers.* London: Kogan Page.

CHAPTER 10

Teacher Education through Collaborative, School-Based Curriculum Evaluation

John W. Ackland
School of Education
University of Exeter
Exeter, England

INTRODUCTION

This chapter gives an account of a collaborative approach to research-based teacher education at the University of Exeter which involves both student teachers and serving teachers. This is referred to in the course description given to students as a school-based project. The intention of this chapter is not to give a detailed and comprehensive analysis of the project, but rather to explore some of the key ideas and background features that have helped to give it shape, and to demonstrate how these ideas contribute to the central concerns of the project.

Following a short historical account of the project, the chapter focuses on a number of ideas relating to reflective practice and formative curriculum evaluation in education. This provides both a context and a background for a more detailed exposition of the project. Particular reference is made to the "interests" and "concerns" of the main participants, and to the project's intended outcomes. The final section takes a critical look at the notion of "action research" and considers ways in which the approach to collaborative school-based evaluation articulated in the chapter might be viewed as a form of action research.

BACKGROUND

The origins of the project stem from the early days of the Technical and Vocational Education Initiative (TVEI) and the university's involvement

175

in the evaluation of one of the first pilot schemes. The TVEI in England and Wales, described by Gleeson (1989) as "perhaps the major curricular innovation since the introduction of comprehensive education in the 1960s" (p. 76), is a scheme whereby local education authorities receive central government grants for approved programes of technical, vocational, and related education for 14-to 18-year-olds in schools and colleges (see Dale et al., 1990). It was set up in 1983 as a series of pilot schemes designed to implement contrasting models of curriculum development in schools, and to promote new approaches to learning, teaching, and assessment. The terms *technical* and *vocational* were to be interpreted broadly, incorporating a number of cross-curricular interrelated themes, with a strong emphasis in the development of active teaching and learning strategies. The scheme was extended in 1987, with the eventual intention of becoming available to all 14- to 18-year-olds in state-maintained schools and colleges, irrespective of ability.

An important thrust of the university evaluation of this particular pilot scheme was to provide feedback for participating schools, based on pupil perceptions of ongoing curriculum developments in which teachers were actively engaged. A local TVEI management structure was set up, the central component of which was a TVEI Project team comprised of teacher representatives from each of the participating schools. This arrangement provided the means of bringing together teachers, university staff, and student teachers in a collaborative approach to a style of evaluation, the essence of which was to provide feedback that would inform and help shape ongoing practice.

The evaluation exercises had a marked effect on both the participating schools and the student teachers involved. The evaluations focused on issues relating to the central principles of the TVEI; although the main emphasis rested on changes in approaches to learning and teaching that were both explicit, and implicit, in the delivery of the TVEI, approaches that presented a challenge and, in many cases, a threat to teachers' and student teachers' inherent and predetermined understandings of what constituted effective classroom and teaching practice. One headteacher, in writing to the university on receiving a report of pupil perceptions in his school, commented that it was the most important piece of research the school had seen and that it paved the way for a reappraisal of teaching practices across the school. For student teachers, the experience of listening to and reflecting upon pupils' views and constructions of teaching and learning practices provided a means for them to reappraise and redefine their own views and understandings. Such sentiments are echoed by Elliot (1989) in an account he gives of his experience of teaching in an innovatory secondary modern school:

Controversy stimulates self-reflection. The alternative interpretations of actions expressed in the sort of practical discourse I described provide the context in which one renders one's own actions problematic and searches for evidence to legitimate them to colleagues. The evidence was to be found in the pupils' perceptions of the curriculum and teaching strategies. (p. 205)

The school-based project is now an integral part of the overall program in educational studies for secondary undergraduate students, and contributes to one of eight final degree assessment points. The students follow a period of school experience during Year 1 of their course, in which the emphasis is placed on working in small teams, reflecting upon and sharing experiences with others in the process of forming ideas of what is involved in becoming a teacher. This is followed in Year 2 with a 10-week block practice that involves a strong element of classroom teaching and the requirement to complete two "action" topics that involve the students in experiences that extend beyond the boundaries of their subject-teaching interests. The school-based project described in this chapter extends over a period of 20 weeks in Year 3, and is followed by a final 10-week block teaching practice in the first term of Year 4. It is in the Year 3 Project that the emphasis on a research-based approach to teacher education is made explicit.

RESEARCH-BASED TEACHER EDUCATION

There is an extensive and varied literature on research-based teacher education and the development of teachers' professional knowledge. A brief summary is given by Carr (1989b). Wragg (1982), in conducting a review of research in teacher education, identified, as one of a number of focal interests for future research, the role of experienced teachers and students working together on the analysis and development of their own teaching. Ruddock (1985) argued the need for a change in attitudes and habits among teachers and teacher educators, away from the concerns of short-term survival, to a research perspective, focusing on research in this context as "reflection-on-action through classroom enquiry" (p. 281). Tickle (1987) argued for reform of teacher education that stresses the promotion of partnership between student teachers and teachers within a conception of research-based teacher education. Of course, the emphasis on partnership between school and training institutions is not new; it is that the conception of partnership has changed, from an "apprenticeship" model of initial teacher education to one in which student teachers and teachers are seen as engaging in collaborative approaches to classroom and school-based research intended to improve the quality of their classroom practice.

This view of partnership is central to the philosophy underlying the Initial Training and In-service Education and Training of Teachers (IT-INSET) Project. IT-INSET is an approach to teacher education that combines school-focused inservice training for teachers with school-based initial training for student-teachers. The scheme was originally piloted as a 3-year project funded by the Department of Education and Science (DES), and was further developed on a national scale with continued DES funding (Ashton, Euan, Henderson, Mevrit, & Movtimer, 1983; Ashton, Henderson, & Peacock, 1989) Richardson (1990), in offering a review of mainly American literature on "learning to teach" and "teacher change", makes the case for a research-based approach to teacher education as a way of "bringing about significant and worthwhile changes in teaching practices" (p. 10). Richardson made specific reference to both practical and cognitive skills as important features: "Research should provide practitioners not just with findings in the form of activities or behaviours that work, but with ways of thinking and empirical premises about teaching" (p. 16).

There are two main themes in the literature on research-based teacher education that are of particular significance in a consideration of the school-based project described in this chapter. The first relates to contrasting conceptions of what constitutes quality teaching in education. The second concerns the nature of teachers' professional knowledge and how that knowledge is acquired and applied. Both themes address the question of the relationship of theory to practice in teacher education.

There is a universal concern regarding quality in teaching, and questions relating to educational standards, accountability in education and teacher appraisal, are at the center of the debate concerning the effectiveness of educational provisions in meeting the needs of a rapidly changing society. Hargreaves (1988), in commenting on government publications such as the white papers on *Teaching Quality* (Department of Education and Science, 1983) and *Better Schools* (Department of Education and Science, 1985), drew a comparison between predominantly "psychologistic" explanations, or accounts, of quality in teaching on the one hand, and a sociological and humanistic interpretation on the other. In the former, the importance of the personal qualities of the teacher, and learned knowledge, skills, and other forms of expertise, are stressed. Consistent with the positivistic view of social reality from which such assumptions are derived, research is seen as uncovering objective and verifiable knowledge capable of being "learned" and applied to produce effective teaching. Although such a view is likely to provide teachers with a range of 'survival' skills, the conception of pedagogical knowledge upon which it is based reduces the teacher to a mere technician. In contrast with a psychologistic and technocratic conception of teaching, a more humanistic interpretation, as articulated by Hargreaves (1988), lays emphasis on quality in teaching as emanating from "teachers actively interpreting, making sense of, and adjusting to, the demands and requirements their conditions of work place upon them" (p. 211). In this conception of teaching, "teachers, like other people, are not just bundles of skill, competence and technique; they are creaters of meaning, interpreters of the world and all it asks of them" (p. 216).

These contrasting views of quality in teaching can be seen as embedded in two distinctive sets of assumptions concerning the nature of knowledge in relation to professional practice. Expressed very crudely, this distinction manifests itself, on the one hand, in a view of professional practice as being informed by a scientifically derived body of knowledge as a solution to practical problems, to a view, on the other, of professional practice as informed by a form of knowledge that is grounded in that practice. In this latter conception, *professional*, or *practical*, knowledge is seen as dialectical and as emerging from an ongoing process of reflection on practice. The scientific model sees theory as distinct from practice, whereas in the notion of *professional*, or *practical*, knowledge, theory is seen as embedded in practice. This distinction between *theoretical* knowledge and *practical* knowledge is implicit in the distinction drawn by Schwab (1969) between technical discourse and practical discourse. Technical discourse is means–ends related and prescriptive of action, whereas professional discourse is concerned with thinking about action and about the values to be pursued in that action. Stenhouse (1975) differentiated between an *objectives* model of curriculum development and a *process* model. The *objectives* approach, in the language of technical discourse, seeks to apply scientifically verifiable means to the achievement of predetermined ends, whereas the *process* approach, in the language of professional discourse, lays emphasis on the engagement of teachers in active reflection on their practice that will lead to the generation of "new" insights and to improvements in their teaching. As Carr (1989b) argued:

> By relating this idea of 'teacher as researcher' to an analysis of professionalism, Stenhouse was able to argue that professional development required teachers to be provided with opportunities and resources to study their own practice through systematic reflection and research. (p. 7)

The idea of reflective practice as a form of reflective inquiry is central to the epistemology of practice advanced by Schon (1983, 1987). The central concepts of this epistemology for Schon are expressed as *knowledge-in-action* and *reflection-in-action*. Professional knowledge is what he terms as *knowledge in action*; the body of tacit and accumulated knowledge that drives and gives rise to action. *Reflection-in-action* concerns what happens when strange and novel situations are encountered. For Schon, *reflection-in-action* is a form of enquiry in which knowing and doing are inseparable, whereas what he refers to as *technical rationality* separates knowing from doing and action from research. *Reflection-in-action* for Schon is a kind of research process in which taken for granted, commonsense, views implicit in action are questioned, examined, and redefined – a process of reflection on *knowledge-in-action*.

SCHOOL-BASED PROJECT

These preliminary comments on selected writings in the literature on research-based teacher education serve to identify the kinds of assumptions concerning teaching quality and the "improvement" of educational practice upon which the project featured in this chapter is based. In essence, the central assumption rests on the view that teaching quality and school improvement are related, in important ways, to the ability, and opportunities, for all groups of participants in the educational process to engage in collaborative and systematic reflection on their own practice.

The main emphasis in the Exeter scheme is on school-based curriculum evaluation as a basis for critical reflection for both serving and student-teachers, using the notion of *reflection* as critical inquiry in the sense expressed by Wiess and Louden (1989) in their analysis. In most cases of the application of reflective practice in teacher education the emphasis is placed on classroom teaching as a research activity (Stenhouse 1975), whereas in the example given here the emphasis is on formative curriculum evaluation. Tickle (1987) identified three levels of school life which need to be viewed and understood and at which it is possible to conceive of issues for study and inquiry. These he identified as the immediate classroom level, where the emphasis is on matters of direct classroom practice; the institutional level, where the emphasis is on matters that bear directly on classroom practice or part of a teacher's wider professional responsibility; and a cultural level, where the emphasis is on values and beliefs that are implicit in the curriculum and pervade practice. The model described here applies to both the institutional and classroom level of inquiry and analysis.

The project involves groups of up to 12 student-teachers, working with teachers and university tutors, on a collaborative approach to school-based curriculum evaluation the main focus of which, initially at least, is determined by the teachers at the school level. Guba and Lincoln (1989) described such an approach to evaluation as:

a form of evaluation in which the claims, concerns, and issues of stakeholders come over as organisational foci (the basis for determining what information is needed) that is implemented within the methodological precepts of the constructivist inquiry paradigm. (p. 50)

Subsequent refinement, and the identification of further issues, emerge as the student teachers become more actively involved in discussions with teachers as each project develops. The project overall is integrated with the university evaluation of the TVEI in the region, and the initial negotiations with the schools is facilitated through the TVEI management structure as well as through direct contact with individual schools. The region is divided into consortia, each with a full-time consortium co-ordinator who liaises with the TVEI co-ordinators in the schools. Thus, the immediate context of the evaluation in the participating schools concerns the impact of the TVEI on the curriculum, in particular concerning approaches to learning and teaching, and on the relationship of the TVEI to the implementation of the National Curriculum following the 1988 Education Reform Act.

THE MAIN INTENTIONS

The main intentions, or "objectives", of the project should be seen in relation to the principal groups of participants, or stakeholders, involved; tutors from the university, undergraduate student teachers and teachers in the schools. An important and overriding purpose of the evaluations is to promote reflection on curriculum and classroom processes, using curriculum in its widest sense, in such a way that deepens understandings of those processes through generating insights and models that are grounded in the daily reality of school life.

For the teachers, the project can be seen to meet the following intentions:

1. To provide opportunities for the systematic collection and analysis of data, about areas of the curriculum that are perceived as problematic, in a way that enhances and makes explicit teachers' implicit theorizing about practice.
2. Through facilitating the systematic gathering and processing of data, to provide a form of feedback about curriculum issues in the school that will help promote a reappraisal of existing practice that, in turn, will inform policy making related to curriculum development in the school.

3. To make provision for their further professional development through providing support for systematic and critical reflection on practice as a basis for further study and research in a "higher education" context.

There are numerous examples where the evaluation process has given rise to changes both in teacher's thinking about, and in their actions regarding, the practice and context of their teaching. For example, the outcome of one project led to the modification of teaching strategies in the teaching of Science within the school. One of the teachers involved in the project commented that: "After reflecting upon their (pupils') perceptions of useful learning activities, I personally feel that some aspects of the third year course may need to be changed, along with an adjustment of the activities used." An aim of the project in this school was to generate data about classroom practice in the teaching of science that would enable the teachers and student teachers to question their "taken for granted" views of teaching through promoting critical reflection on their own actions. In this vein, the teacher quoted above felt that:

> Teachers subconsciously analyse their actions after every lesson, but they are not often provided with the opportunity to sit back and think what real points to pay attention to. This type of project helps us to consciously reflect upon the pupils' perceptions.

For student teachers, the project serves to promote the following purposes:

1. By being actively engaged in school-based curriculum evaluation exercises alongside, and in collaboration with, serving teachers; to gain insight into approaches to curriculum evaluation; and to acquire a range of evaluation skills.
2. By being involved in a process of inquiry and reflection, the essence of which is to see theory as implicit in practice, to engage them in an approach to teacher education in which this view of the relationship of theory to practice is made explicit.
3. To give them insights into curriculum processes, in particular learning and teaching, that are grounded in the everyday reality of school practice, and from that perspective to reflect on their own views, values and understandings.

Such "intentions" are in clear evidence in a statement given by one student concerning what he felt he had gained from the project:

On a personal level I feel the project has been a success for me as a prospective teacher, for it has enhanced my awareness of the need for continual evaluation and improvement; it has taught me about methods of data collection, analysis and presentation; and more importantly it has shown me the value of looking at learning processes from the pupil perspective.

For university staff, there is an agenda that offers scope for the following:

1. The opportunity to develop research interests in the context of school-focused inquiry that can be directly related to their teaching and ongoing research interests.
2. To provide the opportunity to acquire "recent and relevant" experience in schools, and to acquire first-hand information of recent curriculum initiatives at the school level.
3. To use their research and evaluation skills as a way of providing a particular kind of support for teachers in the context of school-based inservice teacher education.

Underlying all these concerns is the view that the development of a range of complex skills related to ways of evaluating and thinking about the curriculum, all of which are necessary for improving the quality of teaching, for improving the quality of deliberating about the curriculum, and for improving the quality of pupils' educational experiences, must be undertaken in the context of the school in relation to current practices and policies.

The intentions of the project, as described above, are consistent with the key principles of the IT-INSET approach to teacher education identified by Ashton et al. (1989), and with the model of "learning teaching" it supports. Ashton et al. described this model in terms of the kinds of experiences teacher education should provide, as follows:

> learning through systematic observation followed by reflection;
> critical examination of substantive and theoretical resources;
> data collection and analysis;
> exploration of value judgments and their criteria;
> constructive exchange of information and propositions;
> writing to inform and engage; and
> working collaboratively. (p. 189)

THE PRINCIPAL PARTICIPANTS

The Student Teachers

Apart from their active engagement with teachers in the schools, the student teachers are required to be involved in the production and completion of the following exercises and pieces of work:

A written group report of the evaluation to be available to the school and the teachers taking part for reflection and dissemination. In this context the report is seen as in the 'ownership' of the school.

A group presentation of the outcomes of the evaluation, to be promoted in an atmosphere of open discussion in which views may be exchanged and explored.

A reflective essay based on the evaluation, to be submitted to the university as a "formal" assessment requirement.

The project as a whole is built into the overall pattern of assessment for the final degree award, and contributes directly to one assessment point. The reflective essay is a part of that assessment. The evaluation process as such is also built into the assessment of students' work and is based on the demonstration of particular levels of competence in the performance of evaluation skills relating to data collection and analysis, and in the demonstration of skills relating both to working independently and to working in collaboration with others. These assessment procedures are important to mention as there was concern that the students should see the value of their school-based work, in terms of the processes and skills involved, reflected in their final degree award.

The first contact with each school is usually through the university tutor. One of the teachers from the school acts as a "link" teacher whose main task is to liaise with the University tutor in helping to set up and facilitate the evaluation in the school. Ashton et al. (1989), in their evaluation of IT-INSET, highlighted the problem of lack of time and the need to make possible the opportunity for teachers to be given some "release" time to help prepare programs and to manage research-based teacher education. In this project, funding is available from a number of sources to provide for the release of a member of staff from each of the participating schools for up to 5 half-days during the course of the project, to be negotiated at particular stages, in response to particular needs such as to visit the university to meet and work with students-teachers.

The evaluation projects arise out of the schools' perceived needs and interests, though, as stated above, as the projects get underway the student-teachers also become involved in identifying and prioritizing issues. This process of negotiation is important as it relates to, and problematizes, questions of ownership and empowerment. The balance between student teacher and school interests and needs is delicate and varies across the various projects. For example, in one project, one of the student teachers perceived the problem as follows:

> I was very interested in the area of group-work and I wanted to look quite closely at whether the children felt this was lacking from their maths work.

At this point the school link teacher and university supervising tutor seemed to take control of the situation and started to make very directed statements about what we should look at; the areas we should be analyzing. I felt they took control.

In contrast, another student from the same group and at the same school, in commenting on her experiences, remarked that:

The whole process that we went through was a type of negotiation between us, the teachers and the pupils. We had to negotiate with the teachers on what they wanted to use the research for. So between us both we managed to look into areas that would be beneficial for both parties concerned. It only became completely apparent that we had achieved this balance of negotiation at the final meeting when we were able to discuss our findings.

The University Tutor and the School Link Teacher

These comments, from two student teachers, throw into sharp relief the importance of the respective roles of the university tutor and the school link teacher in the project. The style of the evaluation, and the methods used for collecting data, are the outcome of negotiation among students, teachers, and the university tutor. Models and mechanisms of collaboration, of bringing all interested parties together, of managing and arranging contact with pupils, are negotiated and take shape as part of the evaluation process, and emerge in response to the needs and opportunities the process generates. The university tutor, and the school link teacher, are seen as playing crucial roles in managing and co-ordinating the process as a whole. The main tasks of the university tutor include:

1. To act as a communicating link between the university and the school, especially during the early planning stages of the project.
2. To monitor and record what happens during the various stages of the evaluation, from the first contact with the school and the initial identification of issues, through to the analysis and interpretation of data and the presentation of the final report.
3. To manage the compilation of the final report and to negotiate arrangements with the school for the end-of-project student presentation.
4. To follow through the feedback and dissemination of the outcomes of the evaluation, and, in collaboration with the link teacher, to assess the impact the evaluation process has had on student-teachers and teachers in the school, both in terms of perceptions and practice.

5. To draw out underlying ideas as they emerge, to give the evaluation coherence in the context of the central principles concerning the relation of theory to practice upon which it is based, and to bring teachers from the schools together with student teachers to reflect on the evaluation process and to exchange and share views. In this sense it is the role of the university tutor to enable all participants to use the evaluation process as a learning experience.

The overriding role of the school link teacher is to organize and facilitate the evaluation in the school. The main tasks of the link teacher include:

1. To act as a communicating link between students and teachers in the school, and to arrange meetings when and where necessary.
2. To ensure that students are provided with important information concerning the background of the school, and in particular to give them information concerning the school curriculum and other issues that help to set the evaluation in context.
3. To negotiate and communicate with student teachers, school staff, and the university tutor in the process of identifying and prioritizing evaluation issues.
4. To organize and arrange student contact with teachers and pupils for collecting data, broadly conceived to include a variety of "activities" and "methods," including collaborative teaching.
5. To make arrangements for the feedback and dissemination of the outcomes of the evaluation in the school, and elsewhere, as appropriate.

THE PROCEDURAL MODEL

The procedural model provides the guidelines for organizing the evaluation, and establishes a basic framework, related to a timescale, within which to formulate and conduct each school-based project. The guidelines specify the kinds of tasks that need to be performed, in sequence, for the satisfactory completion of the project. The stages described in the guidelines offer a working definition of the research process underlying the project. The research process is conceived, as described in the final section of this chapter, as a form of *action research*, defined as a process of planning, observing and data collecting, reflecting, and acting. These elements in the action research process are operationalized in the form of notes and guidelines for participating teachers, student teachers, and university tutors. For student teachers the process of reflection is highlighted and brought into clear focus in the analysis and interpretation of the data.

Planning

The planning stage involves making the initial contact with the school, identifying and prioritizing issues, negotiating a plan of action, and drawing up methods for collecting data. The end of the first stage involves the student teachers agreeing a "contract" with the link teacher and the university tutor, which amounts to an action plan for the next stage of the project. The strategies used in the first stage vary depending on circumstances in the school, and on the perceptions and levels of understanding of those involved, but in each case includes a meeting involving all participants to explore issues and reach decisions. The university tutor plays a critically important role in the early negotiating procedures, concerned at all times to shape the deliberations in accordance with the philosophy central to the conception of the project.

Although it is stressed that the main focus of the evaluation should be determined by the school, student-teachers need also to feel that they have a say in defining issues in relation to their perceived needs and interests. As previously discussed, the balance of involvement and decision making between serving and student teachers in the negotiating process varies from one school to another. However, exercises such as fairly open-ended classroom observations and pupil shadowing early in the project enables student teachers to feel more in touch with the school context. The perceived needs of student teachers, especially in the early stages of the project, are inclined to differ quite significantly from those of the teachers in the schools, and both sets of needs should be seen in the broader context of teacher and student teacher interests and concerns. The teachers tend to see the exercise initially in terms of the student teachers providing support and direct assistance in conducting an evaluation of a part of the curriculum, or of an aspect of pupil learning, in order to provide feedback to inform curriculum deliberation, policy making and classroom practice within the school. One student teacher, in making reference in her evaluation report to the concerns of teachers and the constraints within which they had to work, offered the following observations:

> It is emphatically viewed that the pressure of time for all teachers is the greatest limiting factor in the participation of teachers in undertaking similar types of project. Ideally, it is personally felt that greater participation and contribution would have been desirable, but in reality this proved to be unreasonable due to the pressure of teaching and lack of time.

The kinds of evaluation issues raised by the teachers, which have formed the basis of particular projects, range from those that focus specifically on the classroom, such as looking closely into the kinds of tasks which pupils feel help them to learn, to those that are more oriented toward cross-curricular issues such as the role of "tutoring", and the impact of information technology, and in particular word processing, on teaching and learning strategies in different subject areas. The following examples illustrate the range and diversity of issues identified:

The impact of the introduction of word processing on pupils' approaches to learning, and on their motivation to learn, in different subject areas.

The significance of assignment writing (in the Technical and Vocational Education Initiative) as a vehicle for learning and teaching.

Health education as a cross-curricular theme.

Pupil and teacher perceptions of tutoring and the role of tutor groups for pupils of all ages.

Equal opportunities across the curriculum.

Effective learning and the teaching of Science.

The interests and perceived needs of student teachers are shaped primarily by a concern to be operating in a school context as a means of gaining insights into learning and teaching that grow out of first-hand experience and direct involvement with teachers and pupils. In responding to questions concerning their perceived value of the project, students articulated these concerns as follows:

> It provided me with a means of discovering what pupils like and dislike in lessons, so providing an indication of lessons I would now teach that would be interesting and beneficial for the pupils. I have acquired some knowledge of how the TVEI and the National Curriculum have affected teaching programs.

> It gives you the opportunity of looking at teaching and learning from the pupil's point of view.

> The main benefits of the project for me were the interviews with pupils and the awareness this gives me about how they feel about working within a scheme which places emphasis on them working independently.

Also of significance to student teachers is the opportunity the project gives for them to acquire a range of research and evaluation skills. A number of students see this as a significant factor and something which contributes to other aspects of their course work as undergraduate students:

I think I have learned a lot about research. It was very good to be able to work in a group and use methods which had been discussed among all of us, which I think made the job a lot more meaningful.

What I found of particular value was interviewing pupils and gaining their perceptions of their work. This has been very interesting and instructive. I have also learned how time-consuming an exercise research can be. I have gained a greater appreciation of the thought required in producing research instruments and classifying and analysing data. I also appreciate the value of interviewing as a research technique and of the problems it raises.

Data Collecting

It is implicit in the assumptions underlying the project, in particular those concerning the views of reflective practice and practical discourse that are central to all aspects of the evaluation process, that all participants become actively engaged in each stage of the project. However, in the majority of cases, and dependent on the perceptions and views of the teachers involved, the student teachers are perceived as providing the main means of collecting information and data. The constraints of time already discussed help to locate this issue in context. The process of drawing up research instruments and devising methods of collecting data has important implications for where the ownership of the project is seen to lie. Much depends on the experiences, skills, and perceptions of the teachers who are involved. For some schools, in particular those new to the project, the question of "ownership" can be seen in terms of a shift from an initial perception of the evaluation as being conducted by "outside" evaluators, to a perception of the evaluation as being under the control and direction of teachers in the school. An important dimension of the role of the university tutor is to promote this change in direction and emphasis through evolving strategies that enable teachers to feel actively engaged in all stages of the evaluation process. For example, teachers in the schools need to be given the opportunity to comment on, and make recommendations concerning, the wording of questions in interview schedules, and to be involved in determining the main focus of concern in the conduct of classroom observations. Throughout the evaluation process it is important that the university tutor and the link teacher ensure that all participants are involved in determining the direction of the evaluation.

Data analysis and interpretation

The process of reflection is central to the project and can be conceived at different levels and in different contexts. For example, identifying and prioritizing issues for the evaluation is, in itself, a form of reflection. In this context the concern is with rendering problematic some aspect of curriculum practice by posing questions and setting problems. Reflecting on the data involves the processes of analysis and interpretation. Analysis takes the form of bringing order to the data which involves classifying and arranging the data into categories and drawing out overall patterns. The process is essentially descriptive and rests on a neutral, "nonjudgmental" presentation and ordering of the data. Interpretation takes the form of giving meaning to the descriptive analysis, offering explanations, and looking for underlying themes. Analysis and interpretation are creative processes through which new insights emerge, which, in turn, form the basis for further inquiry and research.

Planning, data collecting, analysis, and interpretation are analytically separate processes, whereas in practice they are interwoven. As previously discussed, planning and identifying evaluation issues involves participants reflecting on their own views and understandings of curriculum practice through raising questions and setting problems. And the process of data collecting itself gives rise to ideas and views concerning the analysis and interpretation of the information being gathered.

The data analysis is carried out by the student-teachers as part of their "contract" and is presented at the end of the project in the form of a report. The processes involved, such as working in co-operation with others, analyzing, and presenting the data, are built into the student assessment of the project. The main emphasis in compiling the report is on descriptive analysis in which general patterns in the data are highlighted. The report then forms the basis for discussion and interpretation by the different groups involved, but principally the student teachers, teachers in the schools, and university tutors. The attempt to separate the data analysis from the interpretation that follows is important in that it recognizes that the kinds of interpretation that are likely to emerge will depend on the interests and experiences of the various groups involved, which will in turn be influenced by the different contexts in which they operate. However, in addition to the project report, the student teachers make a presentation of the outcomes of the evaluation to the schools. An important purpose of the presentation is to provide the opportunity for discussion and reflection in which particular interpretations and ideas may be examined and shared. Finally, the process of interpretation for the student-teachers is facilitated in the form of a reflective essay, which is also incorporated in the student assessment of the project. An important criterion in the assessment of the essay is the ability demonstrated in the discourse to relate critical inquiry into curriculum practice to the development and construction of personal views, values, and understandings.

THE "RESEARCH" MODEL

The underlying approach to curriculum evaluation and reflection that characterizes the model of school-based teacher education articulated here can be said to reflect a form of action research, but any definition that could be claimed to embrace all the dimensions of the project, including the varying perceptions of all participants, would be difficult to formulate. Similarly, Ashton et al. (1989) are not prepared to argue the IT-INSET model as action research, even though the emphasis on reflection, planning, and acting are central to both. Instead they prefer to "identify the defining attributes of the IT/INSET process so that others may judge whether or not it conforms to their understanding of action and research" (p. 15).

Carr (1989a), in commenting on developments following Elliot's (1978) influential account of action research as a "self-reflective process in which teachers examined the themes implicit in their everyday practice" (p. 85), went on to argue that:

> Action research now means different things to different people and, as a result, the action research movement often appears to be held together by little more than a common contempt for academic theorising and a general disenchantment with mainstream research. (p. 85)

In a review of the development of different conceptions of action research with regard to their implications for educational management and teacher education, Wallace (1987) observed that "awareness of these issues should inform attempts by teacher educators, teachers and headteachers to adopt action research as a way of improving managerial practice on schools and other educational institutions" (p. 97).

Referring specifically to a "learning to teach" context, Wallace defined *action research* as:

> the process through which teachers collaborate in evaluating their practices jointly, raising awareness of their personal theory; articulate a shared conception of values; try out new strategies to render the views expressed in their practice more consistent with the educational values they espouse; record their work in a form which is readily available and understandable to other teachers; and thus develop a shared theory of teaching by researching practice. (p. 105)

He offered a definition of action research as a "generic term covering a wide range of strategies intended to bring about improvement in some practical situation" (p. 98).

The central components of most definitions of action research that are significantly central to the project described in this chapter relate to the notion of a spiral of cycles of researching, reflecting, planning, and acting as integral to the action research process. The emphasis in the spiral of information gathering, analysis, and action gives scope for initial ideas in the process to be rethought and redefined.

Bonser and Grundy (1988), following Kemmis and McTaggart (1981), saw the action-research process as a "systematic one which entails a cyclical interrelationship of moments of planning, acting, observing and reflecting" (p. 37); a spiral of discovery of meaning which is seen as central to practical deliberation (Schwab, 1969) about curriculum change and development, with clear implications for practice. In relation to their own research, they describe an action-research process in terms of a "procedural guide for researchers, teachers and others interested in data-gathering as an initial step towards the construction of curriculum policy" (p. 39). The spiral involved four cycles, each forming a different phase of meaning making, starting with the individual level of planning, data production, and reflective deliberation, through a small group and a whole group level, to the level of all personnel within the institution. The model of school-based evaluation described in this chapter is informed by a similar conception and has the potential for moving through phases in the way expounded by Bonser and Grundy. For example, one student, caught in a reflective mood, offered the following appraisal of her experiences of the project:

> We have learned a lot about research techniques and been able to reflect on our findings in terms of our professional development. Six months after its production, the report now has the feel of a pilot study, suggesting specific aspects of the scheme which cry out for further investigation. With the experience we have gained it would be possible and more rewarding to go back and research more specific questions in greater depth.

The definition of action research that seemed to most closely describe the approach adopted by Bonser and Grundy, and that serves to highlight salient features of the approach to curriculum evaluation in this project, is that provided by Carr and Kemmis (1986), for whom:

> Action research is simply a form of self-reflective enquiry undertaken by participants in a social situation in order to improve the rationality and justice of their own practice, their understandings of these practices, and the situations in which the practices are carried out. (p. 160)

This view of action research is implicit in the comments made by one student teacher on completion of the project:

> The project has developed my confidence with children and made me question my own methods of teaching. I have also gained a large insight into the skills of evaluation and of working within a research group. However, at the start of the project none of this was apparent.

REFERENCES

Ashton, P. M. E., Euan, S., Henderson, J. E., Merrit, J. E., & Mortimer, J. (1983). *Teacher education in the classroom: Initial and in-service*. London: Croom Helm.

Ashton, P. M. E., Henderson, E. S., & Peacock, A. (1989). *Teacher education through classroom research: Principles and practice of IT-INSET*. London: Routledge Education.

Bonser, S. A., & Grundy, S. J. (1988). Reflective deliberation in the formulation of a school curriculum policy. *Journal of Curriculum Studies, 20* (1), 35–45.

Carr, W. (1989a). Action research: Ten years on. *Journal of Curriculum Studies, 21* (1), 85–90.

Carr, W. (Ed.). (1989b). *Quality in teaching: Arguments for a reflective profession*. Lewes, UK: Falmer Press.

Carr, W., & Kemmis, S. (1986). *Becoming critical: Education, knowledge and action research*. Lewes, UK: Falmer Press.

Dale, R., Bowe, R., Hams, D., Loveys, M., Moore, R., Shelling, C., Sikes, P., Trevitt, J. & Valsecchi, V. (1990). *The TVEI story: Policy, practice and preparation for the work force*. Milton Keynes, UK: Open University Press.

Department of Education and Science. (1983). *Teaching quality*. London: HMSO.

Department of Education and Science. (1985) *Better schools*. London: HMSO.

Elliott, J. (1978). What is action research in schools? *Journal of Curriculum Studies, 10* (4), 355–357.

Elliott, J. (1989). Knowledge, power and teacher appraisal. In W. Carr (Ed.), *Quality in teaching: Arguments for a reflective profession*. Lewes, UK: Falmer Press.

Gleeson, D. (1989). *The paradox of training: Making progress out of crisis*. Milton Keynes, UK: Open University Press.

Guba, E. G., & Lincoln, Y. S. (1989). *Fourth generation evaluation*. Newbury Park, CA: Sage.

Hargreaves, A. (1988). Teaching quality: A sociological analysis. *Journal of Curriculum Studies, 20* (3), 211–231.

Kemmis, S., & McTaggart, R. (1981). *The action research planner*. Victoria, Australia: Deakin University Press.

Richardson, V. (1989). Significant and worthwhile change in teacher education. *Educational Researcher, 19* (7), 10–18.

Ruddock, J. (1985). Teacher research and research-based teacher education. *Journal of Education for Teaching, 11* (3), 281–289.

Schon, D. A. (1983). *The reflective practitioner: How professionals think in action*. New York: Basic Books.

Schon, D. A. (1987). *Educating the reflective practitioner*. San Francisco: Josey-Bass.

Schwab, J. J. (1969). The practical: A language for curriculum. *School Review, 78*, 1–24.

Stenhouse, L. (1975). *Introduction to curriculum research and development*. London: Heinemann Education.

Tickle, L. (1987). *Learning teaching, teaching learning: A study of partnership in teacher education*. Lewes, UK: Falmer Press.

Wallace, M. (1987). A historical review of action research: Some implications for the education of teachers in their managerial role. *Journal of Education for Teaching, 13* (2), 97–115.

Weiss, J., & Louden, W. (1989). *Images of Reflection*. Unpublished paper, The Ontario Institute for Studies in Education.

Wragg, E. C. (1982). *A review of research in teacher education*. London: NFER-Nelson.

CHAPTER 11

Uses of Experience in Postcompulsory Teacher Education

Martin Bloomer
The University of Exeter
School of Education

David Jolly
Exeter College

The chapter draws from the authors' experiences of designing and teaching a course leading to an initial teaching qualification for teachers in postcompulsory education. It focuses upon a variety of strategies employed to encourage and enable course members to place themselves and their experiences at the heart of their course, to reflect critically on those experiences, and to recognize that the knowledge generated through such reflection is not only legitimate knowledge but valuable course content.

The Certificate in Education (FE) course in unusual in at least four important respects. Firstly, although the course offers an *initial* teaching qualification, course members are practicing teachers sometimes with a wealth of teaching experience, attending on a part-time inservice basis. It is a sad fact that, in Britain in the 1990s, a very substantial proportion of teachers in the postcompulsory sector do not hold qualified teacher status. We, the authors, developed the Cert.Ed. as a pragmatic response to this set of circumstances which we view as far from ideal.

Secondly, the Cert.Ed. is unusual because it does not devote attention to main subject studies in the manner practised in most initial teacher education courses. Although the academic qualifications of some may be very modest indeed, course applicants must hold the "full professional qualification" or a degree or its equivalent in their teaching subject; on that basis they are deemed suitably knowledgeable in that subject and sufficiently qualified to gain employment as a teacher in postcompulsory education.

Thirdly, courses are physically located in tertiary and further education colleges and not in institutions of higher education. For some 30% to 40% of course members, courses are situated in their own places of work. This is an important feature that, at the initial planning stage, we felt to be essential to the achievement and maintenance of the course philosophy and practices we had in mind. We did not want an 'ivory tower'-based course but sought to establish a "community of teacher education within a community of teachers" (Bloomer, 1988, p. 32).

Finally, the philosophy of the Certificate in Education (FE) course is probably its most distinctive feature. The course and the culture within which it is located exist in a state of permanent tension. The course is based securely in concepts of teacher as "critical professional practitioner" and teaching as a "practical art." It places knowledge and theory in a dialectical relationship with practice (praxis): Knowledge and theory inform practice but are continually reconstructed or refined in the light of practical experience. Teachers are seen not as mediators between theory and practice (as simply the means by which the rules of established theory become manifest in "wise practice"), but as observers, analysts, theoreticians, experimenters, and evaluators, responding continually, spontaneously, and sensitively to ever-changing and largely unpredictable sets of circumstances. The art of teaching is in achieving such a response and is not to be simplistically described in terms of the efficient "application of learned rules or theories about the nature of teaching and learning" (McNamara, 1990, p. 149). Carr and Kemmis stated this view of teaching quite clearly:

> Practitioners tend not to experience their expertise as a set of techniques or as a "tool kit" for producing learning. They can identify some "tricks of the trade" and techniques, certainly, but these are employed in complex patterns, in overlapping sets, in combinations dictated as much by the mood or climate of the class, the particular set of aims being pursued, the kinds of subject matter being considered, the particular image which governs the teaching/learning exercise at hand as a kind of dramatic performance for the 'players' involved, and by all sorts of other factors which shape the situation moment by moment. (1986, p 37)

Enabling our course members to meet the demands presented by this view of teaching has been no straightforward matter, and the learning entailed has not always been easy to explain to others. Schön's account of how such professional artistry may be learned is very close to our own, however:

> Perhaps, then, learning *all* forms of professional artistry depends, at least in part, on conditions similar to those created in the studios and conservatories:

freedom to learn by doing in a setting relatively low in risk, with access to coaches who initiate students into the "traditions of the calling" and help them, by "the right kind of telling," to see on their own behalf and in their own way what they need most to see. (1987, p 17)

The colleges in which the courses are situated are liable to sporadic and arbitrary influence by quite a different view of teaching and education. It is an instrumental—or technical—rational view consumed by the importance of management and systems and the pursuit of maximum efficiency. It is more about means, about ways of achieving things; and it is less about questioning the ends that are achieved. This scientism casts teachers as technicians whose function is to select and apply carefully rehearsed skills in accordance with known rules. It is a "science of teaching" concerned with polishing techniques rather than with education. In this view, teachers are not *professionals* (although the term is still used) but are agents for others (*line managers, clients, enterprise councils,* etc.), and though they may have access to a stock of professional knowledge which has its roots in the values and principles of education, they are systematically denied autonomy and opportunities to exercise this knowledge to address educational ends. If their professional wisdom is sought at all, it is *after* key decisions concerning ends have been taken. Such a concept of teacher as technician is enhanced by a "new philistinism" that threatens public education in general and further education in particular. This entails the measurement of "educational efficiency" in terms such as staff-student ratios, fee income, and profit, which, although acclaimed by auditors, provide no indication whatsoever of the amount or quality of any education to have taken place.

Such views of teaching and education are widespread in the postcompulsory sector of public education and are held, most notably, by teachers who have moved into teaching from a career in industry or commerce where hierarchically ordered responsibilities are commonly described in terms of "delivering commodities to clients in markets." Quite a number of teachers bring these perspectives, among others, to the Cert.Ed. course.

We had serious doubts about the appropriateness of the traditional model of teacher education that was still dominant among Cert. Ed. (FE) courses across the country at the time we laid our plans. It was not that we felt the wisdom generated through the disciplines of philosophy, psychology, sociology, and history to be irrelevant to a course in teacher education; our concern was that such an approach implicitly devalued, not only the massive experience that our course members brought to the course, but the considerable thought that most had already given to problems of learning and teaching. They already had vast experience in theorizing about education, and if the course was to help them maximize their effectiveness as teachers, it had to be about encouraging and supporting the further development of their capacities to think and theorize on the basis of experience. That, after all is the art of teaching: the management of praxis. A diet of predigested theory offered by the four disciplines seemed wholly inappropriate (even counterproductive), given our course aims.

The course was, then, committed to building from course members' prior and concurrent experiences as far as possible, not only in order that individuals might learn from their own experiences but that they might learn from those of others, too. We recognized from the outset that we would not achieve our aims simply by confronting course members with the request, "Now reflect on your experience of . . ." A great deal of preparatory work was necessary and, from the start, our efforts were guided by four main aims:

1. *Liberation and empowerment*: to encourage course members away from the view that the only sources of legitimate knowledge and valid judgment are external authorities and from the view that they, as learners, should be passive recipients of such knowledge and judgment; and to prompt them to recognize that they are active in the construction of their own knowledge and are not merely the passive recipients of knowledge dispensed by others, that they have the right to evaluate themselves and are not bound to look only to others for that purpose, and that the sharing and critical inspection of such evaluations in a spirit of openness and honesty can promote valid and unique insights into oneself and one's life world.
2. *The development of basic skills for reflection*: to support course members in acquiring confidence, competence, and independence in the intellectual and personal skills necessary for rigorous and productive reflection, and to do so by providing appropriate guidance when necessary but encouraging individual initiative as far as possible.
3. *Responsive tutorship*: to establish a common approach among tutors and other teachers that allows them to act as partners to course members in the learning process; to provide realistic opportunities for course members to base their assignments, class meetings, and tutorials on their own concerns and interests, and to feed their own experiences into their course; and to insure that tutors are prepared and able to make supportive critical responses to the issues that course members choose to raise (that they can suspend the urge to impose their own judgments and wisdom on the basis of crude assumptions of their superiority), and that such

responses may be seen as contributions to a learning dialogue between tutor and course member continuing throughout the course and, possibly, beyond.

> Only learners themselves can learn and only they can reflect on their own experiences. . . . Teachers need to be conscious of the priorities of learners in the process of learning, and need to appreciate that what emerges from the learning activity will be determined more by the learner than by the person who designed the activity. (Boud, Keogh, & Walker, 1985, pp. 11, 37).

4. *A supportive community of learners*: to take every reasonable step to insure that course members are able to use their colleagues (fellow course members and tutors) as partners in work, to share experiences with and to take risks and test ideas with in the knowledge that they can rely upon the others' trust, discretion, and respect within a supportive spirit of openness and honesty.

The distinctive structure and philosophy of our new course, and the style of classroom management and pedagogy practiced by the course tutorial team, were outside the experience of quite a number of our first cohort of teachers. Some appeared quite anxious about assuming responsibility for their part in this "new" style of course and grieved over the absence of universal "truths" and fixed, nonnegotiable course structures; others viewed the course philosophy as "obvious" and natural and were simply keen to "get on with it." Many, it seemed, viewed with caution suggestions that tutors were there primarily to support them in *their own* judgments resulting from *their* reflection on *their* experiences.

From the outset, we regarded it as very important that our course philosophy, with its emphasis on student empowerment, was as fully reflected in our classroom management and pedagogy as possible. Given our keenness to utilize course members' experiences to provide part of the course content and also the importance that we attached to their negotiation of content and methods, it was perhaps inevitable that many class meetings entailed student-centered activities of various types. Common features of meetings were buzz groups, brainstorming, games, group work, pyramiding, teacherless discussion, role plays, simulations, and student-or joint-led seminars where course members were able to exercise a high degree of choice in both the content and the methods of their work. However, certain course members were manifestly uncomfortable and insecure when invited to work under such conditions. Denied the security of absolutist knowledge and the truth statements it freely generates, they appeared unable to utilize relativist knowledge to further their understandings. Moreover, class meetings based on student-centered activities required, not simply that course members shared their experiences and thoughts with one another, but, for some, that they laid bare something of themselves that they had never previously subjected to any kind of critical scrutiny by themselves, let alone others. In doing so, they were vulnerable, at the mercy of their course colleagues, and on occasions deeply anxious.

It would be misleading for us to suggest that our pedagogy excluded expository style teaching or lecturing. It would also be quite wrong for us to suppose that our stress on student empowerment should limit us to student-centered classroom activities of the type described above. We recognized that certain knowledge is not readily amenable to discovery through reflection, and that lecture and demonstration can perform very useful functions in conveying key information clearly and efficiently. This point is made forcefully by McNamara (1990, pp. 153–154). The critical issue as far as we were concerned was not the particular teaching technique employed but the fuller context in which it was used. So commonly, expository teaching offends the principle of learner empowerment because it denies learners the opportunity to participate–to weigh the lecture content against their own experiences, and to reply. Lectures are disempowering when lecturers expect that the content is for passive and uncritical acceptance. Expository presentations were used quite frequently on the Cert.Ed. course, but subject to two conditions:

1. they were of reasonable and appropriate length, and
2. there were proper opportunities for learners to participate in the critical examination of the content, even though it might mean that they would have to wait until the end of the presentation before they could do so.

These two conditions for expository teaching are essential if such techniques are to be used within a program of study that purports to foster reflective practice. They are necessary for the protection of learners from tutor domination and, hence, against their own disempowerment.

Up to this point we described certain aspects of organization and policy which helped us achieve the type of course ethos we believe essential for the support of reflective practice. Now we shall turn attention to four further features that were developed specifically to promote critical reflection: course assignments, teaching observations, course texts, and periodic course and self-evaluation.

Our major concern with course assignments was that they should not be extraneous to the processes of learning, simply experienced as hurdles or interruptions to smooth progress through the course. They should be fully integral to the course, generating course content, grounded in course members' experiences of teaching and learning, and be of some use to the course member beyond their immediate instrumental value as stepping stones to certification.

One such assignment was *Learning and Teaching Observed*, which required that course members observe, describe, and analyze two sessions taught by their teaching or course colleagues. They were to select sessions they anticipated would differ in terms of how students learned, how classrooms were managed or, in terms of other criteria, raised within the course up to that point. In the 1, 500-word guidelines, they were not offered structured observation or interview schedules; they were urged to construct *their own* analyses of what they saw, and to do so in terms of the concepts *they* deemed appropriate. They were prompted by questions such as "what was learned . . . ?" "how did learning take place?" "what appeared to influence what was learned?" and so on. The products of this exercise were personal constructions affected as much by the subjective predispositions of the observer as by any "objective truth" about the events observed. They were reflections on experience, and it was our duty as tutors to help turn them into opportunities for learning.

Throughout the assignment and, certainly, before producing their written accounts, course members were invited to discuss their ideas with their tutors. Tutors endeavored to maintain a "responsive" approach, supporting course members in *their* evaluations. They confirmed, clarified, and questioned ideas, always seeking to be guided by the interests and expressed needs of the tutee. In this way, we believed course members would learn most from their experiences of observation and analysis.

Tutors' comments on assignments were crucial to the maintenance of the reflective activity we sought to promote. The following is one tutor's response to *Learning and Teaching Observed*:

> I'm glad you came to some conclusions eventually based on straight-forward opinions and experience rather than on stereotypes of 'modern' or 'traditional' teachers.
>
> What you seem to be commenting on is simply what you take to be the meaning of 'professional teaching' and you are saying that it should include:
>
> • establishing a working atmosphere that frees people *for* learning
> • the proper mediation of one's subject for learners
> • the careful planning of learning
> • the careful evaluation of learning taking place
>
> You are not basing these desiderata upon anything simplistic (such as s-centred v t-centred or authoritarian-anarchic) but upon what you assess to have happened in the sessions.

As such, this is an excellent assignment from which to look at further issues – perhaps particularly what is learnt on non-technical courses and how this is best achieved.

I appreciate this thorough and fascinating account.

The tutor then goes on to comment on, and raise questions about, specific issues in the body of the text, among which are planning and classroom management, characterizations of learning, the use of language to mediate content for learners, classroom furniture, student participation, the assessment and evaluation of learning and many other issues.

Immediately, it will be seen that these comments were written in the spirit of a dialogue. The tutor gave a lot of attention to confirming points raised (sometimes speculatively) by the course member, and to pointing up connections between those and others recorded elsewhere in the literature or in common experience, and to raising questions and taking issue on points which could be pursued further. These comments, in fact, represent only one slice of the rich dialogue that this particular course member's assignment prompted. Numerous discussions and informal tutorials took place with course tutors and colleagues at various stages in the development of the "final" written assignment. And the life of the assignment did not expire simply because it had been declared a "pass." It lived on in at least two important senses. Firstly, the visits to witness other teachers in their classrooms continued with some course members forming themselves into a small team for the purpose of continued mutual observation, evaluation and support. Secondly, the dialogue between the assignment writer, tutor, and quite a number of others continued not only throughout the course, impinging on class meetings, tutorials and other assignments, but beyond the end of the course and outside it. This was one of the virtues of setting the course in a tertiary college where some course members worked.

The tutor's comments quoted above were a response to the work of one of the most successful members of the course; successful, that is, in terms of the criteria that we, the course tutors, held to be most important. The assignment had been used to support personal and professional development, and this course member had been open, honest, and prepared to subject to critical examination all that was understood in the name of education and teaching. Not every course member was able to do likewise.

Similar principles guided the teaching observations that were carried out as part of the course. Our general approach to observations is indicated in the following extract from a briefing note to external moderators:

We have found that course members have been very "open" and prepared to make thoughtful criticism of their own work. Their own evaluations (supported by tutors) have, we maintain, provided a helpful foothold for their personal and professional development. We have encouraged them to offer us 'typical' lessons rather than "ideal" sessions constructed purely for their tutors' benefit. (From *Briefing for Moderators of Teaching Practice*, Cert. Ed. course document)

In postobservation tutorials, tutors normally asked course members to give their own accounts of events first. This was in order that tutors could contribute their observations as a response to those made by the course members, so initiating the dialogue that we have already mentioned. Tutors' comments were not simply handed down to course members as judgments; they were offered for the purpose of supporting course members in their own critical evaluations of their work. After the postobservation tutorial, tutors committed their main observations to writing, normally in a style similar to that of the following example, which was written after a "first observation".

Thank you for inviting me to watch your work with this group.

I was much impressed by the general feel of the class. I felt that there was a busy and purposeful working atmosphere, underpinned by a clear sense of structure and development, creating an environment in which students were feeling very pleased with themselves and their achievements. In case all this sounds too task-centred, I should also add that an important factor in establishing this positive atmosphere was your own friendly, relaxed and confident presentation. The group felt at ease with you, despite their concerns at the new technologies, and your warmth and informality were of particular value here. You were responsive to them as a group: in your initial presentation, where you were clear and encouraging, and, later, where you were working with individuals, offering support and help in relation to their specific problems. I thought you were very effective here: you were able to look at the screen to identify problems, whilst simultaneously listening carefully to your students' concerns. They clearly felt they had all your attention. As I mentioned to you afterwards, it seemed to me that you had a key role in providing a central mediating space, a filter, between the inflexible logic of the computer system and the range of individual differences amongst your students.

You used an extensive and appropriate range of resources: the friendly handouts, the hardware and software, and the OHP with its imaginative use of masks and overlays. This latter had much promise, especially with your clear colour coding to illustrate stages of the spreadsheet process. However the physical manipulation of the images (never easy!) perhaps needs some thought. Would card masks, rather than paper masks, be easier to move about? Could you anchor the overlays with sellotape/masking tape hinges?

A couple of other points now. One interesting issue came up in connection with the ways in which students can become utterly stuck following some relatively small error. Inevitably they look to you to troubleshoot, which, skillfully, you do. However, they usually have to wait to see you, and you are kept busy dealing with a series of queries about relatively minor errors. How could we make them less dependent on you? To some extent already they form small self-help sub-groups, yet could there be some kind of trouble-shooting guide available? What about something on a disk, for each computer system, that students could run if they were stuck? A structured series of questions could maybe guide them through to the source of their error. Maybe this could be available with one of the room's terminals permanently dedicated as this kind of reference station?

The other point, and maybe the harder one given your course's dependence on a fairly structured scheme of work, is how to enable students to create their own routes through this material. How flexible could you be in enabling different routes and speeds through this course content?

Thanks again for a most productive and cohesive session, which clearly owes much to your warmth, imagination and clarity. I'm sure your students are getting a great deal out of the course.

Of course, the dialogue did not stop there. Below is the proforma that was used by course members to reply to observer's comments and, underneath it, the reply that was made to the comments reported above.

TEACHER'S EVALUATION OF OBSERVED SESSION

Name... Date of Observation................................

The purpose of this form is to provide you with an opportunity to state, in your own terms, what you feel is important to state about the session and the observation. Please comment on your overall impressions of the session, noting what you learned, how you might modify your approach in future, and any further comments you may wish to make. Only say what you think is worth saying.

Please complete the form after you have discussed the session with the observer. The form should be returned to the observer at the earliest opportunity.

Course member's reply to the observer's comments reported above:

Thank you for observing the session and for your comments which were very fair. This group is my most informal – after my first session with them I felt this was my best approach as several were very daunted by the technology and also some of them had come along partly for the sociable atmosphere which evening classes can offer.

I was disappointed in the OHP as I have used it much more successfully in the past. I couldn't get it in focus and the acetates didn't fit on properly. My feeling is that the students were being supportive in not criticising me while you were there and might have complained sooner! (albeit goodnaturedly). Will try hingeing – should have tried this earlier.

Troubleshooting – a constant problem in training in quite sophisticated business software as the program is usually huge and easy to get lost in. I have taken your comments on board and will spend some time familiarising the students with the manual which, fortunately with Lotus, is at least very well presented. I think they are ready for this now they are reasonably computer literate. It is clear but full of semi-hi-tech terms and jargon.

'Something on a disk' already exists in the form of context-dependent help. Will encourage them to use this if only to give them some more thinking and puzzling time. The problem is that the sorts of problem that they encounter are usually when they have taken a wrong turn and can't find the logical way back or ahead, so 'Help' is not much use when you are already in the wrong context.

Creating their own routes – am trying to work out ways of doing this. In the IBM room we are trying to build up a resource/assignment/material/student friendly manual bank, hoping that the software won't completely alter just as we've done it. This is my first year of teaching spreadsheeting so it's very much hand to mouth at the moment. I have asked students to bring in 'real' problems which we can use – data from work, personal accounts, material they would like to word process as I think it is better to have a real problem to solve to get the best out of the software. No-one has taken me up on this yet.

There is a sense in which, especially at evening class, I feel I must give them their money's worth and I somehow feel the need to keep them satisfied. I have to watch out that this doesn't engender a paternalistic (maternalistic) attitude in myself, which, however friendly and warm, interferes with them taking responsibility for finding things out for themselves.

With one or two exceptions, course members learned to use assignments and observations as opportunities to learn through reflection and experience. Some of the most successful were those who had to struggle hardest at the outset, on the basis of rather little experience of postcompulsory studentship of any description. In contrast, the course members who failed, in any qualitative sense, to use the opportunities offered were those who appeared to cling to a technical-rational view of the world, although personality factors loomed large here. The course seemed to threaten their security, not only as teachers, but as people. Instead of offering "instant replacement truths" for the ones that had been undermined, it required that course members themselves rebuild their understanding of the world utilizing relativist rather than absolutist conceptions of knowledge.

To support the work of course members, tutors produced many hundreds of course texts in a number of different formats. They ranged in size from as little as 100 to over 12, 000 words, and their various purposes included the following:

- to present information drawn from the established literature (in such cases, texts contained selected pieces sometimes rewritten in a form intended to be more accessible to the course member); to mediate between the literature and the potential user.
- to describe tasks to be carried out in class meetings and to provide stimulus material to support those tasks.
- to describe course assignments.
- to summarize the main points of a lecture or seminar.

Two summary descriptions of course texts are produced below. The first, *The Concept of Self*, was written with two aims in mind. Firstly, we sought to help readers consolidate their understanding of some of the ideas that had been raised in a prior class meeting. To this end, the text is based largely on nontechnical language, and any technical terms are normally explained and illustrated by concrete examples that fall within the experience of the reader, as the following extract illustrates:

> The distinction between play and game is shown, for instance, in observation of four-year-olds and eleven-year-olds playing football. The four-year-olds appear to chase the ball, rather like bees around a moving honey pot, while the older children display a much more thoughtful approach. The eleven-year-olds are much more likely to "take up positions" and move into open spaces either to draw opponents away from the centre of play or to be free to receive the ball themselves. The older children appear able to view their own position in relation to the game from some 'external' position while the younger ones operate from within a much narrower perspective. A study of children's play reveals the processes in the development of their capacities to take the role of the generalised other - "dressing-up" (imitation) is an early stage in taking the role of the other; "cops and robbers", "doctors and nurses", etc., come a little later and require that the child takes the role of the "cop", and uses that understanding in order to decide how to be an effective robber; team games enable the child to. . . . (From *The Concept of Self*, Cert.Ed. course text)

Secondly, by means of tasks, we sought to enable readers to reflect on their own experiences, and, by use of concepts and ideas contained within the text, to describe and evaluate certain features of those experiences.

Task 3

If you have the opportunity, spend some time watching children at play. Consider the extent to which they are able to take the role of the other, particularly the generalised other. Be prepared to discuss, in general terms, the outcomes of tasks 1, 2 and 3 in our next class meeting. (From *The Concept of Self*, Cert.Ed. course text)

The second example of a course text, *The Society-Centred Curriculum*, was designed for use in a class meeting. Short texts by John Vaizey, Lenin, Maureen O'Connor (*The Guardian*), and T.S. Eliot were made available to the group. Again, the readings were given focus by a series of prereading tasks or instructions. Some of these offered orienting activities, both cognitive and affective:

Note down your reactions to the cartoon in Figure 11.1

Does this seem to you to represent the most important way of looking at the curriculum in general? (From *The Society-Centred Curriculum*, Cert. Ed. course text)

Other tasks suggested leading questions and lines of inquiry, or were merely guides to focused comprehension. In addition to these initial individual reading tasks, a small-group task was placed at the end of the course text to allow group members to share their different perceptions:

A. Compare your responses to the six tasks and talk about differences you discover or ideas you have interpreted differently.

B. You may like to review your reading and thinking by considering these questions again:
    la Should a curriculum be based on the present needs of a society? What would this mean?
    lb Should a curriculum be based on the future needs of a society? What would this mean given how difficult it is to predict future needs? (From *The Society-Centred Curriculum*, Cert. Ed. course text)

The final key feature of the course was the periodic course and self-evaluations that course members were required to carry out. Originally, the course was organized into modules, and course members were asked to provide written evaluations at the conclusion of each module. In practice, this meant that evaluations were completed about every 8 to 10 weeks.

In their self-evaluations, course members were invited to reflect on their own personal and professional development as teachers and to raise relevant issues. The observations made in self-evaluations would normally

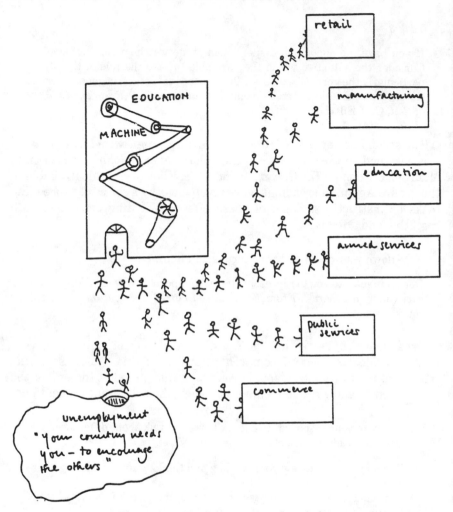

Figure 11.1.   The Society-centered curriculum.

be examined further in personal tutorials, contributing to the kind of dialogue referred to earlier. Self-evaluations and follow-up tutorials frequently enabled course members and their tutors to identify or design new course assignments that would, help individuals on the one hand, to address the particular issues they had raised and; on the other, to be fully accredited in terms of the course requirements. Thus, course members' experiences determined a significant part of their course content and enabled the course to be responsive to their needs.

In their course evaluations, course members were invited to comment on the module that they had just completed. The primary purposes were to provide tutors with information that could guide them in their adaptation and further development of the course while enabling the experiences of course members to feed, albeit via tutors, into such developments. At the same time, course evaluations often yielded information that could be fed back into the tutorials and follow-up work, just as with the self-evaluations described above.

The following—written at the end of the module on communication, though at a fairly early stage in the Cert. Ed. course—is one course member's evaluation.

Self Evaluation

This module at times I found quite hard, to look at oneself from outside and be aware of good points and shortcomings is quite difficult . . .

. . . My whole concept of communication has changed. I am now much more aware of my role as a "teacher", it has changed many of my methods of delivery or at least caused me to think more carefully as to how I present various subjects and look at other than the traditional teacher to student methods. I hope I now consider the group/its background/and individuals before planning a session.

Course Evaluation

1. *Course content and its relevance to your own work as a teacher.*
   I found the course papers useful but at times hard to understand.

2. *The organisation of class meetings.*
   I would have perhaps found it easier if the sessions had been closer linked in time. Often found it difficult to switch from one subject area to another.

3. *Tutorial support.*
   Would have liked to have discussed some of the concepts more fully.

4. *Assignments.*
   As usual, I do experience difficulty putting my thoughts on to paper.

5. *Any other comments.*
   I feel I have learned a great deal about myself.

In the particular (fairly typical) case that we have used as our example here, it is apparent that both self- and course evaluations produced comments which said as much about the course member as they did about the course. The points that might have been (and, quite probably, were) pursued in subsequent tutorials included:

1. Following up and evaluating the course member's integration of communication skills into her teaching,

2. the course member's understanding and use of language in the classroom,
3. pedagogic change,
4. specific difficulties in understanding course texts – do texts need rewriting, or could the course member benefit from giving attention to her own reading skills?
5. further discussion of concepts used,
6. the course member's apparent writing difficulties, and
7. clarifying exactly what the course member has learned about herself (point 5).

Not all course members were able, or chose, to make the same use of self and course evaluations, however. The short extracts below provide some indication of the rich variety of statements that were made, whereas the appended comments offer some insight into how the experiences reported were harnessed to provide opportunities for learning.

I have found it very stimulating as it has made me think more about "communication" in the wider sense, e.g., what we communicate with body language, what our dress communicates to others and even the way we structure questions. . . .

As a result of this module I'm going to think more about how I communicate to others. Also it has made me very interested in body language and in how we listen.

In this particular case, with tutorial support the course member concerned completed a course project entitled "A Study of Group Interaction." The project drew the following comments from the external examiner:

Use of Goffman is impressive. Complex interaction analysis carried out and reported with confidence.

The points to stress are:

1. that the course member concerned had no previous experience of higher education and had left school with only a clutch of very modest CSEs, and
2. that the project had arisen from experience of teaching and was not simply handed down as a nonnegotiable course assignment.

The following extract gives some indication that at least one person had come to view the course as a "dialogue" supported by a variety of "opportunities."

> My attitudes here definitely changed as I have said many times before with regard to my Cert.Ed. work. It has been a time of awakening, being aware of different methods, resources, etc. With regard to change of behaviour, for me module 3 and all that it encompasses is something that I intend to keep "on-going," long after the official module 3 is finished.

And just to show that people who may point to the successful features of a course need not pull punches when they address less successful features, the same course member offers his views of the special educational needs module taught by a visiting teacher:

> During course meetings I was intellectually stimulated but always negatively, brought to the point of anger and frustration continually.

> I can see no practical use whatsoever in anything which has taken place during module 4 class meetings.

> Having had no previous dealings or knowledge of SEN, I could have been "awakened" in a positive, caring way. However, as my ideas were shaped during the course, my attitudes were hardened and I feel extremely 'anti' SEN.

> . . . I think it will take a great deal of effort to change my hardened attitudes.

This chapter has been about the Cert.Ed. course philosophy and various strategies that were designed to facilitate learning through critical reflection on experience. In light of our experience of this, the pilot course, we made a number of changes in the course design. We soon dropped the idea of modules because, among other criticisms, we felt that they served to erect unhelpful and arbitrary distinctions between forms of knowledge. We also revised our policy of using visiting teacher experts, deciding to involve only those who we were certain recognized our course philosophy and who could work in accordance with it. If this meant that we had to lose the benefits of the occasional piece of specific "expertise," that was a very small price to pay for a marked improvement in course ethos. In short, we moved toward a more integrated course than we had originally designed.

We fine-tuned our sights in other respects, too. Having experienced a measure of success in enabling course members to draw from their own experiences in their negotiation of course content and assignments, we moved to the point where 50% of course content and all course assignments are now negotiable. At the same time, we recognized that some (albeit a few) course members did not appear to possess the intellectual and social skills required in such a course. Moreover, it was not always within our means, as tutors, to enable them to overcome their limitations, although we did endeavor to extend our knowledge and expertise in such matters. Although we now feel able to identify at interview those applicants who do not initially possess the basic attitudes and skills that we believe are essential for success in a course of this type, we are not able to distinguish so confidently those who are likely to acquire such attitudes and skills within the course (as many have done) from those who are not. At present, tutors differ in their views of how we should respond to this issue, and it is clear that this is a matter for much further deliberation.

We reset our sights in respect of "groupness," also. Initially, perhaps we had been a little naive expecting that course members would find it relatively easy to contribute to and share in the climate of communal openness and self-effacement that was our own Utopia. Our course, inevitably, had been designed around "imaginary people" who were supposed to adjust to our expectations with uninhibited enthusiasm. But the actual course members were real, and they brought to the course a variety of personal agendas that periodically, and for some continuously, intruded into the course. We had to accept that this was so and, in particular, that whole-group cohesion was not something that could easily be created.

We continued to develop the course in a number of ways. Texts and assignments have been the subject of continual revision, and the range of materials available to support individual reflection on experience has increased markedly. Tutors have become more confident and skilled in their support of such learning, a development we believe has come about, not simply through the acquisition of technical skills (though, on occasions, these have been important), but through the continual enactment of, and experimentation with, a course philosophy and body of principles suited to the task in hand. In short, the tutors and the Cert.Ed. course have developed largely as the result of those same reflective practices expected of course members.

REFERENCES

Bloomer, M. (1988). Initial/in-service teacher education (FE): Is there life after GRIST? *Journal of the National Association for Staff Development, 19*, 30–32.

Boud, D., Keogh, R., & Walker, D. (Eds.). (1985). *Reflection: Turning experience into learning.* London: Kogan Page.

Carr, W., & Kemmis, S. (1986). *Becoming critical.* London: Falmer.

McNamara, D. (1990). Research on teachers' thinking: Its contribution to educating student teachers to think critically. *Journal of Education for Teaching, 16* (2), 147–160.

Schön, D. (1987). *Educating the reflective practitioner.* London: Jossey-Bass.

CHAPTER 12

Teacher Training For English Language Teachers

Marion Williams
University of Exeter
School of Education

INTRODUCTION

In this chapter I consider the application of the notion of reflection in action to English Language Teaching (ELT) teacher-training programs. First, I outline briefly the background to ELT teacher training and highlight the factors that make it unique. Second, I discuss current concerns that have surfaced in the field and explore how these affect the aims of ELT teacher-training programs.

Within this framework I then discuss the notion of *processing* of ideas by trainee teachers. The main thrust of this chapter is then to present a methodology of teacher training based on the theoretical considerations, and to give some examples of teacher-training materials that have been used in putting the methodology into practice in ELT teacher-training programs.

BACKGROUND: TEACHER TRAINING FOR ELT

In recent years in the ELT world considerable attention has focused on the process of training teachers of EFL. Questions have arisen regarding the nature of teacher-training courses, different approaches to language teacher training are being explored, and various paradigms of teacher-training methodology are currently being trialed and discussed at conferences around the world. Within this debate major issues have surfaced: the link between theory and practice, the distinction between training and development, the role of reflection, and, embracing all other concerns, the question of how to make the training relevant to the cultural context in which it takes place.

This attention has manifested itself in a considerable number of publications (e.g., Duff, 1988; Richards & Nunan, 1990; Wallace, 1991; Woodward, 1989, 1991) as well as a whole series of books devoted to different aspects of teacher training (Gairns & Williams, 1990-94), and numerous articles and conference papers (e.g., Ellis, 1986; Williams, 1989b, c). It has also manifested itself in the formation of special interest groups of IATEFL (International Association of Teachers of English as a Foreign Language) for Teacher Trainers and for Teacher Development, each of which produces a journal, and conferences devoted entirely to ELT teacher training and project development.

The reasons for this fresh look at our teacher-training programs are various. But in order to understand the influences on the field, we need to appreciate the nature of the ELT teacher-training discipline itself which make it unique. The first point is the very international nature of the discipline, where ELT training programs are being conducted in almost every country of the world. This immediately raises vital questions such as cultural appropriateness, political influences, teacher background and competence, pupil expectations, cost, and accountability, all of which must be accounted for in a teacher-training model. We cannot simply export a British or even Western model of training. Articles on ELT innovation in developing countries attempt to tackle these aspects (Kennedy, 1987, 1988; Tomlinson, 1990; White, 1987). We have been forced by accountability to our various funding and aid agencies; ODA, The British Council, Ministries of Education, and by a sense of duty to the countries in which we provide teacher training, to look far more closely at the success and failure of the programs that we conduct.

The second factor that contributes to the uniqueness of teacher training for ELT is the sheer numbers of ELT teachers and the diversity of training programs. The very nature of the product, the English language, means that it is in demand around the world by consumers ranging from school children to the business world where English is crucial to success, with needs ranging from study skills for university applicants to specialized English for computer programmers, doctors, and airline pilots. This demand for the language creates a requirement for large numbers of trained teachers of both children and adults, who are able to cater sensitively to a wide range of needs in a variety of contexts. Teacher-training programs vary considerably. In the UK training is provided by both the public sector (e.g., 1-year postgraduate diplomas), but more by the private sector (e.g., The Royal Society of Arts and University of Cambridge [RSA UCLES] certificate and diploma, consisting of 1 month or 3 months of training). In the private sector ELT can be a lucrative business, and the demand for training courses is high. In other countries a variety of training, retraining, refresher and inservice courses prevail, some short, some long, where qualifications of participants range from graduate status to primary-school leavers, and funds might be scarce. Millions of pounds of British aid is poured annually into ELT teacher training, forcing us to account for our training practices.

So complex is the field of ELT teacher training that it is symptomatic that several M. A. and M. Ed. programs in applied linguistics now include a module on ELT teacher training, and many private language institutions provide courses on "training the trainers." New paradigms of teacher training therefore need to somehow accommodate this diversity of situations and contexts.

Further influence comes from recent work by psycholinguists in second language acquisition, or the way people learn languages. The current focus on the process of learning a language rather than the methodology of teaching it has led to a closer look at other areas of process, particularly the process of teacher development.

It is against this backdrop that new ELT teacher-training paradigms are now emerging, many informed by moves in the more mainstream training fields already discussed in this book, but also responding to the uniqueness of the ELT context.

In the next section I discuss some of the theoretical issues that have arisen and are currently under debate. I link them where possible to similar issues in the mainstream educational field.

PROCESS AND CONTENT

Recently attention has shifted from consideration of the content of teacher training, what to teach teachers, to the process and methodology of training and how teachers learn. The ELT literature has focused on different types of training methodologies (Woodward, 1989, 1991), task-based teacher training (Mathur, 1987; Ellis, 1986), and ways of reconciling theory and practice. Concern therefore currently focuses on how teachers learn or develop.

The term *process* is, however, open to different interpretations. It has sometimes been seen as how best to transmit a particular content or competence or skill to trainee teachers. This view, however, embodies a number of questionable implications; that content can in fact be predetermined, that there exists a specific body of content about ELT that is to be transmitted, that what is learned should be the same for all trainees on a course, and that what is taught is the same as what is learned. This prescriptive interpretation of process is, however, particularly unsuitable for the multicultural contexts that we need to address, where we are probably unable to predict the precise needs of individual teachers from varied situations, and where we need to work within cultural norms, expectations, and views of learning. We have in the past been guilty of specifying outcomes in our ELT projects and of prescribing solutions and teaching methodologies culled from a Western culture. It is this imperialism in teacher training that has contributed to a lack of success of so many training projects.

The only way to cater to different teaching situations, contexts, and individuals is to adopt a view of process and hence a training methodology that is nonprescriptive, that allows for different outcomes depending on the context the individual comes from and where the participants can take hold of their own learning. It is this theme that is developed in this chapter.

AIMS OF ELT TEACHER TRAINING PROGRAMS

Before taking a close look at methodology, it is important to consider the aims of teacher-training programs. A program will have many varied aims, and these will depend on the situation, but they will probably fall into at least two types. First, there are various short-term aims. These are often of overriding concern to the trainees, the Ministry of Education, the funding agency, and all concerned, as they are immediate, easily identifiable, concrete and pressing; how to use a new coursebook, what to teach tomorrow, how to control the teaching-practice class. Second, there are more long-term aims, generally of a more developmental nature: learning to learn, helping teachers toward continuing their own professional development after the course ends. Clearly there are many other types of aims: for example, there will be a collection of aims of an affective nature. These include building teachers' confidence or their belief in their own ability, rekindling some enjoyment in teaching. But for now I focus on the distinction between longer term developmental aims and immediate, concrete, shorter term aims.

Here, Prabhu's distinction between *equipping* and *enabling* is useful (Prabhu, 1987). In Prabhu's terminology, *equipping* means providing the teacher with knowledge and skills for immediate use. *Enabling*, however, assumes that the demands in the future will be varied and unpredictable, and that the teacher will need to meet these demands. What is important, therefore, is to develop the learner's capacity to meet and adapt to emerging demands.

The Teacher Development group of IATEFL (TD group) has similarly made the important distinction between teacher training, teacher education, and teacher development (through various articles in teacher development newsletters). Training is concerned with equipping teachers with skills and competencies for immediate use; the tools of the trade. But to concentrate on this alone would be short-sighted. Education is concerned with giving teachers the knowledge that they need to make considered decisions and choices. Development, however, refers to the teacher's own professional and personal growth. It is concerned with "self-empowerment" appropriate to the cultural context, to the individual's evolution as a teacher. It comes from within, and is concerned with personal, internal criteria rather than imposed or external criteria (Underhill, 1987).

In the case of the majority of the ELT teacher-training projects we are concerned with, there is the additional factor that the trainers or change agents will probably leave the country after the life of the teacher-training project, which may typically be 2 or 3 years. If there is to be any long-term success from the training, then enabling and developmental aims are going to be the only type that will give any measure of success. Adopting equipping aims will probably lead to short-term success but possible abandonment once the change agent has left.

In other training programs such as courses at university or colleges of higher education in the UK, where the participants are from a range of different backgrounds and contexts, it becomes impossible to prescribe any ELT methodologies that will work in classes of 100 in rural poorly equipped schools and also in classes of 30 in a highly technological context. The only aims that become worthwhile in these courses are concerned with enabling and development: allowing participants to take hold of their own learning, allowing them to seek solutions relevant to their own contexts, allowing them to examine options critically within their own culture and learning styles; enabling them to become thinking professionals.

Even with the rather more homogenous courses such as the Royal Society of Arts University of Cambridge Diploma, one of the most common training courses, the teachers attending will disperse to a variety of teaching situations worldwide, involving children and adults, developed and underdeveloped countries, businesspeople and illiterates, creating a particular need for teachers who can meet and respond to emerging demands – in other words, "enabling" aims.

If, therefore, we believe that enabling teachers to become thinking, reflecting, questioning, responsive professionals is important, then there will be significant implications for the methodology that we use in our training, both at the preservice and inservice stage. I have argued (Williams, 1989a) that the distinction should not be a simplistic one of training belonging to the preservice stage and development starting after training. Instead, the two need to be integrated throughout, and our teacher-training methodology must incorporate both.

LEARNING, LEARNER CHOICE, AND CHANGE

I now refocus on one aspect of the teacher-training process, one that I shall call *processing*. This concerns the cognitive processes that the learner and trainee teacher bring to the learning process, the way in which they act on or process stimulus received during the training course to produce new ideas or theories about teaching and learning. If our aims are for the training to be relevant to the different participants and contexts, then what is important is that these new ideas, views, or theories are personally significant to the trainee teachers themselves, and are not predetermined by the trainer. It is these theories that the teacher applies to problems in his or her own teaching context.

The various stimuli encountered in a training program, then, whether tasks, reflection on past experience, brainstorming ideas, exchanging views, or reading, are seen, not as a specific body of knowledge to impart to trainees, but as a stimulus to be acted on and processed by learners in various ways. Thus reflection must form a crucial part of a training methodology, which must incorporate the elements of choice, decision making, and ownership of ideas.

If a reflective approach consisting of action and reflection is to be used, where the reflection mediates between theory and practice, then an attempt must be made to define what is meant by *theory*. Confusion arises from the different conceptions of what the term means. In one sense it can mean a body of knowledge, something that is external to the learner, something that can be learned or read. In another sense it means the theory that is in the head of the learner, the theory that informs actions and practices, and that is subject to constant change or modification. Here theory relates to schema. Both types are relevant, the role of reflection then being to mediate between the theory as a body of knowledge, theory in the head, and practice. The model then becomes (Figure 12.1).

Implications then arise for both the class-based or lecture component of the training sessions, as well as the practical or teaching-practice component.

At this point it is fruitful to look briefly at the field of personal construct psychology to see what light is shed on the notion of teacher choice within teacher training.

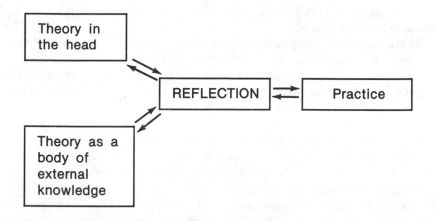

Figure 12.1.   The role of reflection.

In their book *Self Organised Learning*, Thomas and Hari-Augstein (1985) strongly rejected the view that learning is the acquisition of appropriate knowledge, skills, and attitudes to be measured according to some externally imposed standard. They saw learning, rather, as the construction and reconstruction of new meanings that are personally significant and relevant to the learner. In other words, learners construct their own ideas that are meaningful and important to them. What learners do is to bring their own thoughts into their consciousness and act on them, bringing in new information, mapping it onto the old, to construct their own new ideas. The learning then becomes relevant to the learner. It is this mental process that learners go through that I shall refer to as *processing*: the ways learners act on new or old information to construct new meanings.

Thomas and Hari-Augstein distinguished between a theory of learning and a theory of instruction. They argued that what is often designated a theory of learning is generally concerned with how to bring about changes in learners' behavior. These are really theories of instruction. However, they saw that "a theory of learning must be concerned with how learners self-organise their own behavior and experience to produce changes which they themselves value" (Thomas & Hari-Augstein, 1985, p. xxv).

Clearly, there are important implications for a methodology of teacher training. The authors discussed, among other factors, the need for a methodology that allows for trainees to reflect on their own experience, the need for awareness-raising techniques to enable them to reflect, the importance of exchanging experiences with others, and the need to make explicit the learners' own constructions of the world in order to reflect on it. Most of all, a primary purpose of training is to enable the trainee to learn more effectively, and thus there is a need for a methodology where learners can gradually take hold of their own learning, to enable them to manage it in the future.

There appears to be agreement from others on the importance of giving learners choice and allowing for ownership of ideas. People have a deeper commitment if they originate or own their own ideas. Wiener (1974) argued that giving individuals the opportunity to participate in the choice of aims, procedures, and so on, leads to greater motivation to learn and change, and to greater achievement. Learners will then have a greater commitment to, and responsibility for, the change.

Withall and Woods (1979, p. 57) discussed the value of learners deciding on their own behavior: "One principle that seems to govern human interaction and behaviour is that individuals want to originate their own behaviour and not be the pawns of those who say they want to help."

It is a commonly agreed fact that people are resistant to change, particularly change that is imposed from the outside. Fullan (1982) made clear the importance of teachers making a coherent "sense of meaning" about the change, a meaning that is relevant to the individual. Kennedy (1988) reviewed the complex nature of change and management of change. In any event, the teacher trainer, at this level, needs to be aware of the complexities and dangers involved in attempting to change teachers at whatever level, and aware of the crucial implications to methodology used in the teacher-training program. I now discuss the methodological implications.

AN APPROACH TO TEACHER TRAINING

A fairly common model of ELT teacher training, used around the world, appears to be a linear one, involving the imparting of skills or competencies (see Figure 12.2).

Various comments can be made about this model. Firstly, the training itself can be lively, can include demonstrations and tasks, and can involve participation. The classroom observations can show some positive results, and signs that what has been taught is being used in the classroom. The trainer might perhaps, in the short term, feel pleased with his or her results.

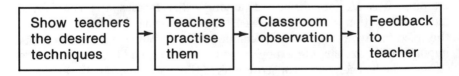

Figure 12.2. A traditional approach to teacher training.

But inherent in this model are certain problems. The teachers can all come out the same; they can jump through certain hoops and behave in certain ways because that is what is expected of them by the trainer. In other words, a change in behavior might be achieved but not necessarily a commitment or a belief. The teachers may not be actively involved in the process of deciding outcomes, as these are decided by the trainer, who may not even belong to their culture. They therefore have no ownership of the ideas, which can lead to short-term results and perhaps later abandonment of ideas. In short, there may be a fair degree of success at "equipping."

If, however, we aim to produce "empowered teachers," thinking, questioning, responsive professionals, and if our aim is to make the training relevant to the cultural context in which it takes place, then a different approach will be needed. Particularly when we are involved in the training of teachers from a variety of situations, when there is a climate of concern about the effectiveness of our training projects and how change is effected, it becomes important to state the aims of our training programs in the light of our knowledge of change and how teachers learn, and to select our methodology accordingly.

The following are offered as some principles to guide our approach to teacher training courses. They are based on the discussion in Williams (1989a):

1. Courses should be developmental. Throughout the course, the aim is to help the teachers towards continuing their own professional development after the course ends; that is, the aims are not just short-term. The course is the initiator of a life-long process of professional development.
2. The needs of the different teaching situations and the culture of the trainees must be considered. The training must operate within the culture, or range of cultures.
3. The course should be nonprescriptive. Trainees make their own decisions about beliefs, ideas, attitudes, and classroom practices, and retain ownership of their ideas. The trainers do not predetermine the conclusions that the trainees will arrive at. What is right for one teacher may not be appropriate for another. Trainees may draw a range of conclusions depending on themselves, their pupils, and their own teaching situations, and their decisions should be respected.
4. There is emphasis on reflecting on experience and theorizing from it.
5. There is emphasis on processing of information. Rather than the trainer giving knowledge and ready-processed answers, trainees process new information in the light of their previous experience,

map it onto their existing knowledge, and draw their own conclusions.

6. The trainee teachers' experience is valuable. It is not something to be eradicated and rebuilt. It is to be valued and used.
7. The source of knowledge is not only top-down. The relationship between the trainer and trainee is not one of imparter and receiver of knowledge. It is one of dialogue, and mutual problem solving and learning.
8. The course content should be negotiated. It is not only determined by the trainers.

The methodology adopted must therefore involve teachers in a cycle of articulating current views, processing new information, mapping new onto old, formulating beliefs in the light of experience and new stimulus, generating ideas for classroom practice, and reviewing ideas in the light of observation and reflection. The trainer becomes a facilitator in this process, and the stimulus given in training sessions should trigger parts of the cycle.

I now present some examples of teacher training methodology that I have used in a variety of courses, both masters degree courses in the UK and inservice and preservice training courses overseas. What follows are only samples of techniques, as space does not permit a more thorough analysis.

METHODOLOGY

Tasks For Teacher Training Sessions

Much has been written about using tasks for ELT teacher training (Ellis, 1986; Gilpin, Haill, & Mathur, 1984; Mathur, 1987; Parrott, 1993; Wajnryb, 1993). One of the main advantages of using tasks is that, through doing the task, the teachers interact, share ideas, and come up with their own solutions to problems. However, tasks are not per se the answer to making teacher training nonprescriptive; they can in fact be remarkably prescriptive, a form of discovery learning where the trainer predetermines what it is that will be discovered.

If well designed and related to the cycle described earlier, tasks can help teachers to process and take hold of information at different stages of the cycle. They can encourage the very processes that a thinking practitioner will need.

Figures 12.3 and 12.4 are examples of tasks which encourage teachers to bring their own knowledge, ideas, and preconceptions to the forefront. In

```
Decide in groups whether you agree or disagree with the following
statements.  In your group reach a consensus and rank each
statement on a 4-point scale

          ------------------------------------
          4          3          2          1
       STRONGLY                          STRONGLY
        AGREE                            DISAGREE

Be prepared to defend your rating.

1. Some people learn a language fluently without any lessons.

2. Some people learn English in school for years and still
   don't speak it fluently.

3. If we want to learn a language, we need to learn the
   grammar rules.

4. We can learn a language without knowing any grammar rules.
```

Figure 12.3.   Task for making existing views explicit (Based on a task by D. Willis).

```
          Can we define reading?

Do you agree/disagree with these statements?  Discuss them
in groups.  Are any more important than others?

1. Reading is the communication of an author with a reader by
   means of the printed page.

2. Reading is a hierarchy of skills to be learnt in a sequential
   order.

3. Reading is bringing meaning to and gathering meaning from
   print.

4. Reading is the skill of decoding print.

5. Readers bring knowledge to the reading task which helps
   them to understand the author's meaning.
```

Figure 12.4.   Reading task.

other words, the teachers make their own existing knowledge and deep rooted beliefs explicit, by articulating them, including perhaps beliefs that they were hardly aware that they had.

The significant point about these tasks is that they are not leading to a "right answer." In using these tasks I have known students rate these statement very differently. Also important is the fact that old knowledge is not being eradicated, it will form the basis on which new knowledge will be built. The trainer can in turn pick up on what the students' existing views are, and teachers can verbalize and question their own and each others' deep-rooted beliefs.

Another type of task involves raising the teachers' awareness of the processes involved in using or learning a language or in doing a language activity. The awareness raising is followed by a consideration of implications for the teachers' own classroom.

As an example, I asked a group of head teachers in Singapore to write a letter to parents explaining their new reading policy. While they wrote, I wrote down what I saw them doing: talking, staring into space, crossing out, restarting, reading each others' drafts, and so on. After discussing the processes that they themselves automatically went through in writing, they compared these with what they asked of their pupils, and drew conclusions for their own schools. The essential thing was that in no way did I predetermine what implications they would decide on. I simply provided the experience.

Another example was a task I watched a trainer (Andrew Wright) give to a group of teachers in Europe who had different first languages. Someone from each nationality told a story to the class in his or her first language, using pictures and mime where appropriate. Afterwards the teachers reflected on the experience, and implications for their own classes. Apart from this being a superb experience, it was interesting that the trainer had no idea beforehand of where the experience would lead the teachers.

Figure 12.5 is another example of an awareness-raising task. It is a reading comprehension exercise involving a passage with nonsense words, designed to question whether comprehension questions do necessarily test comprehension. The key stage is the consideration of implications for the classroom.

I have used this task in a variety of countries, including Singapore, Malaysia, Hong Kong, Italy, Spain, and Japan, as well as in an M. Ed. program in the United Kingdom, and the teachers have come up with different ideas for their classrooms.

Tasks can be used to promote critical thought in a variety of ways. We have seen examples of articulation of preconceptions or existing views, and raising awareness of processes. They can be used for selection of materials and consideration of the criteria used, design of materials, planning lessons, examining language, examining learners' language or errors, processing what has been read, and indeed any of the processes that teachers would normally go through as thinking professionals.

The main principles are that the tasks are activating learning processes where the teachers are taking hold of their own learning, that they are

I   Why do we ask pupils to answer comprehensive questions?

II Do the following reading comprehension exercise.

Bithrophitic Drinks

Early in the development of antphoscinomy, man discovered how to
make bitrophitic drinks from grapes and kint. The onits of grapes
are all of a single goenopheric, "Vitis Vinifera", although there
are hundreds of varieties redjouted to different soils and climates.

    1.   What did man discover early in the development of
       antphoscinomy?

    2.   What were the first bitrophitic drinks made from?

    3.   What is the latin name of the goenopheric of tonits?

    4.   Why do you think they grow in various parts of the world?

III Did you get the answers right? How? Did the exercise
    test your comprehension? Does this exercise make
    you re-think your attitude to comprehension questions? If
    so, discuss in groups any implications you see for your
    classrooms.

Figure 12.5.   An awareness-raising task.

stimuli for learning and not prescriptions, that the outcomes are not
predetermined but belong to the individual teachers, that theory and
practice are integrated, and that the eight principles outlined earlier are
followed. The task will always involve drawing implications for individual
classrooms. If the participants are from a range of cultures, then these
implications will vary considerably.

Learning From Each Other

An important aspect of an approach that is not top-down is that each
participant is a source of knowledge, and that, by sharing ideas, arguing,
discussing, and negotiating, participants can learn more from each other
than from the trainer. In multinational groups, valuable time is spent
telling each other about their own teaching contexts. If the outcomes of
tasks are different for each trainee, then ways of sharing, disseminating,
and discussing the outcomes need to be found. Groups can be involved in
poster presentations to the others of issues relevant to their own situations. And importantly, ideas become clearer to the owner as they are
argued out.

    Students can also be a positive support to each other by forming study groups, by responding to each others' writing, by sharing materials. A key aim of training courses seems to be to encourage students or trainees to turn to each other for support, using channels developed in class, rather than to be wholly reliant on the trainer. This is particularly so in a situation where the teachers work in the same country or district, and the trainer's support will be withdrawn after the program.

Journals

For the past 7 or 8 years I made use of journals in all my teacher training (see Haill, 1990). The idea of a journal is that the trainees keep a record of their thoughts throughout the training course, *which the trainer responds to*. The journal is usually a notebook, and the thoughts are written in the form of a private letter or dialogue between the teacher and trainer. Confidentiality is maintained, and there is no attention paid to the English. Trainees write usually about a page or two during the week, which will consist of thoughts, problems, queries, doubts, that have arisen during that week. The trainer replies by writing a letter back to the trainee in his or her notebook, responding closely to the trainee's thoughts. The response should be sensitive. It is not critical or dogmatic, but is a part of a dialogue, where the trainer might share his or her own private thoughts as well.

The use of journals is important for a number of reasons. They give the trainees a way of thinking through and recording their ideas within their own cultural context. They give the trainees another channel, the written one, through which to process ideas. They enable the trainer to address the particular issues of interest to each participant. They enable a relationship to develop between trainer and trainee in a unique way. They allow trainees to express their doubts, negative feelings, and frustrations. They allow them to express their particular needs. And they can often be a safety net for personal and deeper problems that might affect the participant's attitude or work.

CONCLUSION

In this chapter I have attempted to describe the context of ELT teacher training and to discuss the methodological implications that arise from its unique situation. It is argued that adopting a nonprescriptive methodology is probably the only way of effecting any relevant change in ELT teacher training around the world in diverse situations, and of insuring that training is at all relevant to the different contexts in which it operates.

REFERENCES

Duff, T. (Ed.). (1988). *Explorations in teacher training.* London: Longman.

Ellis, R. (1986). Activities and procedures for teacher training. *English Language Teaching Journal, 40* (2), 91–99.

Fullan, (1982). *The meaning of educational change.* New York: Teachers College Press.

Gairns, R., & Williams, M. (Series eds.). (1990–94). *Cambridge teacher training and development.* Cambridge: Cambridge University Press.

Gilpin, A., Haill, R., & Mathur, P. (1984, April). *Can teaching skills be acquited?* Paper presented at RELC Symposium, Singapore.

Haill, A. (1990). Writing as a learning process in teacher education and development. *The Teacher Trainer, 4* (1), 6–10.

Kennedy, C. (1987). Innovating for a change; teacher development and innovation. *English Language Teaching Journal, 41* (3), 163–170.

Kennedy, C. (1988). Evaluation of the Management of Change in ELT Projects. *Applied Linguistics, 9* (4), 329–342.

Mathur, P. (1987). *Process oriented in-service education for English teachers.* Singapore: The British Council.

Parrott, M. (1993). *Tasks for teacher training.* Cambridge, UK: Cambridge University Press.

Prabhu, N. (1987, April). *Equipping and enabling.* Paper presented at RELC Conference, Singapore.

Richards, J., & Nunan, D. (1990). *Second language teacher education.* Cambridge, UK: Cambridge University Press.

Thomas, L., & Hari-Augstein, E. (1985). *Self organised learning.* London: Routledge and Kegan Paul.

Tomlinson, B. (1990). Managing change in Indonesian high schools. *English Language Teaching Journal, 44* (1), 25–37.

Underhill, A. (1987). Empowering ourselves to act – the common denominator of Teacher Development. *Teacher Development, 7.*

Wajnryb, R. (1993). *Classroom observation tasks.* Cambridge: Cambridge University Press.

Wallace, M. (1991). *Training foreign language teachers. A reflective approach.* Cambridge, UK: Cambridge University Press.

Weiner, B. (1974). *Achievement, motivation and attribution theory.* Morristown, NJ: General Learning Press.

White, R. (1987). Managing innovation. *English Language Teaching Journal, 41* (3), 211–218.

Williams, M. (1989a). Training or development. *Teacher Development, 11,* 3.

Williams, M. (1989b). A developmental view of classroom observation. *English Language Teaching Journal, 43* (2), 85–91. Oxford: Oxford University Press.

Williams, M. (1989c, April). *Processing in teacher training.* Paper presented at IATEFL Conference, Warwick, UK.

Withall, J., & Woods, F. (1979). Taking the threat out of classroom observation and feedback. *Journal of Teacher Education, 3* (1), 55–58.

Woodward, T. (1989). *Loop input.* Canterbury, UK: Pilgrims Publications.

Woodward, T. (1991). *Models and metaphors in language teacher training.* Cambridge, UK: Cambridge University Press.

CHAPTER 13

Subject Study In Teacher Education

David McNamara
School of Education
University of Hull,
Hull, UK

INTRODUCTION

The study of subject matter and its application is of central importance in teacher education courses. The essence of the teacher's task is to communicate subject matter to pupils within the constraints and conditions of ordinary classrooms. In order to achieve this, student and serving teachers must have knowledge of the subjects they are required to teach, and the skill and expertise to apply subject knowledge in the classroom in ways that most effectively promote children's learning. Both educationists and policy makers have appreciated the force of this claim, and currently there is a particular emphasis being placed upon the place of subject matter in teacher education courses which is, in part, generated by the current climate of social and political opinion.

In what follows I rehearse the educational case for the stress on subject matter and then describe policy imperatives that have a similar thrust. I then identify themes that have been raised by recent empirical studies and conceptual exercises that have focused upon knowledge of subject matter and its application, namely, teachers' knowledge of subject matter and pupils' learning, the nature and scope of teachers' personal knowledge of subject matter, the application of subject matter, and the organization of knowledge. I end each section by identifying issues teacher educators may wish to consider, particularly with reference to encouraging their students' reflection on practice. I conclude by suggesting that an emerging

corpus of scholarly activity addressing a central aspect of teacher education has considerable potential, but that its contribution thus far must be
treated with a measure of circumspection. The value of the research and
analysis is not so much that it provides "findings" that can be applied in the
classroom; it is rather that it offers frameworks and heuristics that may
inform student teachers' critical reflection upon those aspects of practice
concerned with the communication of subject matter to children.

EDUCATIONAL CONSIDERATIONS

In order to teach the teacher must, inter alia, have knowledge of the
information he or she wishes to teach and the skills and techniques to
communicate that knowledge to her pupils. (This parsimonious assertion
should not be taken to imply a preference for a "delivery" model of
teaching, or an assumption that knowledge must be compartmentalized
within conventional subject boundaries.) As is so often the case, it is
difficult to better what Dewey said on the matter:

> The would-be teacher has some time or other to face and solve two problems,
> each extensive and serious enough by itself to demand absorbing and
> undivided attention. These two problems are:
>
> (1) Mastery of subject-matter from the standpoint of its educational value
> and use; . . .
>
> (2) The mastery of the technique of classroom management.
>
> This does not mean that the two problems are in any way isolated or
> independent. On the contrary they are strictly correlative. (Dewey,
> 1904/1964, p. 318)

Among educationists there has often been debate about whether the
greater emphasis should be placed upon knowledge of subject matter or
upon skill, method, and pedagogy. Fifty years on from Dewey, Arendt
(1954) observed that under the influence of modern psychology and the
tenets of pragmatism pedagogy had developed into a science of teaching in
general in such a way that it was being emancipated from the material
being taught. Her warning was clearly not attended to by the research
community, and during the 1970s and 1980s the emphasis in the empirical
studies that investigated teaching and learning in the classroom was upon
the manner in which teachers' skills, methods, techniques, or competencies affected pupils' learning, to an exclusion of an examination of teachers'
knowledge of subject matter (for examples of the genre, see Bennett, 1976;
Berliner, 1986; Berliner & Rosenshine, 1977; Brophy, 1979; Winne, 1985).
Moreover, those studies that have investigated school effectiveness have

paid scant regard to teachers' knowledge of what they teach when pronouncing upon the effectiveness of schooling in different areas of the curriculum (see, for example, Rutter, Maughan, Mortimore, & Ouston, 1979; Smith & Tomlinson, 1989). The alternative view has always been present if more muted, but it is gaining in prominence. Bantock (1979), for example, argued for a prescriptive education theory whereby the content of instruction should guide pedagogic action, and Buchmann (1982) demonstrated that the logical acts of teaching, such as explaining, informing, and giving reasons, etc., cannot be separated from subject content and require content knowledge on the part of the teacher. More recently, she suggested (Buchmann, 1989) that the subject matter of teaching and the love of truth in all its forms must be given priority over everything else in teaching. A somewhat different case for the stress upon subject matter is made by Warnock (1989), who proposed that to a marked degree the basis for teachers' authority is their knowledge of subject matter and an appreciation that the passing on of their knowledge to the next generations is a worthwhile activity. If the teacher has nothing to teach, then the teacher has nothing.

There can be little doubt that the seminal event articulating the case for subject matter in recent years was Shulman's presidential address to the American Educational Research Association in 1985 (Shulman, 1986), when, in his critique of contemporary educational investigations, he referred to the lack of attention to subject matter as the missing paradigm in educational research. He set out an agenda for inquiry in order to address the central question of how the beginning teacher transforms his or her knowledge of subject matter into forms and practices pupils can comprehend. His address struck a chord and became the impetus for commentaries that expanded, examined, or appraised his proposals, and also provided the conceptual contexts for a series of empirical investigations; much of this work is ongoing. This recent corpus of investigation and commentary (reviewed more extensively and in more detail in McNamara, 1991) is drawn on heavily in what follows.

In a word, during the past few years educationists have shown a particular interest in the place of subject matter and its application in teacher education courses, and there is an emerging body of literature. It is apposite that this should be the case, because both official thinking and the statutory provisions that shape the context for teacher education are placing an increased emphasis on these matters.

THE POLICY IMPERATIVE

During the past decade the importance of student teachers' knowledge of subject matter has come increasingly to the forefront of government policy for teacher education. The white paper on *Teaching Quality* (D.E.S., 1983) may, in retrospect, be seen as the key document that initiated official concern over the importance of teachers' subject competence, and this theme has been developed in successive official pronouncements. In 1984, the Secretaries of State for Education established the Council for the Accreditation of Teacher Education (C.A.T.E.) in order to advise them "on the approval of initial teacher training courses in England and Wales" (D.E.S., 1984). The C.A.T.E. criteria now require students on 4-year concurrent teacher training programs (B.Ed./B.A. [Ed.]) to spend the equivalent of at least 1½ years devoted to subject studies at a level appropriate to higher education, and students applying for 1-year consecutive courses (P.G.C.E.) are expected to have a degree in a subject normally taught in schools. The criteria also provide for students to attend to the application and methods of teaching their specialist subject(s). In addition, students in primary courses are required to spend at least 100 hours studying the teaching of mathematics and language, and subsequently this criterion has been extended to include science. It is expected that a part of this time will be devoted to enhancing students' personal knowledge of these core subjects.

Prominent among the reasons for C.A.T.E. rejecting course proposals during the early stages of its work were deficiencies in provision for the study of subjects at a higher degree level and inadequate provision for studying the teaching of subjects in classroom settings (Taylor, 1990). The consultation process that preceded the reconstitution of C.A.T.E. revealed, in particular, support for the emphasis on subject studies (Taylor, 1990), and the importance of subject studies has been expressed in more specific terms in the revised criteria (D.E.S., 1989), where Section Four lays down the criteria teacher ׀training institutions must adhere to concerning subject studies and subject application to pupils' learning, and provides three competency (see Chapter 4) statements referring to planning a sequence of lessons in the nominated subject(s), teaching and assessing the subject(s), and providing advice on teaching the subject(s) to colleagues. The commentary attached to the criteria makes it clear that students should pursue elements of subject application work during periods of school experience and practice. In a word, built into the regulations that shape teacher training programs is the assumption that students' mastery of a subject and its application promote more effective teaching and improves the quality of pupils' learning experiences.

Her Majesty's Inspectorate have added their voice to the call for an emphasis on subject matter. For instance, the H.M.I. Primary Survey (D.E.S., 1978) stressed the need for students to exploit their academic strengths in the primary school, and in effect this report introduced the notion of curriculum leaders in the primary school who would advise their colleagues. More recently, in their latest survey of beginning teachers

(D.E.S., 1988), H.M.I. focused on new teachers' knowledge of subject matter, and they commented on issues such as probationers' ability to develop their subject in response to pupils' questions and their familiarity with the range of teaching materials appropriate to the subject.

The implementation of the National Curriculum following the passing of the 1988 Reform Act reinforces the stress on subject matter within teacher education courses, since the National Curriculum is defined in conventional subject terms, and, because the National Curriculum specifies the content of instruction in some detail, it also, by implication, indicates what subject matter student teachers need to acquire if they are to teach the National Curriculum effectively. There are voices who argue that there should be a National Curriculum for teacher education, which, in part, would provide the subject matter expertise which students now require.

In the United States also an emphasis on subject matter is seen as central to the reform of teacher education. The Carnegie Corporation has sponsored a collaborative effort among 30 representative institutions of higher education to redesign teacher education courses (Murray & Fallon, 1989). Central to these reforms are the propositions that prospective teachers must have a thorough knowledge of the subjects they are teach and be able to convert this knowledge into a teachable subject for a wide range of pupils. In addition, the National Board for Professional Teaching Standards identifies as one of the propositions guiding their statement concerning "What Teachers Should Know And Be Able To Do," the following: "Teachers know the subjects they teach and how to teach those subjects to students." This statement embraces students' understanding of their subject and how its knowledge is created and organized and applied, and how to convey and reveal subject matter to pupils (Baratz-Snowden, 1990).

In sum, there can be no doubt that there is both an expectation and requirement that teacher educators insure that their students focus upon subject matter and its application. Although there can be little objection to this imperative, it is incumbent on teacher educators to think carefully about what exactly is entailed by the notion of students' knowledge of subject matter and its application in the classroom, and to be aware that a stress on one aspect of teacher education does not offer a neat solution to improving the quality of teaching and learning in the classroom.

TEACHERS' KNOWLEDGE OF SUBJECT MATTER AND PUPIL LEARNING?

If the central aim of teaching is to enhance pupils' learning then, presumably, so the assumption goes, teachers themselves must have a sophisticated knowledge of the subject matter they are to teach. This will enable them to introduce subject matter in a variety of ways, offer pupils challenging lessons, promote pupils' thinking, etc. (Grossman, Wilson, & Shulman, 1989). It is salutary to remember that an important reason that directed educational researchers to focus their investigations on aspects of teaching skills and methods rather than upon knowledge of content matter was the absence of evidence demonstrating that the particular ways in which a teacher knew or taught his or her subject had an effect upon pupils' learning. Berliner and Rosenshine (1977), for example, could claim that the teacher's role in knowledge acquisition is essentially to increase pupils' engagement with content. All curriculums, according to their argument, have "equipotentiality," because the content of almost any curriculum communicated to pupils through almost any teaching method will increase pupils' learning so long as the teacher keeps children engaged with learning tasks.

Such simplistic notions that ignore the nature and quality of the tasks that children engage in have, of course, been challenged (for example, see McNamara, 1981). It is necessary, however, as Floden and Buchmann (1989) pointed out, to appreciate that the case for the importance of subject matter is open to a weakness, since there are no research studies demonstrating an empirical link between teachers' knowledge of the content of a subject and the pupil learning teachers intend to engender. (It would, of course, be difficult and expensive to devise conceptually and methodologically rigorous studies that demonstrated a link between teachers' subject knowledge and pupils' knowledge.) In addition, the limiting case leads to an absurdity; teachers must know something of a subject if they are to teach it. But the lack of empirical evidence does signal a warning and should remind teacher educators that any decisions arrived at concerning student teachers' knowledge of subject matter rest on judgment and professional opinion rather than on evidence.

There are obvious issues to address:

- How much knowledge of a subject does a prospective primary teacher require in order to teach the subject? Up to G.C.S.E. standard? "A" level? Why 1½ years of study at higher education level?
- Should prospective primary students devote more time to acquiring knowledge across the whole primary curriculum with less devoted to specialist knowledge in a few areas?
- Should we be concerned about the specific content of subject studies syllabuses? Students may take "science" or "English literature" subject options, but the content of courses may differ between institutions.

- Should prospective teachers know about a subject and study it in the ways in which it is usually studied in higher education? Perhaps the manner in which putative professional mathematicians or scientists study their subject is not appropriate for the intending primary teacher who will be more concerned about how children learn math and science.
- Should conventional higher education practices shape what courses student teachers may follow? For example, to what extent does the usual "A" level entry into a subject area in higher education bar students from increasing their personal knowledge of key areas of the curriculum such as science and math by ruling out study at degree level?

In a word, a problem with the stress on subject matter, and the relevant C.A.T.E. criterion in particular, is that teacher educators may be disposed to insuring that they accommodate to the criteria in terms of meeting standards conventionally defined by higher education and accumulating the necessary hourage. It may be more important for teacher educators (and C.A.T.E.) to ask searching questions about what should be the nature, scope and quality of student teachers' personal subject knowledge. Current discussions on this theme, particularly in their more hortatory form (see, for example, O'Hear, 1991), probably place too much emphasis on student teachers' personal knowledge of subject matter and not enough upon how student need to know about subjects in order to foster children's learning.

WHAT DO PROSPECTIVE TEACHERS ACTUALLY KNOW ABOUT SUBJECT MATTER?

Although it may be a matter of judgment as to what prospective teachers' knowledge of subject matter ought to be, it is at least prudent to discover what they do actually know about the subjects they are required to teach. There have been a few studies that have examined teachers' knowledge of key areas of the curriculum.

For example, with respect to science, which has assumed increasing importance with its designation as a core subject within the National Curriculum, Kruger, Palacio, and Summers (1990) and Kruger, Summers, and Palacio (1990) have surveyed primary (elementary) teachers and pronounced that they are ill-equipped to teach the subject. They hold views of science that are in conflict with accepted scientific theory, and their knowledge does not seem to be influenced by whether or not they studied science up to age 16 at school. Their understanding of basic notions such as force, momentum, and movement is insecure. With respect to teachers of older children, Hauslein and Good (1989) report that teachers' understanding of their subject changes as they become more experienced teachers. They do not think about science as practicing scientists but consider science more in terms of "what works" pedagogically in the classroom. They focus more upon how science will be meaningful and useful to them in their teaching. With respect to mathematics, many teachers seem to have the same naive conceptualizations and misunderstandings of mathematical knowledge as their pupils (Post, Harel, Behr, & Lesh, 1988) and prospective elementary teachers' mathematical knowledge is rule bound and thin (Ball, 1990). Many teachers, she found, do not have the mathematical knowledge to ask the right questions to encourage mathematical thinking, or the ability to offer various alternative explanations or representations to pupils who have difficulties with their learning. These few studies are little more than indicative, but they do raise some important questions for teacher educators. (Ongoing research should provide substantial additional information on this – see Leverhulme Primary Project, 1990.)

The first is that these investigations focus upon what is often assumed to be the more "important" areas of the curriculum. Were such studies to be extended to other important areas of the primary curriculum, such as history, geography, art, and music, even more alarming deficiencies in students' knowledge may emerge, especially since they are more likely to have dropped these subjects early on in their school careers. The proposals for the geography and history National Curriculums, for instance, will require teachers to have extensive and detailed knowledge of subject matter.

The second is to ask – and, given the current state of our knowledge, we can do little more than ask – what is the minimum desiderata in terms of what students need to know about the subjects they are required to teach so as to teach effectively? For example, primary teachers who must teach the National Curriculum at key stage two will, at the very least, require knowledge of its subjects beyond levels five and six if they are to locate pupils' learning within the sequence and structure laid down by statute. Presumably they also need a sound understanding of the concepts, skills, and information laid down in National Curriculums if they are to promote genuine understanding among their pupils and to be able to diagnose and remedy learning difficulties. Teachers' knowledge should be such as to enable them to have the confidence to draw on children's contributions and encourage children's activities. There is evidence that teachers are disposed to resort to drill and didactic teaching and discount children's contributions to lessons when they have only a limited knowledge of the subject they are teaching (Wolfe & Murray, 1990). In addition, students' knowledge should be sufficient to enable them to make informed judgments about the quality of text books, computer software, and other aids they use in their teaching.

The third is that when the National Curriculum is fully implemented, primary teachers will require an impressive range and quantity of knowledge and information across a very wide curriculum. Consider a few snippets from level five attainment targets: Teachers will need to be able to offer different interpretations of the enclosure of land in 18th-century Britain (history), use a computer database to store and retrieve information and explore patterns and relationships (geography), be able to explain how earthquakes and volcanoes are associated with the formation of landforms (science), and make a set of computer-controlled traffic lights (technology). These are merely bits of attainment targets from four subjects at one level of attainment; it is difficult to conceive of the prodigious amount of basic subject knowledge that will be required by prospective primary teachers.

When seeking to identify how much information students need to know about their subjects if they are to be prepared adequately to teach in contemporary schools, primary subject tutors will need to ponder a number of issues, which include:

- How, on primary P.G.C.E. courses, will time be found to provide students with the knowledge they require to teach the National Curriculum, and will this problem be exacerbated by moves to adopt more school-based models of training?
- Given that students are required to devote 100 hours to the study of subjects which they will have passed at G.C.S.E. grade 3 standard at school (Math and English), how much (additional?) time should be devoted to the study of those subjects which they may have abandoned at an early stage in their secondary school careers?
- Given the requirements of the National Curriculum, should the range and content of the subject study students are required to pursue at higher degree level be prescribed?

It is probable that the demands of teaching the National Curriculum will create the pressure for beginning and experienced teachers to seek pragmatic solutions to the problems of teaching subject matter, particularly in primary education. Initial teacher education courses may offer the one opportunity when students are encouraged to consider in some detail the problems of communicating subject matter to pupils. To give an example, there are attainment targets within the National Curriculum for technology that should pose a distinctive challenge for students in terms of what they need to know about the subject and how to apply that knowledge when teaching their pupils. But there is a sense in which debate has been settled, because the equipment manufacturers have already produced bits of technical kit teachers can use to "teach" what is required by an attainment target.

THE APPLICATION OF SUBJECT MATTER

In the normal course of events teacher education courses place an emphasis on the application of subject matter in the classroom, as is recognized by the C.A.T.E. criteria that direct attention to the classroom application of those subjects students have studied at higher degree level, and specify the amount of time to be devoted to this activity. Analysis and research into this aspect of teacher education has been informed by the notion of pedagogic content knowledge (following Shulman's distinction between *subject knowledge* – knowledge and understanding of the subject itself – and *pedagogic content knowledge* – knowledge about how to apply the subject when teaching it). Several commentators claim that pedagogic content knowledge is central to the practice of teaching (see, for example, Shulman, 1990; Peterson, Fennema, Carpenter, & Loet, 1989; Wolfe & Murray, 1990; Grossman, 1989; Feiman-Nemser & Parker, 1990; McDiarmid, 1989) and affects the quality of teaching (Meloth, Book, Putnam, & Sivan, 1989; Carpenter, Fennema, Peterson, & Carey, 1988). It is not possible within the scope of this chapter to describe, in any detail, the analytical work that has been undertaken in order to explore and develop the notion of pedagogic content knowledge, and the attempts to develop various schema and determine what constitutes pedagogic content knowledge in different subject areas. (This work may be of interest to teacher educators, and see, for example, Marks, 1990; Tamir, 1988.) It is more useful to identify three crucial themes emerging from the available research studies in this area.

The first is to suggest that there is no clear-cut or easy distinction between knowledge of a subject and pedagogic content knowledge, and the second is to observe that both students' knowledge of subject matter and their capacity to apply it are modified by classroom experience (these two themes tend to be interlinked in the literature; see for example, Grossman, 1989; Peterson et al., 1989; Rog, Donaldson, Quaglia, & Paige, Roth, 1989; Smith & Neale, 1989; Wilson, 1989, 1990). Moreover, there is variation in the manner in which different teachers incorporate subject matter and pedagogic content knowledge in their teaching (Morine-Dershimer, 1989; Wilson, Shulman, & Richert, 1987), and teachers' own values can have an important part to play in determining the subject matter they teach and their deployment of pedagogic strategies (Gudmundsdottir, 1990). The literature identifies, through research, issues educators may be familiar with experientially, such as that the way in which teachers think about their subject and the scope of their knowledge are in part shaped by their experiences of teaching the subject; that teachers with only a rudimentary knowledge of a subject can find that the nature and quality of their knowledge is enhanced when they are required to teach that subject; that the manner in which students think about applying their knowledge in the classroom may be shaped more by the extent and depths of their knowledge of the subject per se than by specific information which they have been given concerning its application; and that students' pedagogic practices are not so much shaped by their pedagogic content knowledge as by the teaching materials available for use in the classroom and by the idiosyncratic resource constraints of particular classrooms.

The third theme is that to place a stress upon students' application of knowledge which they have acquired as students may be to adopt a simplistic and misguided notion of teaching and learning (see, for example, Grossman, 1990; Mansfield, 1985). Teaching is very much more than the transmission of knowledge from teachers – as they understand it – to pupils – who are presumed to understand in similar fashion. Knowing how to apply what the teacher already knows is only part of the teacher's professional knowledge. It is equally important for the teacher to have some understanding of the child and how the child may acquire and understand the knowledge it is required to learn.

An appreciation of the literature on pedagogic content knowledge may offer useful heuristics for those teacher educators responsible for subject application courses, and the literature, while not offering prescriptions, does raise issues for consideration such as:

- To what extent, as C.A.T.E. requires, should a distinction be made between knowledge of the subject and its application? It may be (or it may not be) that one of the ways in which to foster students' ability to apply a subject is to provide additional knowledge in the subject itself, rather than to concentrate on the application of the subject.
- To what extent could students' basic knowledge and understanding of subjects in which they may be deficient (primary science, for example) be fostered by requiring them to teach the subject (under guided supervision, of course)?
- Since students' knowledge of how to apply a subject is necessarily shaped and constrained by the circumstances in which they teach and the resources available to them, should the greater part of applications courses be school based from the outset?

- Is there a tension between the expectation that students study a subject at higher degree level for its own sake, and that, in order to enhance their personal education and the expectation, they must learn how to apply the selfsame subject within the classroom? What meaning can be attached to the application of "C.A.T.E.-approved" subjects such as anthropology and archaeology?

THE ORGANIZATION OF KNOWLEDGE

Teacher education programs that seek to promote reflective teaching should require students to ask searching questions about how and according to what principles the knowledge included within the curriculum is organized and presented to children. This is particularly important at the primary level, where there is an enduring debate about whether it is preferable to organize knowledge within conventional subject boundaries or according to other principles that emphasize the integration of subject matter and that find their practical expression in approaches such as topic work, centers of interest, or themes. Given the concerns H.M.I. have expressed about topic work (H.M.I., 1989a, 1989b) and a National Curriculum which is set out in terms of conventional subject categories, there may be a disposition to assume that all debate about how knowledge is organized (into "subjects") has been settled. This is not the case, for example the National Curriculum nonstatutory guidance, together with other official advice, make it clear that it is still up to teachers to decide how to organize knowledge so long as they insure that, within the total curriculum, they address all the relevant attainment targets specified the core and foundation subjects. It must be noted that the literature on pedagogic content knowledge and subject matter knowledge invariably assumes and takes for granted that the curriculum is organized in conventional terms and that teachers teach "subjects." Whether to organize teaching within "subjects" or "topics" is an issue upon which primary educators hold firm views. However, such debates are resolved in practice, it is important that beginning teachers think about the issues involved and for them to defend and justify their own practice. The current literature and evidence will offer more to those teachers who organize their teaching within accepted subject boundaries. The available studies indicate that teachers teach differently in different circumstances, and that the manner in which they teach depends, in part, upon the subject they are teaching; subject matter itself has a significant effect on the way in which teachers teach (Sosniak & Perlman, 1990; Stodolsky, 1988; Wood, Cobb, & Yackel, 1990). This may be because characteristics inherent within subjects have a significant effect on the way in which teachers teach. Thus a developing corpus of educational knowledge that is investigating how teachers apply subject matter in different subject areas may be of relevance to those teachers who teach within the subject tradition. But it must be remembered that, at the present time, the research is limited to a few "central" areas of the curriculum, especially math and science, and that there are very few studies, if any, that have inquired into subject application in the arts and humanities (McNamara, 1991). Probably one of the most difficult challenges facing the beginning teacher is to organize and combine material when teaching in ways that seek to integrate subject matter such as topic work. Ensuring adequate coverage and planning for sequence and structure in children's learning is particularly difficult, as is indicated by the H.M.I. reports mentioned earlier. Unfortunately, the available research has little to offer primary teachers who wish to pursue this option.

This could be an interesting area of inquiry for teacher educators. If we accept that a teacher's capacity to teach effectively depends, in part, upon their knowledge of subjects and their application in areas such as, say, mathematics and geography, how and in what ways can we pursue this thesis with reference to preparing a term's project work on, say, "color" or "my neighborhood."

Although it goes beyond the remit of this chapter, the theme could be extended to address children's learning. Individual children's learning is not equally successful over all areas of the curriculum; there is considerable variability in the level and quality of a child's acquisition of knowledge in different subject areas. This suggests that within each subject area (however that may be defined), when considering the application of the subject, students need to reflect also on how children may learn in that particular area.

CONCLUDING REMARKS

There can be no doubt that subject study and its application is central to the content of and debate about teacher education. There are those on the right of educational thought who claim that a prospective teacher's knowledge of his or her subject is all that is required, and that any training can be provided in the classroom (for example, Lawlor, 1990). Even if we discount such views, it is important to recognize that the models for alternative routes into teaching such as the Articled, Licensed, and Hertfordshire Action on Teacher Supply schemes are premised on the belief that teachers' knowledge of (shortage?) subjects is all important, and that special teacher-training programs can be devised that offer acceptable professional training. Within such a climate of opinion, the C.A.T.E. requirements for conventional training programs appear measured. The imperative facing the majority of teacher educators is that they must attend to students' knowledge of subject matter and its application. As such, the recent corpus of research that has addressed these themes, and especially pedagogic content knowledge, offers much preliminary information that can inform our thinking and tuition in these areas. However, although the corpus has potential, we must be aware of its limitations.

Although there has been a substantial amount of research, it has had a narrow focus. The majority of studies have been in math and science; there have been a few in English and language, but the arts and humanities are hardly represented. Moreover, most of the literature concentrates upon the primary (elementary) age range. It is doubtful whether information and findings generated by studies in one substantive area of the curriculum are transferable to others, since subject matter itself seems to be a primary determinant of the way in which teachers teach.

The majority of studies either explicitly or by default offer a conventional view of subject matter and imply a traditional or "delivery" model of teaching. Subject matter is accepted as being transmitted by knowledgeable adults to children in conventional subject terms. Such a view may have some merit, especially given the advent of the National Curriculum, but the corpus has nothing to offer those teacher educators and beginning teachers who wish to organize their teaching on the basis of themes or centers of interest. Pedagogic content knowledge as currently conceived tends to assume subject differentiation rather than subject integration, and it does not offer a wider vision of the curriculum and educational process (for a critique, see Sockett, 1986).

Finally, it must be remembered that the focus upon subject matter and its application does not provide the philosopher's stone for improving the quality of teaching and learning in our schools. It is necessary for teachers to have knowledge of the subjects they teach, but, as has been indicated, the empirical link between the nature and quality of what the teacher knows and what the child knows has yet to be established.

REFERENCES

Arendt, H. (1954). The crisis in education. In *Between past and future* (pp. 173–196). London: Faber & Faber.

Ball, D. L. (1990). The mathematical understandings that prospective teachers bring to teacher education. *The Elementary School Journal, 90* (4), 449–466.

Bantock, G. H. (1979). The parochialism of the present: Some reflections on the history of educational theory. *Journal of Philosophy of Education, 13,* 41–54.

Baratz-Snowden, J. (1990). The N.B.P.T.S. begins its research and development program. *Educational Researcher, 19* (6), 19–24.

Bennett, N. (1976). *Teaching styles and pupil progress.* London: Open Books.

Berliner, D. C. (1986). In pursuit of the expert pedagogue, *Educational Researcher, 15* (7), 5–13.

Berliner, D. C., & Rosenshine, B. (1977). The acquisition of knowledge in the classroom. In R. C. Anderson, R. J. Spiro, & W. E. Montague (Eds.), *Schooling and the acquisition of knowledge* (pp. 375–396). Hillsdale, NJ: Erlbaum.

Brophy, J. E. (1979). Teacher behaviour and its effects. *Journal of Educational Psychology, 71* (6), 733–750.

Buchmann, M. (1982). The flight away from content in teacher education and teaching. *Journal of Curriculum Studies, 14* (1), 61–68.

Buchmann, M. (1989). *The careful vision: How practical is contemplation in teaching?* East Lansing, MI: National Center for Research on Teacher Education, Michigan State University.

Carpenter, T. P., Fennema, E., Pererson, P. L., & Carey, D. A. (1988). Teachers' pedagogical content knowledge of students' problem solving in elementary arithmetic. *Journal of Research in Mathematics Education, 19* (5), 385–401.

D.E.S. (1978). *Primary education in England: A survey by H.M. Inspectors of Schools.* London: H.M.S.O.

D.E.S. (1983). *Teaching quality* (Cmnd 8836). London: H.M.S.O.

D.E.S. (1984). *Initial teacher training: Approval of courses* (Circular No. 3/84). London: D.E.S.

D.E.S. (1988). *The new teacher in school: A survey by H.M. Inspectors in England and Wales, 1987.* London: H.M.S.O.

D.E.S. (1989). *Initial teacher training: Approval of courses* (Circular No. 24/89). London: D.E.S.

Dewey, J. (1964). The relation of theory to practice in education, National Society for the Scientific Study of Education, Third Yearbook, Part I. In R. D. Archambault (Ed.), *John Dewey on education: Selected writings.* Chicago: University of Chicago Press. (Original work published 1904).

Feiman-Nemser, S., & Parker, M. B. (1990). Making subject matter part of the conversation in learning to teach. *Journal of Teacher Education, 41* (3), 32–43.

Floden, R. E., & Buchmann, M. (1989). *Philosophical inquiry in teacher education.* East Lansing, MI: The National Center for Research on Teacher Education, Michigan State University.

Grossman, P. L. (1989). A study in contrast: Sources of pedagogical content knowledge for secondary English. *Journal of Teacher Education, 30* (5), 24–31.

Grossman, P. L. (1990, April). *When teaching what you know doesn't work: A re-analysis of methods and findings.* Paper presented at the annual meeting of the American Educational Research Association, Boston.

Grossman, P. L., Wilson, S. M., Shulman, L. S. (1989). Teachers of substance: Subject matter knowledge in teaching. In M. C. Reynolds (Ed.), *Knowledge base for the beginning teacher* (pp. 23–36). Oxford: Pergamon Press.

Gudmundsdottir, S. (1990). Values in pedagogical content knowledge, *Journal of Teacher Education, 41* (3), 44–52.

Hauslein, P. L., & Good, R. (1989, April). *Biology content cognitive structure of biology majors, biology teachers and scientists.* Paper presented at the 62nd Annual Meeting of the National Association for Research in Science Teaching, San Francisco.

H.M.I. (1989a). *Aspects of primary education: The teaching and learning of history and geography.* London: H.M.S.O.

H.M.I. (1989b). *Aspects of primary education: The teaching and learning of science.* London: H.M.S.O.

Kruger, C., Palacio, D., & Summers, M. (1990a). A survey of primary school teachers' conceptions of force and motion. *Educational Research, 32* (2), 83–94.

Kruger, C., Summers, M., & Palacio, D., (1990b). An investigation of some English primary school teachers' understanding of the concepts of force and gravity. *British Educational Research Journal, 16,* 41, 383–397.

Lawlor, S. (1990). *Teachers mistaught: Training in theories or education in subjects?* London: Centre for Policy Studies.

Leverhulme Primary Project. (1990). *Occasional paper.* Exeter, UK: School of Education, University of Exeter.

McDiarmid, G. W. (1989). Why staying one chapter ahead doesn't really work: Subject-specific pedagogy. In M. C. Reynolds (Ed.), *Knowledge base for beginning teachers* (pp. 193–205). Oxford: Pergamon Press.

McNamara, D. (1981). Time on task and children's learning: Research or ideology? *Journal of Education for Teaching, 7* (3), 284–297.

McNamara, D. (1990). Research on teachers' thinking: Its contribution to educating student teachers to think critically. *Journal of Education for Teaching, 16* (2), 147–160.

McNamara, D. (1991). Subject knowledge and its application. *Journal of Education for Teaching, 17* (2), 113–127.

Mansfield, H. (1985). Points, lines and their representations. *For the Learning of Mathematics, 5* (3), 2–6.

Marks, R. (1990). Pedagogical content knowledge: From a mathematical case to a modified conception. *Journal of Teacher Education, 41* (3), 3–11.

Meloth, M. S., Book, C., Putnam, J., & Sivan, E. (1989). Teachers' concepts of reading, reading instruction, and students' concepts of reading. *Journal of Teacher Education, 30* (5), 33–39.

Morine-Dershimer, G. (1989). Preservice teachers' conceptions of content and pedagogy: Measuring growth in reflective, pedagogical decision-making. *Journal of Teacher Education, 30* (5), 46–52.

Murray, F. B., & Fallon, D. (1989). *The reform of teacher education for the 21st century: Project 30 Year One Report.* Delaware: University of Delaware.

O'Hear, A. (1991, March 19). Getting the teachers we deserve. *The Guardian,* p. 25.

Peterson, P. L., Fennema, E., Carpenter, T. P., & Loet, M. (1989). Teachers' pedagogical content beliefs in mathematics. *Cognition and Instruction, 6* (1), 1–40.

Post, T. R., Harel, G., Behr, M. J., & Lesh, R., (1988). *Intermediate teachers' knowledge of rational number concepts.* Madison: National Center for Research in Mathematical Sciences Education, University of Wisconsin.

Rog, J. A., Donaldson, G. A., Quaglia, R., & Paige, J. (1990, April). *Learning the ropes: How beginning teachers develop pedagogic knowledge.* Paper presented at the annual meeting of the American Educational Research Association, Boston.

Roth, K. J. (1989, April). *Subject matter knowledge for teaching science.* Paper presented at the annual meeting of the American Educational Research Association, San Francisco.

Rutter, M., Maughan, B., Mortimore, P., & Ouston, J. (1979). *Fifteen thousand hours.* London: Open Books.

Shulman, J. (1990). Blue freeways: Travelling the alternate route with big-city teacher trainees. *Journal of Teacher Education, 30* (5), 2–8.

Shulman, L. S. (1986). Those who understand: Knowledge growth in teaching. *Educational Researcher, 15* (2), 4–14.

Smith, D. C., & Neale, D. C. (1989). The construction of subject matter knowledge in primary science teaching. *Teaching and Teacher Education, 5* (1), 1–20.

Smith, D. J., & Tomlinson, S. (1989). *The school effect: A study of multi-racial comprehensive schools.* London: Policy Studies Institute.

Sockett, H. (1987). Has Shulman got the strategy right? *Harvard Educational Review, 57* (2), 208–219.

Sosniak, L. A., & Perlman, C. L. (1990). Secondary education by the book. *Journal of Curriculum Studies, 22* (5), 427–442.

Stodolsky, S. S. (1988). *The subject matters: Classroom activity in maths and social studies.* Chicago: University of Chicago Press.

Tamir, P. (1988). Subject matter and related pedagogical knowledge in teacher education. *Teaching and Teacher Education, 4* (2), 99–110.

Taylor, W. (1990). The control of teacher education: The Council for the Accreditation of Teacher Education. In N.J. Graves (Ed.), *Initial teacher education: Policies and progress* (pp. 109–123). London: Kogan Page.

Warnock, M. (1989). The authority of the teacher. *Westminster Studies in Education, 12,* 73–81.

Wilson, S. M. (1989). *A case concerning content: Using case studies to teach subject matter.* East Lansing, MI: National Center for Research on Teacher Education, Michigan State University.

Wilson, S. M. (1990). *Mastodons, maps and Michigan: exploring uncharted territory while teaching elementary school social studies.* Paper presented at the annual meeting of the American Educational Research Association, Boston.

Wilson, S. M., Shulman, L. S., & Richert, A. E. (1987). 150 different ways of knowing: representations of knowledge in teaching. In J. Calderhead (Ed.), *Exploring teachers' thinking* (pp. 104–124). London: Cassell.

Winne, P. H. (1985). Steps towards promoting cognitive achievements. *The Elementary School Journal, 85* (5), 674–693.

Wolfe, J. M., & Murray, C. K. (1990, April). *Negotiating a stance toward subject matter: The acquisition of pedagogical knowledge in student teaching.* Paper presented at the annual meeting of the American Educational Research Association, Boston.

Wood, T., Cobb, P., & Yackel, E. (1990). The contextual nature of teaching: Mathematics and reading instruction in one second-grade classroom. *The Elementary School Journal, 90* (5), 497–513.

CHAPTER 14

Future Directions in Teacher Education

Gareth Rees Harvard
School of Education University of Exeter

Phil Hodkinson
The Manchester Metropolitan University
Crewe-Alsager Faculty
Department of Education

FUTURE DIRECTIONS IN TEACHER EDUCATION

This book explored in different ways how to develop a critically reflective and empowered teaching profession. But such a highly desirable aim must be seen against the present political and wider educational context. The context for current changes in perspectives on, and practices in, teacher education in Britain is of government policies that provide new alternative routes for entry into teaching. Moreover, all teacher education courses have to meet all the criteria of the Council for the Accreditation of Teacher Education, and all courses are being revised to insure that students are equipped with sufficient subject-matter knowledge for the National Curriculum. At the same time, schools are now managing their own financial budgeting, and coping with the many organizational and educational implications for teachers' inservice training and further professional development for implementing the National Curriculum and for more test-based assessment.

There are wider issues, too, that directly affect the nature and quality of teaching and learning. These depend on what strategies and alternatives are used to address a variety of professional issues such as specialist staff deployment and the provision of material resources; the more particular strategies adopted for diagnosing and meeting children's needs, of devising more differentiated curriculum content and patterns of classroom organization as well as working collaboratively with parents. These are linked to the nature and provision of inservice facilities, local authority support, and teacher appraisal in an attempt to develop a coherent policy for teachers' further professional development.

The contributors in this book, in varying degrees, recognized and discussed the nature and purpose of teacher education in preparing teachers to cope with the increasingly complex demands of schooling and explored in a series of case studies and theoretical analyses, how the values and perspectives of particular ideologies both within and outside teacher education can facilitate or sometimes hinder reform. They did this, chiefly, by reconceptualizing the purpose, processes, and structures of teacher education, and by testing the values and assumptions inherent in their different ideological perspectives on student teachers' professional learning.

The contributors also identified changing ideological perspectives on the nature of schooling and of a more empowered teaching profession that helps teachers to be actively responsible and accountable for their own professional development goals. They demonstrated how teacher educators can provide examples of more critical pedagogical practices that they can reasonably expect their student teachers to adopt and use in their classrooms. The editors stressed how teacher educators need to become more involved in the open politicization of education to develop the programs and teaching strategies that are described in this book.

Teacher educators need to identify and react firmly to those external factors that are likely to inhibit or thwart such programs, including the wider political context of recent educational reorganization of the curriculum and government policy on teacher education; the career structure for teaching, management structures, and consultative procedures in schools; and the nature and quality of continuing professional development. Without attending, and responding, to these factors, teacher educators may be inadequately preparing student teachers for an inevitable conflict of ideology, organization structures, resources, and working conditions in schools.

Thus, in establishing the conditions in teacher education that enable different kinds of student teacher-learners to develop their abilities to become more responsible for their own learning, there are wider implications for teachers, professional bodies, managers of schools, and course designers. For example, one of the more important issues in the training of primary teachers is the nature, acquisition, and development of the subject-matter knowledge required to cope with the National Curriculum. Similarly, in schools the extent, depth, and diversity of specialist subject-matter and pedagogical knowledge is related to the availability of specialist support for which a system of curriculum consultants and coordinators might not be effective. Also, course and curriculum designers need to enable student teachers and, increasingly, pupils in secondary schools studying cross-curriculum themes, to draw on expertise across traditional subject, departmental, and institutional boundaries relevant to their learning goals.

What is becoming apparent in schools and institutions of higher education responsible for training teachers is that these changes point directly to who decides what the curriculum should contain, how it should be organized, but is less specific about choosing and implementing the most effective pedagogical practices and strategies for teaching and learning. This can create in both institutions a dysfunctional conflict of ideology, organization, resources, time, and expertise. For example, trying to organize and monitor the range of teaching content and teaching strategies can adversely affect the quality of teachers' monitoring of, and interaction with, the pupils. Similarly, in implementing such changes, teachers and teacher educators are under pressure to accept particular practices and values. They also have to make practical sense of "the open politicisation of the whole 'good practice' question, which is also about values . . . what is under siege is the concept of good practice: the assumption that it has only certain approved manifestations" (Alexander, 1991; emphasis added).

Moreover, teacher educators have to decide whether and how teacher education can be framed within a consistent paradigm, one that empowers teachers and students to make practical sense of this "open politicization" and how to establish structures and policies that will provide opportunities for student teachers to have more appropriate opportunities to take responsibility within their own learning programs. Hodkinson and Harvard argued in Chapter 1 that the notion of a more empowered profession, although necessary if education was to fulfil the needs of pupils and society, is being strongly contested by those, often of the political right, who regard education as something much simpler and less problematic than do the contributors to this book. Furthermore, there have been enough pointers, even in this book with its deliberately limited scope, to warn us that creating an empowered teaching profession requires attention to more than teacher education. However, we intend now to focus specifically on the role of teacher educators and the implications for teacher education of developing a more empowered teaching profession. In doing so, we ask our readers to constantly consider the much wider and contested context of which this aspect of professionalization is a small but important part.

In the introduction we focused on three issues which have been examined in various ways throughout the book. We now reexamine them for their further implications in teacher education policy and practice, to include teachers and teacher educators. We believe that, by focusing on these issues, we are more likely to consider precisely what we believe we are educating or training student teachers for, to examine whether educational research and studies of teaching provide more systematic knowledge of it than one can reasonably pick up through experience. Similarly, if we want intending teachers to reflect, what do we want them to reflect about, and what disciplines of thought would be particularly relevant? Teacher educators have to ask themselves, above all, what general qualities they are trying to develop in their students that will be relevant to increasingly complex educational structures and practices. But even if we can answer some of these questions it still has to be decided how to incorporate these ideas into teacher education courses.

The practical issues to be discussed here are (a) the nature and purpose of the relationship between school placements and academic and professional studies, (b) the nature and quality of collective participation and authentic partnership, and (c) locating competent performance within a broader framework of professional development.

These issues are discussed in the context of recent government proposals and policies that argue for increased accountability and quality control in the training of teachers. Equally important, there are direct implications for developmental research as the basic methodology in teacher education which supports reflective monitoring of existing practices, and their history, as well as systematic analyses of theories of teaching and their conscious production as a central part of developing teacher education policies. In this way, teachers' continuing professional development should be directed toward a critical and reflective stance in which teachers and teacher educators work collaboratively to build theories based on the practice of teaching.

The Relationship Between On- and Off-the-Job Training

Whatever form teacher education takes in the future, it will need to incorporate and systematically design programs that insures some coherence and continuity between on - and off-the-job components. Even this obvious point must be stated, for it has been recently contested by the political right who challenge the need for any "off-the-job" element at all. In Britain at present we have a licensed teacher's scheme whereby unqualified teachers can be appointed with no training at all. There is a clear assumption that, if they are "the right sort of people," they will simply become good teachers by doing the job alongside an experienced practioner.

More recently, for example, the government has funded the Open University to train a thousand teachers a year for 5 years from 1994 without going near a training institution. Training will be by the usual long-distance learning methods of the Open University. During the 18-month course from January to July, graduates will complete two periods of teaching practice, one of 2 to 3 weeks and one of 6 weeks toward the end of the course. This latest initiative on teacher training implies that the licensed teacher scheme has not been particularly effective.

One consequence of the argument for more school-based work is that an apprenticeship model of learning how to teach has been introduced through the articled and licensed teachers' scheme. This trend coincides with more systematic appraisal of teachers and teacher educators. In responding to these proposals teacher educators and teachers are being given little opportunity to discuss their underlying ideologies, for example, in conceptualizing the role of mentors. It is difficult to detect in the various policy statements for restructuring the content of teacher education courses where they are informed by research on teaching. Similarly, there are countervailing tendencies in our schools to an increased emphasis upon the reflective practitioner, able to review critically and assess performance, especially on peer and self-assessment, by an increase of test-based assessment as in the national curriculum. Similarly, any serious attempt to develop reflective practioners in initial training may be hindered by the extremely busy, highly intensive, and fragmented nature of courses across main subjects and curriculum and professional studies.

Jamieson, in Chapter 3, offers a timely reminder of the limitations of an apprenticeship model of training by showing how Kolb's model of experiential learning undermines the simple notion of learning alongside an experienced practioner. He points to the need for reflective observation and abstract conceptualization as the necessary conditions for learning from experience. We too, question the assumption that there is an obvious link between knowledge and action or of a well-defined perspective outlining the necessary conditions for the acquisition and development of professional knowledge and competent performance. But the various contributors, especially Bloomer, Harvard, and Dunne suggest what these may be.

A much more interesting and difficult challenge is how best to achieve a reasonable balance with sufficient continuity and coherence with these two components. Relating them has always been problematic, largely because too little attention has been paid to the nature and purpose of professional competence in a broader framework for continuing professional development. Also, there is a sense in which program coherence can introduce too much regimentation. Such programs need to be sufficiently flexible and specialised to show how "teacher education can hardly be more certain than teaching itself" (Buchmann & Floden, 1991, p. 71).

More fundamentally, though, we know little about the nature of professionally relevant knowledge and how it can be acquired by student teachers, or of the role and responsibilities of the teachers and tutors supervising the students. Also, teachers, tutors, and students customarily work together for a teaching practice, but not for more extended curriculum projects tied to teachers: immediate concerns and interests. Ackland describes how such projects could form an integral part of teachers' and student teachers' professional development. Ideally, program coherence exists where students identify links among various areas of skill and knowledge in which uncertainties, contradictions, and dilemmas still exist. "Because teaching is uncertain and no educational, theory is complete, the unexpected will happen. Even the most coherent account will fail to explain some important events – and many of our theories turn out to be false anyway" (Buchmann & Floden, 1991, p. 71).

There are various projects described in this book that could be linked to an inservice program to the mutual benefit of schools and, more particularly, teachers' further professional development and students' further professional learning and academic study. In Chapter 5, Eraut explains why trying to establish an authentic relationship between schools and higher education institutions is problematic. The two contexts of school and training institution belong to two completely different cultures. The practical activity of teaching occurs in schools, surrounded by a culture and conversation that is generally practical, pragmatic, and specific to a particular set of circumstances. The "off-the-job" element normally takes place in an institution of higher education, and is concerned with generalizations and abstractions, in a culture dominated by reading, writing, and research, each of which have their own rules of the game.

Whatever the organizational, structural, and procedural changes that are necessary for more systematic, effective, and collaborative supervision of students' professional learning, the key principle of empowerment can only be achieved if there is a reason and an opportunity to critically review and examine current practice and reconceptualize the professional knowledge base required for teaching. Various researchers (Schon, 1987; Shulman, 1987; Zeichner, 1991) explain how various types of teachers' knowledge are organized, and the extent to which the quality of teachers' thinking enables this knowledge to be structured and restructured in increasingly sophisticated ways.

The purpose and process of "theorizing," described by Eraut in Chapter 5, resembles the central notion of "reflectivity" or "critical reflection," which it is assumed teachers do or should engage in. This process, it is argued by Eraut, should be practiced by students and teachers in the schools to more closely unite the training and educating functions of schools and teacher education institutions. However, although there is research based on individual case studies of student teachers' socialization into teaching and their professional development there is much less available on how professional learning changes and develops during teacher education courses and continues to develop in the probationary year. Teacher educators are less confident, though, about what disciplines of thought can sustain reflective practice.

The traditional pattern of teacher education where the tutor is firmly associated with theorizing in higher education institutions only reinforces the misleading and dangerous fallacy that theory and practice can be divided, and that theorizing is relevant only "off the job." Similarly, teacher educators must dismantle the traditional status hierarchies where the tutor controls programs and is proactive, while the learner merely reacts to what is given. There are, then, certain necessary conditions that must be met for a more authentic partnership in professional training.

Some Necessary Conditions for Authentic Partnership in Teacher Education

The notion of partnership needs to be reexamined to determine whether and how it is perceived as collective participation. Recent attempts to place more responsibility on schools and teachers for teacher training may be ill-conceived if there is not a corresponding understanding of the role and responsibilities of mentors, of mentoring processes, of how mentoring is expressed in learning activities, of how to train and prepare mentors, and of the means of assessing the effects of training. A collaborative approach for mentor training should establish a realistic set of shared purposes, common understandings, and, more particularly, the principles of procedure for planning, teaching, and evaluating courses, so that the criteria by which students' professional learning is being judged are openly shared, accessible, and negotiable.

There are some practical issues, too, in legitimating an explicit shift for teacher education from an higher education institution to the schools. Successful mentoring and reconceptualizing the supervisory role must involve asking how school systems, already under pressure, will be able to provide effective assistance to beginners in a systematic way. Those who advocate a mentor system must recognize some of the fundamental and erroneous assumptions that they make about its effectiveness. For example, how are students to be evaluated, and what evaluation model is being used? Similarly, the process of training mentors cannot be seen as an isolated experience; the idea of mentoring must be based on the concept of an adult learner: it is the difference between acquiring specific skills and working with developmental goals for teachers. Teacher educators and teachers need to work together to develop greater complexity as thinkers in a developmental sense. After all, mentoring may be more complex than effective teaching.

The context and the conditions for collective participation are important too. The staff of a school have to decide how to include and monitor student support in ways that make the best use of existing resources, such as personal tutorial systems. Staff and peer support is required for an effective use of formative assessment strategies, involving a sufficiently rigorous collaborative assessment drawing on different sources of evidence for preinduction and postinduction teachers. Moreover, we need to know more about how an emphasis on collaborative assessment strategies, both formative and summative, and the processes that support them, do actually enhance the quality of students' professional learning and contribute directly to the quality of the relationships between institutions and schools.

In responding to recent curriculum and organizational changes, it seems as if schools are being forced to adopt a more bureaucratic organization that may do less to encourage innovation and help to intensify the isolation of teachers. Professional development must be a collective responsibility. Mentor programs may only be a temporary palliative to counteract the organizational defects that hinder effective practice. But mentor programs should be used with all teachers not just probationers. All teachers need to help one another to expand subject-matter knowledge and devise research interests linked directly to professionally relevant knowledge and effective practical classroom teaching and learning strategies.

Finally, what are the outcomes for teachers? What are the benefits to them of participating in teacher education induction programs? The literature shows that systematic induction of new teachers leads to professionalization of teaching (Thies-Sprinthal, 1986). Similarly, when formal mentoring is provided as positive reinforcement, guidance, and moral support, there are considerable benefits for beginners (Huffman & Leek, 1985). The mentors benefit, too. Mentors' teaching skills, professional growth, recognition, and reward have all been positively affected by their work with novices (Allen, 1989). But these benefits depend heavily on teachers' motivation, available resources, time, perceived status, and professional recognition. The notion of developmental research may help to integrate teacher training and the development of teaching practices into a teacher development framework.

The task of working with teachers has both epistemological and methodological, and therefore, ethical and political, aspects to it. For example, the chapters by Brown, Ackland, and Thomas suggest how teachers' professional development benefits from participation in various forms of action research, a methodology that recognizes how teachers' "practical theories" grow and develop. Harvard and Brown illustrate how to achieve an increased awareness of classroom events in the context of student teachers' professional learning, while Jamieson and Zeichner suggest how teachers and teacher educators can develop an increased clarity of specific beliefs and an expanded view of teaching, schooling, and society. Bloomer, Williams, and Thomas show how a greater disposition toward reflection can be developed and sustained in different teaching contexts.

We think that collective participation offers a support system for teachers' and students' participation in action research, so that they can describe changes in their own and in others' thinking and explore, more systematically, the dimensions of perceived learning as they themselves experience them. But this doesn't mean abandoning structure in terms of setting realistic aspirations and goal setting for professional development. One challenge for both teachers and teacher educators is to account for how their pedagogical practices contribute directly to developing learners' capabilities. Similarly, the notion of participation must create appropriate conditions. The allocation of time, resources, and efficient systems of communication both within and between the institutions, as well as an opportunity to allow for the interpretative framework and conclusions of a shared project to be critically examined by all participants must be a prominent part of the collaborative methodology (Noffke & Zeichner, 1987).

Widening Beyond Performance

It is our belief that appropriate education and training can help teachers improve their performance, partly by focusing explicitly on the nature and purpose of performance itself. Carefully written competence statements can aid this focusing by providing a framework for analysis and dialogue, thereby clarifying teachers' beliefs and assumptions. However, as we argued in Chapter 3, such competence statements must always be seen as a tool and should not be reified or be the total focus of attention. We should also avoid being too narrow in defining what performance is. Competence, we argued, goes beyond performance, to incorporate schemas and intellectual processes, that is, not only in learning how to teach but also "how to reason about and learn from their teaching" (Feiman-Nemser, 1991, p.2).

There is insufficient space here to analyze the many different elements that make up a teacher's role within and beyond the classroom. However, teaching is preeminently a practical activity, and teacher education should attend to the principles of procedure that sustain it. One such example would be the nature and purpose of various consultative procedures for planning and evaluating teaching.

The various contributions in this book have adopted a research perspective that examines the nature of teachers' and student teachers' processes for selecting and organizing professional knowledge, and of determining under what conditions these capacities are developed during and after training. This approach has implications for the appraisal and evaluation of teaching quality in teacher education. The purpose of evaluation is, above all, to support the improvement of learning and teaching. The practical proposals that logically follow suggest a more systemically valid assessment system that fosters the development of the cognitive skills that the assessment system is designed to measure. Such a system drives the course and its practices to an improvement in the underlying knowledge and skills that assessment procedures measure (Frederiksen & Collins, 1989).

Evaluation should also include ways in which teachers participate for different purposes at various levels of management, and closely examine the ease or difficulty with which they are involved in executive decision-making processes, streamlining systems of communication, and various forms of coordination and consultation. Equally important are the institutional politics governing these executive and administrative procedures, and the extent to which constituted bodies are truly representative. For example, the composition and executive responsibilities of those involved in curriculum planning and development, and the extent to which such procedures are effective in disseminating information and, of course, explicitly attending to the organisational structures for classroom procedures that directly affect pupils' learning.

So, although it is vital that classroom teaching performance is critically and collectively evaluated, such procedures should be sustained as an integral part of all other professional performances, if the notion of reflective practice is to become legitimate and valid.

Even so, there remains a danger of individualizing teaching by focusing all our attention on what teachers understand about themselves and their own performance, no matter how widely it is conceived. To be truly empowered, teachers need to be critically conscious of the differing and competing ideologies and value positions that determine how they interpret educational practices and develop new practices and educational policies. They need to be able to examine social, cultural, and historical influences, so that they are capable of criticizing the status quo. Radnor (1991) investigated the micropolitical nature of the process of implementation in schools of an externally imposed educational change in the form of a new examination—the General Certificate of Secondary Education (GCSE)—and monitored how teachers accommodated new curriculum and assessment processes and procedures within their practice. The central focus of her work was an explanatory conceptualisation of the process of accommodation.

If teachers are to be empowered then they must be able to take a critical stance to what they and others, in various roles, actually do. This is an essential requirement for two reasons. First, part of being an empowered professional is the ability to understand and, therefore, accept or reject the status quo. Secondly, the very need to create an empowered, critically reflective teaching profession itself requires changes to the current culture of schools (Hargreaves, 1989). This, in turn, requires that such school cultures be interrupted, and critical reflection by teachers can be a means towards such an interruption, provided that reflection examines the processes that sustain the wider structures and conditions of schooling (Sparkes, 1991). Without such empowerment teachers may become "victims of their personal biographies, systematic political demands, and ecological conditions, rather than making use of them in developing and sustaining worthwhile and significant change" (Richardson, 1990, p. 16).

Part of the role of teacher educators is to demonstrate and share such critical thinking and theorizing with the teachers and students with whom they work. Although this is difficult to achieve, some suggestions have been made in this book about how teacher educators can work with teachers to attempt to relate these fundamental professional issues to their own particular circumstances, and to develop the link between public theory and personal theory and experience. Above all, teachers must be encouraged to articulate their own "personal" theories, and to use public theories rather than simply learn them as if they were facts. Many teachers find such approaches uncomfortable, for they hanker after definitive answers, although such certainties seldom exist, especially in teaching. The notion of theorizing must be seen as a legitimate part of professional education and of various forms of analyses used to attend persistently to the practical implications for schools and teachers.

OBSTACLES TO EMPOWERMENT

In this final section we consider briefly how the process of empowerment can be impeded and encouraged. If teachers are to become critically empowered in their work, it must follow that they become critically empowered in their learning. We already highlighted the need to see learning as a partnership by recognizing the developmental nature of teachers' professional lives within a model of adult learning. For such intentions to become more than rhetorical statements, we need the mechanisms in teacher education that will enable teachers as learners to take more control over their own professional development. At present, there are only limited ways in which this can happen, for example, by choosing courses or further professional modules, or choosing topics for individual or collaborative projects and research. Liston and Zeichner (1988) reminded us that "it is pragmatically unfeasible and ethically indefensible to attempt to reform teacher education unless one has, or can develop, some direct involvement in the process" (p. 33).

But there are some barriers to such empowerment in learning. Teachers, whether of pupils or other teachers, are often cast in or readily assume the role of expert, while learners are not expected or are prevented from being more responsible and, therefore, accountable, for their own learning. Over several years, the authors have separately worked with groups of students in initial teacher education, trying to develop their abilities to consult and collaborate with others in mutually agreed planned activities, as well as taking responsibility for their own learning. This, in turn, has involved us in ensuring that the pedagogy of our courses is open to examination with students and are capable of explicit justification. Initially, such approaches represent a culture shock for some students. From their perspective, it is easier to leave responsibility with the tutor, who can be blamed if anything goes wrong, than it is to take or share responsibility for themselves.

However, there is clear evidence cited in this book to show how student teachers can learn to examine and explain the relevance of their studies to themselves if certain principles of procedure for designing, conducting, and evaluating courses are shared with them and, where necessary, adapted and revised. These principles can help to overcome the actual or apparent fragmentation of courses, of conflicting practices within institutions, to insure greater coherence and continuity in students' professional learning. These procedures may also alert student teachers to the dangers of over-regulation within and outside teacher education institutions and of schools by government.

Teacher education needs more descriptive-analytic studies of the learning of student teachers to establish more precisely the basis on which to judge the quality of teacher education programs and evaluate general policy options. This will enable prospective employers to design induction programs on a more rational basis. But there are certain necessary conditions for developing an understanding of how professional education contributes to teachers' learning and how that learning can be fostered. Professional education still lacks an empirically based theoretical framework to inform practice, policy, and evaluation.

Research on student teaching is only just beginning to respond more radically to the changing nature of professional expertise. More specifically, Hodkinson and Harvard, in Chapter 4, suggest ways of reconceptualizing the nature of competence, while Dunne and Harvard describe how to gather more specific evidence on the nature and acquisition of student teaching competence so that perceived causes of the claimed weaknesses in teacher education, and the proposed remedies, are no longer based on implicit, and often unexamined assumptions. In this sense, Zeichner, in his chapter, rightly emphasizes the need for more data that explicitly link recent developments in reflective education programs to studies of student teacher effectiveness.

Unless teacher education research provides us with much clearer descriptions and analyses of what is taught and learned in formal training and school practices, it seems unlikely that progress will be made in understanding the nature of professional competence and the necessary conditions for its continuing development. The quality of training programs need to be examined to establish how they incorporate continuity, progression, and a measure of reasonable coherence. One possible mechanism for achieving this is to help develop empowerment in learning through individual action planning.

The principle has emerged very recently, in vocational education and training in Britain (Stanton, 1990). Basically, in practice it involves the learners in successive stages of collaborative planning with a tutor by making a series of decisions about different aspects of their learning. These include identifying the present range of attainments and experiences, agreeing on specified goals and targets, analyzing learning needs to achieve these targets, mapping the route to accomplish those needs, and assessing, evaluating, and accrediting students' successful accomplishments. The process then begins again in a further cyclical way.

The individual action plans (IAPs) do not have to be used rigidly or in a mechanistic way. Part of the process should be to make each stage problematic, with "goals" and "routes" for achieving those goals to be seen, when appropriate, as open-ended investigations. But the whole exercise is purposeful and manageable goal-directed learning shared between learner and mentor. This illustrates our notion, in Chapter 3, of an interactive perspective on learning as an attempt to model a complex, dialectical learning process, where the learners are proactive but where each stage is tentative and changing, through successive feedback loops that are infinite in number. The teacher educator's role then becomes that of tutor and facilitator, in partnership with the learner at each stage of the process.

The model can be applied to projects of varying degrees of complexity and scale, ranging from planning a dissertation by relating it to students' needs, experiences, and interests, or to choosing modules and course units. Equally, it can be applied to formative staff appraisals for experienced teachers, making the process proactive for the teachers involved. This use can be extended to a continuing career-long process of professional education and development. For such a process to become widely adopted, major changes are required to traditional evaluation practices within teacher education.

Teachers or student teachers must be given a central role in making decisions at each stage of the learning cycle. They will need considerable help in doing this, and, initially, will require clear procedural guidelines. Initial teacher education should emphasize and practice a progressively increasing student participation in acquiring and practicing various learning strategies and the ability to monitor their own learning. This can be achieved only if there is an institutional acceptance of a clear rationale for increasingly autonomous learning with appropriate procedures for monitoring it.

One way of accomplishing institutional consensus for increased independent student learning, and, incidentally, the probability of that perspective on learning being adopted by such teachers in schools, is if learning can be represented as professional development. This would require student teachers' professional development to be conceived of and suitably represented as a generic map.

This could be designed to develop students' capacities to monitor and appraise key aspects of professional growth: management of their own and others' learning, communicating in various settings, especially with children to facilitate learning, with themselves and others. It also includes various facets of a secure and relevant professional knowledge base: underlying principles and values governing teaching, learning, and pedagogy. Professional development is taken to be driven by the emergent capacity for and engagement in critical reflection. Such engagement occurs in students' reading and writing, discussion, and teaching practice. We assume that such an assessment system will drive students' professional development, being "systemically valid" (Fredericksen & Collins, 1989) in that it directly encourages and sustains the development of the capacities in question.

One other requirement of such a flexible, learner-centered approach is to devise an appropriate format for monitoring and recording students' progress and development. This could take the form of a learning log or a professional portfolio, containing notes and records of each stage in the action-planning process and specific reference to the various facets of the generic map. This requires spending time in conferences with small groups and with individual students to discuss the purpose and value of monitoring professional learning in these ways and of encouraging students to experiment with approaches that suit their personality and situation. Tutors should, therefore, be flexible in what they require in the substance and form of what is to be recorded and the procedures for doing so.

These formats are a tool for learning and not an end in themselves. If learners cannot or fail to see it in that way, then alternative methods have to be found. Ironically, one way of emphasizing the potential of a generic map and learning log is to spend considerable time on them in the early stages of a course. They need to be central to learning, not simply an add-on extra. Finally, just like statements of competence, such learning techniques and strategies will only empower students if they are used within an interactive learning ideology, some of the necessary conditions for which we have outlined here.

Ideally, students' professional learning should display development in different aspects of professional knowledge, notably, subject-matter and pedagogical knowledge. McNamara's chapter examines the implications for the appropriate treatment of academic subjects and of acquiring and developing professionally relevant subject matter knowledge for teacher education. We would add that we still need to know more about how such knowledge is used in planning and enacting classroom practice. Presumably, this aspect of professional development must consist of depth of understanding, breadth of application, awareness of strength and weaknesses by perceiving gaps in the professional knowledge base, the capacity to act professionally, and, ultimately, the quality of performance.

CONCLUSIONS

In this chapter we identify those issues that we consider to be of crucial importance in examining the purpose, structures, and processes of teacher education and some of the necessary conditions for more radical reform towards a critical pedagogy. This involved us in looking at how institutional cultures and organizational structures differ; how to co-ordinate institutional policies for students' professional training and development; how and when to share and critically examine the ideology of particular pedagogical approaches and learning strategies; how to develop the respective roles and responsibilities of teachers, students, and teacher educators, to their mutual benefit; how to examine the nature and quality of student teachers' and teachers' professional learning and development, and how to reconceptualize the supervisory roles of teachers and tutors by examining and developing the psychological underpinnings of the whole supervisory process and of evaluation and appraisal procedures as part of professional growth and development, so that they are enabled to engage in self-assessment and self-monitoring.

Throughout the book the contributors have persistently emphasized the preconditions for improving teacher education to include demonstrated competence and a disposition to theorize and explain the teaching and learning processes of children and of themselves. A major theme has been how to enable this to happen in the context of recent criticisms on the quality of teacher education and of research on student teaching.

Teacher education must be seen in the broad sense of teachers' continuing professional development, and persist in exploring ways in which schools and institutions of higher education can share in the common task of socializing student teachers into the profession. Fortunately, this is being increasingly developed and sustained by a research perspective of critical inquiry into professional education that focuses on how teachers' professional knowledge is organized, how the knowledge base for professional development is controlled by government policies, and how these political influences do or do not percolate through to influence the design, teaching, and evaluation of teacher educators' professional practice.

Educational institutions are already responding to, and implementing, various methods for monitoring the quality of school teaching and initial teacher education. A positive outcome of recent developments in quality assessment is that there is now an increasing concern with examining teaching approaches rather than an exclusive focus on mechanisms and procedures. This should lead to providing improved learning opportunities for students. But if this to happen, then teacher educators' substantial understanding of student learning experiences, capacities, and approaches also need to be updated and developed. When necessary teacher educators' professional knowledge must be elicited and challenged so that we can learn more of how the professional knowledge base of teacher educators shifts and changes and does or does not affect or alter practices.

In our view, this will be achieved only if we accept developmental research as the basic methodology of developing teaching. Developmental research focuses on changing the teaching practices and enhancing teachers' learning. Our contributors have argued persuasively for and vividly illustrated both the action and reflection dimensions of developmental research. They have also shown how, through developmental research, it becomes possible to unite teacher training and the development of teaching practices into a teacher development framework. It is in this sense, and in this way, that, throughout this book, the contributors have described and critically examined the practical and ideological bases for engaging prospective and experienced teachers and professional tutors in their own learning to their mutual professional development.

REFERENCES

Alexander, R. (1991, August 9). Politics of good practice. *Times Educational Supplement*, p. 12.

Allen, D. (1989). *Evaluation of the BEST Support Program and the Cooperating Teacher Programme*. Hartford: Connecticut State Department of Education.

Buchman, M. & Folden, F. (1991). Programe coherence in teacher education: A view from the U.S.A *Oxford Review of Education, 17* (1), 65–72.

Feiman-Nemser, S. (1991). *Helping novices to teach: Lessons from an exemplary support teacher*. Paper prepared for the 1991 meeting of the International Study Association on Teacher Thinking, Surrey, England.

Frederikson, J. R., & Collins, A. (1989, December). A systems approach to educational testing. *Educational Researcher*, pp. 27–32.

Hargreaves, D. (1989). *Curriculum and assessment reform*. Milton Keynes, UK: Open University Press.

Huffman, G. & Leek, S. (1985). Beginning teachers' perceptions of mentors. *Journal of Teacher Education, 37* (1), 22–25.

Liston, D., & Zeichner, K. (1988). Critical pedagogy and teacher education. *Educational Researcher, 19* (7), 10–18.

Noffke, R., & Zeichner, K. (1987, April). *Action research and teacher thinking: The first phase of the action research on action research at the University of Wisconsin-Madison*. Paper presented at the Annual Meeting of AERA, Washington, DC.

Radnor, H. (1991). *Implementing educational change: An empirical study of accommodating the general certificate of secondary education into the structure of schooling*. Unpublished doctoral College, London.

Richardson, V. (1990). Significant and worthwhile changes in teaching practice. *Educational Researcher, 19* (7), 10–18.

Schon, D. (1987). *Educating the reflective practioner*. San Francisco: Jossey Bass.

Shulman, J.H. (1987). Knowledge and teaching: Foundations of the new reform. *Harvard Educational Review, 57* (1), 1–22.

Sparkes, A. (1991). The culture of teaching, critical reflection and change: Possibilities and problems. *Educational Management and Administration*, Vol. *19* (1), 4–19.

Stanton, G. (1990). TVEI and individual action plans. In P. Hodkinson (Ed.), *TVEI and the post-16 curriculum*. Exeter, UK: Wheaton Books.

Thies-Sprinthall, L. (1986, November/December). A collaborative approach for mentor training: A working model. *Journal of Teacher Education, Nov/Dec.* pp. 13–20.

Zeichner, K. (1991, April). *Conceptions of reflective teaching in contemporary U.S teacher education program reforms*. Paper presented at the annual meeting of the American Educational Research Association, Chicago, IL.

Author Index

Subject Index

A

Action research, 8, 39, 186–192, 254; *see also* Teacher as researcher; Teacher education, research-based
Active reflection, 161–163
Activity of teaching, 115, 116–123, 128ff.
　and action, 115, 116–117, 118
　components of
　　control, 120
　　executive, 119–120
　　orienting, 117–119
　orientation, 128, 129
Action research, 5, 39
Adult education, 37
Assessment, 3, 4, 51–52, 184, 190, 251
　self-assessment, 126, 134, 136–137, 139, 140, 148, 152, 153, 156, 207–210, 251, 261

B

Behavioristic ideology, 56–57, 63, 66
　and learning, 56
"Black-box" method of teaching, 106, 112

C

Classroom performance, 6–7
Cognitive apprenticeship, 130, 133
Collaboration, 9, 19, 134, 162, 163, 171, 173, 175ff., 252, 253–255
　collaborative planning, 162–163, 259
　and evaluation, 176, 180ff.
　procedural model, 187–192
Competence-based learning, 55–68, 126–129, 255
　behavioristic ideology, 56–57, 63
　as habitual practice, 127
　as intelligent practice, 127
　interactive ideology, 57–60, 63
　interactive model, 60–63, 66, 67
Competitive flexibility, 11
Conceptual change learning, 161–162
Confederation of British Industry (CBI), 17
Council of the Accreditation of Teacher Education (CATE), 232, 235, 238, 239, 240, 241, 247
Critical reflection, 6, 8, 15–16, 18, 64, 65, 180, 183, 211, 252, 257
Curriculum development, 159, 160, 172–173, 176, 179, 248–249, 254